BERNHARDT AND THE THEATRE OF HER TIME

Edited by Eric Salmon

Contributions in Drama and Theatre Studies, Number 6

GREENWOOD PRESS
Westport, Connecticut • London, England

The essays in this book originated as
papers read at a conference, "The
International Stage in the Bernhardt
Era," held at the University of Guelph,
Ontario, Canada, in May 1977.

Library of Congress Cataloging in Publication Data

Main entry under title:

Bernhardt and the theatre of her time.

  (Contributions in drama and theatre studies, ISSN
0163-3821 ; no. 6)
  Papers presented at a conference held at the
University of Guelph, Canada, in May 1977.
  Includes bibliographical references and index.
  Contents: Palmy days at the opera / by Douglas
Arrell—The stage techniques of Sarah Bernhardt / by
Robert Horville—Sarah and Coq / by Marguerite Coe—
[etc.]
  1. Bernhardt, Sarah, 1844-1923—Congresses.
2. Actors—France—Biography—Congresses. I. Salmon,
Eric. II. Series.
PN2638.B5B44   1983   792'.028'0924   83-1439
ISBN 0-313-23755-7 (lib. bdg.)

Copyright © 1984 by Eric Salmon

All rights reserved. No portion of this book may be
reproduced, by any process or technique, without the
express written consent of the publisher.

Library of Congress Catalog Card Number: 83-1439
ISBN: 0-313-23755-7
ISSN: 0163-3821

First published in 1984

Greenwood Press
A division of Congressional Information Service, Inc.
88 Post Road West
Westport, Connecticut 06881

Printed in the United States of America

10 9 8 7 6 5 4 3 2 1

Copyright Acknowledgments

Grateful acknowledgment is made for the kind permission given to reprint the following:

The essay ''Mademoiselle Rhea—An American Bernhardt?'' by Alan Woods (Chapter 8) has been published previously. It appeared in the November 1980 issue of *Theatre Survey* and is here reprinted with permission of the American Society for Theatre Research.

''Sidgwick and Jackson for extract from ''Amaranth'' by John Drinkwater.''

A. E. Housman: Extract from Poem XXXII from THE SHROPSHIRE LAD with the permission of The Society of Authors as the literary representative of the Estate of A. E. Housman, and Jonathan Cape Ltd., publishers of A. E. Housman's COLLECTED POEMS, World excluding U.S.A.

From ''From far, from eve and morning'' from ''A Shropshire Lad'' - Authorized Edition - from THE COLLECTED POEMS OF A. E. HOUSMAN. Copyright 1939, 1940, © 1965 by Holt, Rinehart and Winston. Copyright © 1967, 1968 by Robert E. Symons. Reprinted by permission of Holt, Rinehart and Winston, Publishers.

for
JANET
with love always

Contents

Plates

BERNHARDT AND THE THEATRE OF HER TIME

Introduction

Eric Salmon

Sarah Bernhardt was born in 1844 and played her first professional rôle in 1862. The theatre of the time was changing, a change more immediately noticeable in Germany and England than in France but ultimately affecting France as well and all Europe. As Douglas Arrell points out in the first chapter of this book, the change was of a very radical kind, involving the abandonment of one theatre aesthetic and the eager adopting of another. Bernhardt, both in the vicissitudes of her own career and in the nature of her temperament and her approach to the craft of acting, provides a particularly fascinating example of the way this change operated and the way it affected individual performers and what audiences expected of those performers. What this present book attempts to do, therefore, is to re-examine Sarah Bernhardt not only as an individual performer but also—and more particularly—in comparison with other performers, other styles and other approaches and objectives in the theatre.

Techniques and practical methods apart, there were actually two main changes going on in the theatre of the nineteenth century. One was the continued movement from classicism to romanticism which had begun in literature in the late eighteenth century and in music and painting in the early nineteenth. The other was the gradual transformation of romanticism in the theatre from the lush and—in retrospect, at any rate—rather simple verities of Victor Hugo to the dark, complex but no less romantic visions of Ibsen, Strindberg, Chekhov and Shaw. The former of these changes Bernhardt literally personified; the latter she helped—inadvertently—to provoke. She began as a classical actress, trained for and attached to a firmly-entrenched and conservative institution—the Comédie Française. Her very first part there was that of Iphigénie in Racine's *Iphigénie en Aulide* and her most famous rôle in the early part of her career was Racine's Phèdre, both of them parts which, until the transformation which Bernhardt began to work upon them, had always been played in the style which Professor Arrell, aptly following Shaw, describes as "palmy" and compares with *bel canto* (as contrasted with more "realistic" singing in the operas of Wagner and the *verismo* school). Bernhardt, if contemporary comment is to be believed (and in this connection Robert Horville's fascinating and important account, in Chapter 2, of the responses of various contemporary critics is invaluable to us), from the very start began the process of romanticising (I mean this word in a strict sense—converting into the romantic mode) the way the great classical rôles were played, thereby effectively changing the plays themselves. This, in certain senses, was a much more drastic change when applied to Racine than was the change, during the nineteenth century in England, in the style of Shakespearean playing. To abandon a purely classical mode in favour of a romantic one in a Shakespeare play is a move with some logic in it since Shakespeare himself is a great romantic and the vision of the world reflected in his plays is a wholly romantic one. But Racine's world-view is classical and to superimpose a romantic style of playing upon him, while it may—and in Bernhardt's case certainly did—produce a marvellously striking theatrical occasion, nevertheless represents a distortion of the central senses of the play. This is the point that Gabriel Boissy was making when he criticised her playing of *Andromaque* in 1873: "it is a character from de Musset or perhaps Marivaux; never from Racine."

Where did it come from, this romantic urge which challenged the spirit of the very plays to which it was applied? Not, of course, from any mere desire to be perverse or "different". It was in the air of the times; the whole cultural climate of the nineteenth century was full of it and Sarah Bernhardt instinctively responded to it and echoed it. And alongside the new, romantic style of playing there was growing up a vast literature of romantic *writing* for the theatre. In this, Bernhardt in the later stages of her career was to find her spiritual home.

Bernhardt, however, though by any ultimate analysis a child of romanticism and not of classicism, retained until quite late in her career something of her classical approach to the theatre's purpose. Though she loved melodrama and a sensation, both on the stage and off, the "purpose of playing" remained for her the creation of that elusive, indefinable quality of "beauty" about which Douglas Arrell talks. Both Robert Horville and Marguerite Coe (in Chapters 2 and 3) emphasize this, especially with regard to vocal quality—the use of verse in the theatre as an incantation designed to convey a sense of beauty, rather than as a statement designed to convey information (and as Horville also points out, she consciously strove for abstract beauty of *posture* also, "introducing into the theatre"—as Professor Horville says—"an aesthetic dimension", the visual counterpart of the *bel canto* of which Douglas Arrell speaks). Perhaps what this demonstrates, however, is that the romantic and the classical apprehensions are always co-existent and that, in any artist or in any work of art, the division between them is a matter of degree and emphasis rather than a matter of absolute definition.

Victor Hugo's famous dictum, in his preface to *Cromwell*, that art must no longer select for its subjects only the consciously beautiful but must combine the beautiful with the grotesque, touching and reflecting and revealing all corners of living experience, is in itself a piece of romanticism, though it does not embody the whole compass of the romantic view. It does, however, sufficiently capture one important aspect of it, namely its sense of desperation, its feeling for the necessity of grabbing and clutching every experience, seizing instantly, on the moment, all phenomena as they bombard the senses and before they and the world slip from the human grasp. English poetry, for example, in the nineteenth and early twentieth centuries is full of this sentiment; a score of examples spring to mind:

One moment in annihilation's waste,
One moment of the well of life to taste;
The stars are setting and the caravan
Starts for the dawn of nothing: oh, make haste!

* * * * *

Now—for a breath I tarry
Nor yet disperse apart—
Take my hand quick and tell me,
What have you in your heart.

Speak now, and I will answer;
How can I help you, say;
Ere to the wind's twelve quarters
I take my endless way.

* * * * *

Look thy last on all things lovely
Every hour. . . .

* * * * *

And all things we have known for beauty here,
All little things fugitive and forgot,
Quick blossoms that have fallen year by year,
Kisses that even the dawn remembered not
All these are now the judgement that we bring
To know the heart of every lovely thing.

Notice the pun in the Housman verse quoted above: "Take my hand *quick*. . . ". The very essence of being alive ("quick") at all subsists in the speed and readiness with which one reaches out one's hand to grasp experience. Here is no aspiration, such as lies at the heart of the classical mode, toward the calm acceptance of eternal truths, no effort to confine oneself within the modest limits of order; the tumult of the blood is accepted as the heart of the matter and is therefore the pivotal point of the experience and, hence, of the poem. Victor Hugo's definition, while it leaves out much that is most typical of and germane to the romantic mode (the glad embracing of melancholy, for example, and the love-affair with death) does accurately reflect this romantic trait of gulping down experience hectically: and adumbrates, both in its implying of this spiritual impatience and in its explicit emphasis on the grotesque, the outline of another characteristic of romanticism—spiritual and artistic extravagance. At its best, this quality leads to Wagner and Richard Strauss, and to some moments in Coleridge and Swinburne; at its worst, it degenerates into Victorian melodrama, Stephen Phillips and Victorien Sardou (and, some would say, the verse melodramas of Victor Hugo!).

Setting aside her temperamental inclinations, Bernhardt's romanticism is, historically speaking, in the direct line of descent from Victor Hugo and Dumas (père et fils). And all too often, it would seem, it ran to the kind of extravagance, both of subject-matter and of presentation, which, far from being breath-taking with an all-embracing beauty, must have been, even at the time, embarrassing to the discriminating. There is, indeed, plenty of contemporary critical comment to this effect. Just as neo-classicism in decay had tended toward mannerism, empty formalism and an over-emphasis on artistic decorums, so romanticism in decay tends to what, roughly speaking, one might describe as the opposites of these—emotionalism, vulgarity, empty spectacle and an over-emphasis on narrative, especially sensational narrative. And to this kind of decline and decadence much of Bernhardt's later work was prone, both as regards the plays she chose to do (many of them written especially for her) and in respect of her production methods and objectives. There can be no denying, I think, that alongside the acknowledged witchcraft of personality and the superbly-controlled technique there was an unmistakable streak of coarseness and triviality. It was this aspect of her work, and similar manifestations in the work of other leading actors and actresses of her time, that pushed the nineteenth-century theatre's spirit of romanticism into new and deeper channels; and it is in this sense that Bernhardt unwittingly helped to provoke reactions (in both senses of that word) which would finally have the effect of bringing to an end the kind and style of theatre that she represented. To what extent this response is attributable to Bernhardt personally is, of course, impossible to gauge but M. C. Bradbrook draws attention to the significance of the fact that, at the very time at which Paris was dominated by Bernhardt and Bernhardt's kind of theatre, that city was also the centre and focus of the new burgeoning of radical alternatives.[1] It was the very strength and popularity of Bernhardt's sort of theatre—represented not only by her but by those other spellbinding actor-managers of the time—which compelled the violence and the totality of the response and it is only logical to suppose that the fervour of the response would increase in direct proportion to its closeness to the provoking force. And, of all that force's exemplars, Sarah Bernhardt was the best known, the most powerful, the most avidly followed. Hence it was (or, at least, *perhaps* it was hence) that Antoine, with his naturalistic theatre, Villiers de l'Isle-Adam and Maeterlinck, with their symbolist plays, and Alfred Jarry, with his surrealism, all either sprang from or had very close connections with the Parisian theatre. It is worth pausing for a moment to contemplate the fact that, though all of these represented a rejection of and a revolt against the Bernhardtian theatre, they also represented—different as they were from each other—extensions of romanticism into other areas of experience and other forms of expression. Naturalism itself, which has often been regarded as an anti-romantic force (and, indeed, advertised itself as such at its onset), is in reality the most complete manifestation of the romantic impulse. So far as it has any real place at all in the sphere of artistic expression (as distinct from a purely polemic, didactic or sociological function), that place is an exceptional and anomalous one. For naturalism, as an artistic convention, makes the pretence that there is no convention at all—it is a form of art which says to its onlooker: "This is not a piece of art; this is, directly and without the interposition of any interpretative pattern or medium, a piece of actuality". That it is therefore a contradiction in terms need not be laboured here. But that it is, of all art's anarchies, the most anarchic does need to be remarked, since that is one of the chief signs of its romanticism. At the opposite pole from classicism's insistence upon form as the essence of meaning is this assertion that art can pretend to be not-art and yet somehow retain its identity. The nineteenth-century dramatists, actors and scene designers who espoused the naturalistic method were driven to it, in their search for new artistic contact with truth and reality, by the falsity and shallowness which had taken hold of and vitiated the older forms of the romantic theatre, but they were not driven away from romanticism itself, only from a particular phase and style of it which had served its turn and, in its turn, had died. The Parisian theatre of which M. C. Bradbrook speaks, and which exercised a compelling and decisive influence on all of Europe (and, therefore, on America) was a romantic theatre in its post-Bernhardt manifestations as it had been in the great Bernhardt's hey-day. But her romanticism decayed, a plum rotten-ripe and ready to drop from the tree. And S. Beynon John, in the brilliant essay which concludes this present volume, demonstrates not only the nature of some of the alternative theories (and practices) of theatre that were a part of the rebellion against this decay, but also the reasons why these responses were of so violent and so extreme a nature. His argument leads us, as he himself remarks, to the point at which we recognize the emergence, from the romantic nineteenth-century theatre, of the different and varied theatre of the twentieth century—a theatre which is also deeply romantic in its main *geste*: but that's another story and another case, and it would be inappropriate to pursue it any further here.

Bernhardt's romanticism, one could almost say, had sociological out-croppings and manifestations as well as artistic ones. She was not simply an actress, a presenter of plays and a re-presenter of characters: she was also the founder of a cult and the head of that cult. In fact, she became in a curious way the *personification* of the cult itself. She assumed the position of queen, of demi-goddess, and she maintained that position by exploiting the practice of the grand star tour, a practice which relentlessly occupied the second half of her life and which neither her greed nor her vanity (though both of these were certainly factors) can wholly account for. Clearly, some force more compelling than either of these drove her to those mammoth exertions and this force, I postulate, was in itself an expression of the romantic outlook of the times. Richard Findlater accounts for it, I think, in his deft comparison of Bernhardt with other "player queens" (Mr. Findlater's own felicitous phrase—and the title of one of his books). She behaved like some outrageous, heroic, larger-than-life character in a novel or play of the high romantic mode. Beginning in London (a visit which J. C. Trewin, with his witty, light, unerring touch, sketches deliciously for us in Chapter 5), Sarah set out to subdue the whole of the western world to her cult—and succeeded, in gargantuan theatrical tours to which two of the contributors to this present volume refer as "royal progresses": Queen Sarah visiting her people and being received with flowers, tears, sighs and verses composed in her honour. Unique, atypical, utterly different from the vast majority of her countrymen (or, for that matter, from the majority of people of *any* country) she, oddly, became in the popular imagination the embodiment of the spirit of her country: she was cast by her adorers in the rôle of La France—and she accepted the part hungrily, as if it were one of those preposterous creations especially written for her. Taking Montreal as his sounding board—a perfect choice: Little France away from France—John Hare neatly provides us, in Chapter 6, with evidence of this sociological marvel.

Bernhardt's exploitation of the mystique of the touring international star, and her elevation of that mystique and its practice to undreamed of heights, invited imitation—and got it. From the date of her first American tour until the gradual decay of the whole touring idea in the twentieth century, it became obligatory for all those who were, or wished to be, considered the leaders of the acting profession to lead their forces forth in long, arduous battles with schedules, trains, managers, audiences and the natural elements in journeys that spanned the continents of Europe and North America and made more than occasional forays into South America, Asia and Australia. L. W. Conolly, in Chapter 10, gives us an interesting account of a British variant of the idea, devised by one of its more distinguished later practitioners. A more direct imitation of Bernhardt, by the French-speaking Belgian actress, Hortense Rhea, who turned herself into an English-speaking American actress, is engagingly discussed by Alan Woods in Chapter 8. But though it was Bernhardt who took and glorified the idea of the great international star on tour, and who profited from it hugely in reputation, cult-standing and hard cash, it was not—as Marvin Carlson demonstrates for us in Chapter 9—Bernhardt who invented the device. This could be said to have been done by Adelaide Ristori (1822-1906), the Italian actress who in the 1850s became Rachel's serious rival in the latter's own native city of Paris. Ristori's tours of the United States became the model for the astute Bernhardt, who realised the potential of the device in a way that Ristori had not done, or had done only embryonically.

Not everyone succumbed to the Bernhardt magic, however; Shaw's high-spirited demolishing of her is well known and is referred to in several of the following chapters. Less well known but equally perceptive (and equally characteristic of their source) are the critical comments of Chekhov on Bernhardt's performances. He first saw her in 1881, when he was twenty-one. Laurence Senelick, in Chapter 7, gives us a generous sampling of the young Chekhov's newspaper articles about the great French actress and uses these effectively to demonstrate the contrasts and differences between the Russian and the French approaches to theatre in the late nineteenth century.

Contrast and difference, indeed, might well be taken as the *leitmotif* of the whole of this book, not only as between Bern hardt's kind of theatre and several other kinds but also within the scope of Bernhardt's craft itself. "Miss Rehan[2], who is coming next week", wrote Shaw on June 22, 1895, "will expose the musical emptiness of Madame Bernhardt's habit of monotonously chanting sentences on one note, as effectually as Duse has exposed the intellectual emptiness of her Magda."[3] But we should not take only Shaw's word; nor only Chekhov's, when he says: ". . . she has none of the spark that alone is capable of moving us to bitter tears or ecstasy." We must also take into account Henri Fouquier's description, quoted by Robert Horville, of Bernhardt's stage presence as "the poetry of an impersonal, mythical being" and Jules Truffier's view of her acting as "a harmony beyond interpretative meaning". Comments of this kind have nothing to do with sociological causes, nor are they responses to Bernhardt's well-known *penchant* for publicity stunts. Fouquier and Truffier—like many others—were responding to Sarah the artist: and at her best she must have been, as all really great actors are (and decent, everyday actors are not), artist as well as craftsman, a creator as well as an interpreter. Even if one mistrusts—as one should—Bernhardt's panache and dislikes her flamboyance, even if one discounts—as one should— the rhapsodical ecstasies of the more sycophantic commentaries, there still remains too much sober, responsible and considered commentary to allow us to believe that her success and her appeal were all only a conscious trading on and delight in a public personality. There was more to it than that. She *was* the kind of woman that Dante Gabriel Rosetti called (and not entirely flatteringly) "a stunner", but she was much else besides. Our purpose in this present volume is to explore the relationship between the art and the craft, between the art and the artist, between the celebrity and the achievement, between the romanticism of Bernhardt's theatre and the expressions of the romantic impulse in other (and, as it turned out, more important and more influential) theatres and theatre forms of the Bernhardt era.

NOTES

1. In a paper called "Paris as the Workshop of Drama in the Bernhardt Era". The paper was read at the Guelph Conference in 1977 but was, unfortunately, unable to be included in this present volume for copyright reasons. It is included in volume 2 of *The Collected Papers of Muriel Bradbrook* (Brighton: Harvester Press, 1982).

2. Ada Rehan (1860-1916), famous American actress, of Irish descent.

3. The chief character in Sudermann's *Heimat (Home)*. In English the play was performed under the title *Magda*.

1

Palmy Days at the Opera: Traditional Performance Style at Covent Garden in the 1890s

Douglas Arrell

On May 21, 1776, after one of David Garrick's last performances as King Lear, the prompter Hopkins noted in his diary:

Human nature cannot arrive at greater Excellence in Acting than Mr. Garrick was possess'd of this Night. All words must fall far short of what he did & none but his Spectators can have an Idea how great he was.[1]

The truth of this last remark is something that theatre historians do not like to admit. We do not like to remember that we are in the position of blind art historians, or tone-deaf musicologists, that the least attentive member of Garrick's audience that night is in a far better position to talk about his acting than are we who have sifted through every scrap of historical evidence on the subject. We can simply never know how great Garrick was. The experience about which we are centrally concerned is forever lost to us.

The frustration is particularly great in the case of actors prior to the mid-nineteenth century because most of us, I think, have a sense that the whole nature of acting has changed immeasurably since then. Not only can we say nothing about the merits of an individual like Garrick, but one becomes more and more aware as one reads the evidence carefully that we do not even understand what the eighteenth century meant by the term "acting". The kind of experience theatre provided in those days is one that is quite foreign to our theatres; there was no doubt as much difference between the Lear of a Garrick and that of a Scofield as there was between the painting of a Reynolds and that of a Picasso. Imagine trying to study the history of art with no paintings available but the works of twentieth-century artists! And yet this is precisely the position of the theatre historian.

In this chapter I would like to present a method for alleviating the frustration of this position that I have personally found useful. Perhaps I should begin by quoting the first paragraph of an article written in 1886 by the young George Bernard Shaw, called "Palmy Days at the Opera":

When old-fashioned people deplore the decadence of the modern theatre, and regret the palmy days of the drama, superstitious ones are apt to take the desirability of palminess for granted, without troubling themselves to ascertain the exact conditions which constituted it. On inquiry, we are led to infer that long runs, elaborate scenery and dresses, efficient performance of minor parts, and prose dialogue, are degenerate; but that prompters, changes of program every night, poster playbills printed in blue color that adheres to everything except the flimsy paper, and "historical" costumes—*i.e.* costumes belonging to no known historical epoch—are palmy. Between the merits of these things, the young London play-goer can hardly judge; for he has no experience of palminess. There are many persons of culture still under thirty who are familiar with the palmy flat, vanishing from the scene with the scene-shifters' heels twinkling at its tail; who have touched the orchestra palisade from the front row of a palmily stall-less pit; who have seen the creations of Shakespeare enter and quit the scene to the strains of Handel; and whose fingers have been a sorry sight after smudging the playbill for three hours. But these experienced critics are from the country, and began their playgoing careers whilst palminess and stock companies still lingered there, as they do, perhaps, to this day. But the West Londoner, who only visits first-class theatres, has only one way of studying palminess. He must go to the opera, where he will soon get quite enough of it to convince him that the theatre in John Kemble's time, when it was carried on much as Italian opera is now, had quite enough drawbacks to reconcile a reasonable man to the changes which have since taken place.[2]

We should note that Shaw's qualifications for making this comparison are remarkably good. He was himself one of those "young persons of culture under thirty" who had had a taste of the palmy school of acting in a provincial theatre where the old methods lingered on. In addition, he had been raised in an environment saturated with operatic music, and he later attended Covent Garden regularly as a music critic. He knew, then, the old style of acting and the contemporary style of opera singing as well as any one man could probably know it. But I believe Shaw's greatest qualification was his schizophrenic artistic sensibility. For while he was one of the creators of the modern theatre, the theatre of Ibsen and Wagner, he had a special appreciation for the theatre which was diametrically opposed to the tendencies of these innovators. This appreciation is exemplified by Shaw's admiration for that provincial barnstorming tragedian, Barry Sullivan, who was certainly one of the last relics of the palmy days, and who in his old age Shaw remembered as one of the greatest actors he had seen:

Such acting I had never seen or imagined before, nor was its impression weakened, when, much later on, I saw the acting of Salvini and Ristori, the last of the great Italians, from whom I gathered what else I know of acting.[3]

Thus Shaw, the arch-modernist, was one of the few of his contemporaries who had any real sympathy for the kind of theatre that the modern theatre was replacing; he was in a uniquely good position to understand the virtues of both the old theatre and the new.

Now as it happens we are in a position even today to know a good deal more about the Covent Garden opera Shaw refers to than we are about the Covent Garden of Kemble. Many of the singers Shaw saw on the stage during his tenure as a music critic were able a few years later to leave to posterity a generous sampling of their artistry in the form of gramophone records. Although to the uninitiated these records seem impossibly dim and scratchy, record collectors know that with patience one can learn to attune one's ear to their low fidelity, and that when one has done so one can be astonished at the living artistic presence they project. Recent advances in the processes of transferring these recordings to modern long-playing records, which now include the use of a computer to compensate for the distortions of the original recording techniques, promise to make the singers of the turn of the century even more vividly accessible to us. We can actually *experience* them in a way that is denied us for the actors of the Kemble or Garrick periods. And what is more, there is no doubt that the experience they provide is unique, extraordinary, something almost as totally absent from the opera house of today as it is from the modern theatre. It is an experience which spontaneously brings to my mind descriptions of Siddons or Kean, and would do so even without Shaw's word that the world of these legendary performers and the world of the opera singers of his time were somehow comparable. If it is indeed the case that there is a remarkable parallel between the theatre of the eighteenth century and the opera of Shaw's time, that in fact the latter was a kind of living theatrical fossil preserving an older theatrical aesthetic, then these recordings are documents of the most valuable kind, since they may provide the theatre historian with some tenuous access to the kind of experience that must have been enjoyed by the audiences of the pre-modern theatre.

The aim of this chapter will be to verify Shaw's perception of the parallel between the two types of performing art. It will begin by examining analytically the resemblance Shaw mentions between the "palmy" theatre of the Kemble or Garrick periods and the opera of his time. It will attempt to describe how the former was transformed into the kind of theatre we are familiar with today, and explain why the opera in England avoided this transformation. Then it will take a close look at Shaw's criticism of opera and demonstrate that the features he singles out for critical blame are precisely the features he attacks also in the palmy theatre, while the quality in opera he praises is that which he admires in Barry Sullivan and other traditional actors. The truly paradoxical nature of Shaw's theatrical sensibility will be revealed when we examine his criticism of the new Wagnerian singing, where he is visibly torn in two directions by his attachment to the virtues of the modern and pre-modern theatres. In the course of this discussion, the justification for regarding Golden-Age opera-singing and classical, pre-modern acting as manifestations of the same performing aesthetic, and the unique features of this aesthetic will, I hope, become clear.

The most significant of the features that Shaw finds to be common to both the late-eighteenth-century theatre and the late-nineteenth-century opera house is the repertory system. Both theatres changed the bill almost every night during their seasons and presented works drawn mainly from a pool of accepted productions built up over the years and well known to their audiences. By contrast, the ordinary theatres of Shaw's time generally relied on the long-run system, in which a single work, a new play or a specially-produced old one, was repeated night after night to audiences who were not expected to be familiar with it. The existence of the repertory system in both the opera and the eighteenth-century theatre indicates a fundamental similarity between them in the nature of their audiences. The repertory system is essentially a theatrical means of coping with a very small potential audience; this audience must be enticed to the theatre very frequently by a constant change of bill, and since it is humanly impossible for a company to produce a constant stream of new works, the productions presented must generally be old ones. It is this small, habitual audience which dominated the eighteenth-century theatre and the opera house that is the key to understanding many of their other similarities. According to Samuel Foote, the canny manager of the Haymarket in Garrick's time, the potential London audience in the mid-eighteenth century was only about twelve thousand and this figure is confirmed by modern research.[4] If we assume an average of 50 percent attendance at the two patent theatres, this figure means that the average playgoer in the eighteenth century must have attended the theatre about once a week. The opera in England in the late nineteenth century had a similarly habitual audience; its primary social function was to serve as what Shaw called a "fashionable post-prandial resort" for the highest levels of society during the London social season, which lasted from mid-April to July.[5] This class maintained its hegemony over the opera by a number of means: high prices, mandatory evening dress, and a subscription system which allowed the same people to take a box for the whole season year after year—their names were inscribed in gold on the box doors.[6] As Harley Granville Barker points out, the eighteenth-century theatre was more like an "unruly club" than a public theatre in the modern sense,[7] and the nineteenth-century opera house atmosphere was also that of a club, though of a more exclusive kind.

A theatre with a small, habitual audience is likely to be a highly conventional theatre. That is to say, it is not likely to be a place in which the audience expects to receive an abundance of new information, as it does in the modern theatre. Rather, it will not expect to see anything that is unfamiliar, anything about whose nature it has not already agreed. This means most obviously that the theatre will use many theatrical conventions—devices whose effectiveness depends on their prior acceptance by the audience, such as soliloquies, blank verse, apron stages and proscenium doors. It means that the audience will recognize certain elements in the performance as important and others as unimportant; it will have learned where to focus its attention. But most important, it will accept as given most of what may be called the *content* of the production, that which in the modern theatre occupies the bulk of our interest. It has agreed upon the stage representation of a king, of a villain, of a chambermaid; it has agreed upon the stage image of grief, anger, love; it has in fact agreed upon the stage representation of Hamlet and King Lear and the other standard characters of the repertoire; it has even agreed on particular details of business, such as the way Lady Macbeth carries her candle in the sleep-walking scene. This agreement is not totally irrevocable, of course; a great actor can make limited changes, as Mrs. Siddons did when she altered the traditional manner of carrying the candle, against the protests of Sheridan.[8] But the tradition, the convention, of such a theatre is not fundamentally altered in spite of a succession of actors whose small innovations seem startlingly "natural" to their conservative audiences.

The true origin of the modern English theatre was the birth of the mass London audience in the early nineteenth century. In 1800, London's population was about one million; by 1850 it had increased to almost four million.[9] At the same time, improving transportation made it increasingly possible for those in the suburbs and provinces to visit the London theatres, and the tourist element became a more and more important factor in London audiences. The effect of this influx of theatrical neophytes was rather like what might be expected in a social club when it is invaded by a body of new members equal to many times the original membership. The convention broke down, in spite of heroic attempts by actors and managers to preserve it, and the theatres fell into disorder. It was not until the 1860s that prosperity returned to the theatre under a completely different system, which bore a relationship to the old system somewhat similar to that of the new mass-production factories to the old craft industries. What the new managers discovered was that traditions and conventions had no meaning to a mass audience; that what this audience noticed was precisely what the old audience took for granted—the content of the performance; and that by making this content new and interesting—not conventional—the mass audience could be attracted to the theatre in a seemingly never-ending stream. Thus, the Bancrofts at the Prince of Wales theatre presented a new play by Tom Robertson in a detailed, realistic *mise-en-scène*, with genteel, unstereotyped acting; Henry Irving at the Lyceum presented a fascinating illustration of a popular story, as detailed and elaborate as an engraving by Gustave Doré. Audiences at these theatres experienced a flood of information about society, about human psychology and about manners, dress and interior decoration. Later, in small experimental theatres all over Europe, a limited section of this audience was exposed to information of a more disturbing kind: new ideas, new insights into the darker corners of human psychology, new criticisms of society. The modern theatre, in both its commercial and its serious or literary manifestations, is founded on this conveyance of new information from stage to audience. Only the opera, which was protected by its special class orientation from the invasions of the mass audience, continued to provide theatrical entertainment of the old conventional kind.

From our modern point of view, then, what strikes us as odd about the eighteenth-century theatre is the audience's relative indifference to the content of the performance; it did not seem to go to the theatre to learn something new. Theatre historians at the turn of the century also noticed this indifference, and it is interesting to note that they often turned to the opera of the period to try to explain the values of the older theatre. In attempting to explain the popularity of the heroic tragedies of the Restoration period, William Archer, for example, reached for an operatic analogy:

We are bound to believe that they must have had, in performance, some element of attraction which is now lost to us. What that element was there can be no question—it was virtuosity in acting, not very different from that of the great singers of today. . . . Imagine a modern actor—imagine even Forbes-Robertson, with his beautiful voice—rendering one of the rants of Almazor, Alexander, or Jaffier as it was evidently intended to be rendered! He could not if he would, and would not if he could. You might as well ask him to go to Covent Garden and sing Verdi's Otello or Wagner's Tristan.[10]

Referring to an eighteenth-century tragedy, Granville Barker says:

One pertinent question remains. How was it that generations of presumably intelligent people were able to enjoy this sort of thing? I think the answer is a simple one. Take, for a parallel, our Italian opera. We enjoy it (those of us that do), if only it is well sung, by some peculiar process of ignoring its obvious absurdities. Audiences, almost to our own day, must have viewed these plays with much the same eyes. The parallel is indeed very close. There was the great actor, as to-day the great singer, and interest was concentrated upon him and upon the fine vocal and emotional effects he could make. The play was so much material for these, and so to be judged.[11]

Compare these statements with a passage from Shaw's writings:

During the career of Mrs. Siddons a play was regarded as an exhibition of the art of acting. Playwrights wrote declamatory parts for actors as composers did for singers and violinists, to display their technical virtuosity. This became an abuse: Wagner was quite justified in his complaint that singers thought only of how they sang, and never of what they were singing. Actors who had learnt how "to bring down the house" with a tirade were quite as pleased when the tirade was trash as when it was one of Shakespear's best.[12]

All three men make the same point: the old actors, like the modern opera singers, were relatively indifferent to the *content* of the plays in which they appeared.

If we examine Shaw's criticism of the performances he saw at Covent Garden, we will see that he often adopts a modernist perspective and attacks them for their indifference to informational content. At the same time we will note how often the conditions he describes can be paralleled with those on the eighteenth-century stage.

The operas Shaw saw at Covent Garden were deficient in informational content above all in that they were familiar; we are no longer as excited by a familiar story, we are no longer as curious about familiar characters, familiar milieux, familiar ideas, as we were when they were new to us, and a theatre in which few works are new to its audience is sure to be a theatre that does not emphasize the values of story, character, milieu and idea. At Covent Garden the foundation of the repertoire was a short-list of favourites of which the audience never seemed to tire—the *Fausts*, *Traviatas*, *Trovatores* and *Carmens* that appeared year after year in the bills. *Faust*, for example, was presented at every single season between the year of its English premiere, 1863, and 1911.[13] And one of Shaw's chief criticisms of Augustus Harris, the manager of the opera season at Covent Garden from 1888 to 1896, is of the "narrow and hackneyed" choice of repertoire,[14] which excluded many great works while presenting familiar ones from which nothing new could be learned.

And, admirably suited as they are to their purposes, the libretti of these works are not high in informational value even to someone exposed to them for the first time. The characters are not deep, the action is not life-like, the language is conventional. What Archer and Granville Barker say of Restoration and eighteenth-century tragedy certainly applies to the libretti of *Lucia di Lammermoor* or *Il Trovatore*. Moreover, they were presented in a language foreign to their audience, and they were not even presented intact. Just as the *King Lear* that Garrick acted was in fact a traditional stage vehicle based on a play by Shakespeare, similarly the *Don Giovanni* and the *Les Hugenots* that Covent Garden audiences heard were not necessarily the works originally created by their composers. Of Meyerbeer's *Les Hugenots*, Shaw says:

Nobody who does not know the score can have any idea of the mutilated state of the work as performed at Covent Garden, or how completely obsolete is the phase of public taste which influenced the mutilators in their choice of cuts.[15]

Often these cuts destroyed the dramatic coherence of the work; even today, Rossini's *Barber of Seville* as presented in many opera houses is dramatically incomprehensible, owing to the cutting of a scene essential to the audience's understanding of the plot. In Shaw's time, the works were further distorted by the addition by the singers of cadenzas and high notes to their arias; the transposition, rearrangement, and cutting of these arias to suit their particular vocal abilities; and the occasional interpolation of completely extraneous songs and ballads into operatic masterpieces. The willingness of audiences to tolerate such traditional desecrations is the result, in part, of their tendency to accept the work as given, not to respond to it freshly as a source of new information.

These values were similarly absent in the production of these works, for here also convention and tradition were dominant. The notion of a coherent production reflecting the unified interpretation of a director was as relatively absent in the nineteenth-century opera house as it was on the eighteenth-century stage. To the dramatic critic who takes such a notion for granted, Shaw says:

How I should like to see him doing six weeks Italian Opera without the option of a fine! There he would find only one period, "the past", and only two places, "an exterior" and "an interior". In costume the varieties might prove more definite and numerous. I have often seen Marta, in which Queen Anne is introduced alive, with the ladies in early Victorian Archery Club dresses, the Queen's retinue in the costume of feudal retainers of the Plantagenet period, the comic lord as Sir Peter Teazle, the noblemen in tunics and tights from Il Trovatore, and the peasants with huge Bavarian hats beneath their shoulders, reminding one of the men in Othello's yarns. As to La Traviata, with

Violetta in the latest Parisian confections, and Alfredo in full Louis XIV fig, that is familiar to every opera-goer.[16]

Although Augustus Harris is credited by historians of Covent Garden with having greatly raised the standard of production there, Shaw frequently criticizes him for the absurdities of his stage management:

He made an initial mistake in engaging five leading tenors and no stage manager. For want of a stage manager, Orfeo was murdered. For want of a stage manager, the first act of Otello was laid waste. For want of a stage manager, Tannhäuser was made a laughing-stock to every German who went to see it, except in the one or two passages which Albani stage-managed. For want of a stage manager, the first scene in Boito's Mefistofele remains so absurd that it is to be hoped that when Edouard de Reszke appears at one of the holes in a ragged cloth, and sends a hearty "Ave, Signor" in the direction of another hole, the audience do not know whom he is supposed to be addressing. For want of a stage manager, no man in Les Huguenots knows whether he is a Catholic or a Protestant; and conversations which are pure nonsense except on the supposition that the parties cannot distinguish one another's features in the gloom are conducted in broad moonlight and gaslight. . . .[17]

It would be wrong to say that Covent Garden audiences cared nothing for production values, for in fact enormous sums were spent on scenery, costumes and supernumeraries. But what Shaw complains of is that these features were treated conventionally; they told the audience nothing about the historical milieu of the drama, the relationships between the characters, the logic of the action. In short, they were another symptom of the opera audience's relative indifference to informational values.

Finally, the performances of the singers themselves were highly conventional:

If Mr. Harris has a fault as an *impresario* it is his too indiscriminate attachment to the traditions of the operatic stage. Instead of making up his mind to a clean sweep of all its barn-storming absurdities, he had cultivated them on the largest scale. He should go to his singers and say gently, "Do not saw the air thus. You think yourselves fine fellows when you do it; but the public thinks you idiots. The English nation, among whom I am a councillor, no longer supposes that attitudinizing is acting. Neither would I have you suppose that all amative young men wear dove-colored tights, and have pink cheeks with little moustaches. Nor is it the case that all men with grown-up daughters have long white beards reaching to the waist, or that they walk totteringly with staves, raising hands and eyes to heaven whenever they offer an observation. The daughters of Albion do not, when in distress, leave off wearing bonnets in the open air, assume mourning, keep their hands continually on their hearts, and stagger and flop about like decapitated geese." And so on. Harris's advice to the opera singers would become more celebrated than Hamlet's to the players.[18]

According to Shaw, some leading artists at Covent Garden seemed to lack "even a superficial knowledge of the stories told in the operas".[19] Their identification with their rôles was never complete, and they were always liable to "come out of a stage faint to acknowledge the applause it evokes",[20] to accept a basket of flowers handed up across the footlights, or to oblige with an encore. They were not even required to look their parts; just as the aged Garrick was accepted by his audience in rôles like Benedick and Hamlet, so the enormously fat Therese Tietjens was accepted as Marguerite in *Faust*, or even in the *travesti* rôle of Leonora in *Fidelio*. All these facts indicate, I think, that the opera audience did not expect the performers to interpret their characters in the way that modern audiences expect modern actors to do; it expected them to do the conventional thing supremely well, and expected relatively little new information about life or about human psychology. And I think most historians would agree that, generally speaking, the audience in the eighteenth-century theatre had similar expectations.

It should be noted that, in spite of his admiration for actors of the palmy school, Shaw criticized them on exactly the same grounds that he attacked contemporary opera singers. Thus Ada Rehan, the American actress, clearly retained more than a touch of the palmy manner, and Shaw expressly compares her to Barry Sullivan. But he criticizes her for her indifference to the content of her vehicles and her isolation from contemporary ideas and culture; as he says: "We admire not what she is doing, but the charm with which she does it."[21] Shaw similarly treats Bernhardt as a representative of the older school of acting, though not, in his opinion, a particularly good one; as in the case of Rehan, he criticizes her for "the commonness and obviousness of the in-tellectual material of her acting",[22] that is, her neglect of infor-mational value. On the other hand, for him Eleonora Duse is the greatest of modern actresses primarily because her acting is uniquely rich in these values.

At this point we can no longer avoid a problem that is central to our discussion. I have said a good deal about what the opera audience did not come to see. But what did it come to see? What positive value compensated it for the deficiencies Shaw de-scribes, which would not be tolerated in a modern performer? Shaw's word for the valuable element in the opera of his time, and in the pre-modern theatre, was "beauty". He was, after all, a member of the generation that produced the Aesthetic move-ment. Shaw never ceased to demand this quality from the per-former; he says that an actor must have:

a sense of beauty—the artistic sense—cultivated to such a degree of sensitiveness that a coarse or prosaic tone, or an awkward gesture, jars instantly on the artist as a note out of tune jars on the musician.[23]

Elsewhere, Shaw writes to Ellen Terry of her reading of a poem:

You brought tears to my eyes, not, you will understand, by the ima-ginary sorrows of the lunatic (sorrow does not make me cry, even when it is real) but by doing the thing beautifully. My whole claim to be a critic of art is that I can be touched in that way.[24]

Similarly, he says in a letter to Janet Achurch:

Anybody can be tragic if they are born so; but that every stroke shall be beautiful as well as powerful, beautiful to the eye and ear; that is what I call art.[25]

There is no doubt that in his dramatic criticism Shaw strongly associates this quality with the older actors, with Barry Sullivan and what vestiges of his style remained on the stage. On the other hand, he frequently deplores the disappearance of beauty among the younger actors; a performer like Janet Achurch, whose pioneer portrayal of Nora in Ibsen's *A Doll's House* made her the best known of the avant-garde actresses, must be exhorted over and over again not to neglect this value: "But Nora may be Nora, and even Norissima—I am not denying that you are Norissima— and yet she may cruelly starve and baffle the artistic appetite— the appetite for beauty and grace."[26]

Thus, for Shaw the virtue of the new theatre is its valuable informational content; it shows us true images of life, conveys provocative ideas, exposes social problems. The virtue of the old theatre is beauty, which does none of these things, but which is somehow valuable nonetheless. If we turn again to Shaw's criticism of opera we find that it is this quality which is the central compensating virtue of the Covent Garden performances, and that it is available there in a way that it no longer is in the ordinary theatres.

The best-known singer of Shaw's time was undoubtedly Adelina Patti; she had been the undisputed queen at Covent Garden in the 1860s and 1870s, and although she now appeared in London only at a few concerts a year at the Albert Hall, she still set the standard of vocal excellence for most opera-goers. Shaw was highly appreciative of some aspects of her singing:

Time has transposed Patti a minor third down; but the middle of her voice is still even and beautiful; and this, with her unsurpassed phrasing and that delicate touch and expressive *nuance* which make her cantabile singing so captivating, enables her to maintain what was, to my mind, always the best part of her old supremacy.[2]

It is to be noted that he praises her for her voice, her technique, her control of the formal aspects of singing; as we shall see, "beautiful" is the word that constantly recurs in this connection. On the other hand, Shaw makes it clear that he finds in her the same deficiencies that he ridicules in most of the opera singers of the period:

If she were a dramatic artist, I should say by all means let her devote herself to Donna Anna, Leonora, and Isolde. But she is not, never was, and never will be. There has not yet been witnessed a dramatic situation so tragic that Madame Patti would not get up in the middle of it to bow and smile if somebody accidentally sprung his opera hat.[28]

The leading artist at Covent Garden in the 1890s was the Polish tenor Jean de Reszke. And Shaw recognized his greatness as clearly as he recognized Patti's. Shaw says of his performances in Massenet's *Werther* and Gounod's *Romeo et Juliette*:

Not a tone nor gesture has a touch of anything common or cheap in it: the parts are elaborately studied and the execution sensitively beautiful throughout, the result, aided by his natural grace and distinction, being in both operas an impersonation not only unflaggingly interesting, but exquisitely attractive. . . . I must admit reluctantly that these performances of Werther and Romeo seem sure of a place in the front rank of my operatic recollections.[29]

But De Reszke was not a good actor as the modern theatre judges actors; as Shaw says, "Except in a character like Romeo, which proceeds on the simplest romantic lines, he creates very little dramatic illusion."[30] Elsewhere, Shaw says:

Though he does everything with a distinction peculiar to himself, there is an exasperatingly conventional side to his posing and playing across the footlights. And though he has the true dramatic instinct, and does really throw himself into his part, yet he is not consistently an actor: for instance, no human being—except perhaps a sexton—ever entered a tomb at midnight in the fashion illustrated by him in the fifth act on Saturday night. . . . The charm of De Reszke lies in the beauty of his voice, his sensitively good pronunciation, and the native grace and refinement of his bearing, all of which make his manliness, his energy, and his fire quite irresistible.[31]

It thus appears that these singers, so admired by Shaw, shared the characteristic approach to acting of their operatic contemporaries; they were conventional rather than freshly interpretative in their approach to their rôles. It was what Shaw calls the "beauty" of their singing that was their chief attraction to their audiences.

By the 1890s a new influence was beginning to be felt in English operatic production that was eventually to modify drastically its traditional aesthetic. The music dramas of Richard Wagner were revolutionary in much the same way that Ibsen's plays were revolutionary; and their increasing invasion of the repertoire was a sign that the values of the modern theatre were beginning to encroach on the opera house. Wagner's works differed from conventional opera in the much greater emphasis they put upon the informational content of the performance. Wagner published his libretti as serious literary works; his devotees found in them the most profound philosophical, psychological, and political ideas. His musical treatment of them was expressly designed to bring new emphasis to the words and to the drama. His complex use of musical *motifs* made it possible for him to give a kind of informational content even to the orchestral parts of the score. And in his search for suitable modes for presenting his music dramas, Wagner brought the techniques of the modern theatre into the opera house; his insistence on the subservience of the singer to the production as a whole, his long rehearsals and detailed *mise-en-scène* designed to reflect faithfully his dramatic intentions, his insistence on a serious, disciplined approach from all concerned, including the audience, his development of his theatre at Bayreuth, which is the prototype of the twentieth-century theatre building with its democratic seating and darkened auditorium, all represented challenges to the conventional mode of operatic production, whose worthlessness (from an informational point of view) Wagner never ceased to denounce.

London held out for a long time against Wagner's influence; it was not until 1892 that a complete *Ring* cycle was presented at Covent Garden; and for it Harris felt it necessary to import singers, orchestra, and productions especially from Germany. This occasion was significant for a number of reasons. For the first time, the house lights were turned out during a performance at Covent Garden, marking the end of another tradition which allied the theatre with its eighteenth-century prototype. But in fact the audience for Wagner was subtly different from the regular Covent Garden audience; there was a special subscription for Wagner, and the breakdown of the old exclusive club-audience had begun. In his history of opera at Covent Garden, Harold Rosenthal notes:

The main body of the subscribers for the German performances was made up of two classes of people who were unable to secure boxes and stalls still largely occupied by "society" for the regular season—city merchants who knew Harris as a Sheriff of London, and the German colony. This new element gradually infiltrated into the Grand Seasons' subscription lists, and so during the period before the first world war there was a subtle change in the character of the opera audiences at Covent Garden.[32]

The upper-class control of Covent Garden may be said to have finally ended after the first world war, when Nellie Melba, one of the greatest of the *bel canto* singers, was outraged to see men in "shabby tweed coats" sitting in the stalls.[33] And perhaps there was more than snobbery in her outrage, for Melba's art, and that of her *bel canto* contemporaries, was inextricably bound up with the old club-like audience at Covent Garden and the destruction of this audience could only mean the end of her school of performing, just as a similar destruction in the early nineteenth century meant the end of the classical school of acting.

Now Shaw was one of Wagner's greatest supporters in England, and some of the latter's increasing dominance at Covent Garden may have been partly the result of Shaw's influence. But a careful reading of his criticism reveals that at least one aspect of the changes attributable to Wagner greatly disturbed him; this was Wagner's influence on singing. The new breed of singers who specialized in Wagner's operas had all the qualities Patti and De Reszke lacked. That is to say, they made an effort to understand Wagner's meaning and convey it to the audience; they were conscientious in their acting and avoided breaking the illusion by acknowledging the presence of the audience; they used their voices to achieve dramatic and emotional as well as musical effects. But they also neglected the perfect vocal beauty that was the aim of the *bel canto* singers. And Shaw, as he sits on the hard seats at Bayreuth and listens to the conscientious declamation of the Wagner singers in *Die Meistersinger*, cannot help sighing "more than once for ten minutes of Covent Garden":

Not, of course, for the Covent Garden orchestra, or the conductor, or the cuts, or the stalls and boxes, or the late hours, or the superficialities, or the general cloudiness as to the meaning of the stage business, or the pointless Italian verse. But I could have borne a stave or two from Jean de Reszke and Lassalle with a tranquil mind. It is true that Herr Gudehus understands the part of Walther much better than De Reszke: he acts with humor and intelligence, and sings by no means without fervor and power. . . . Again, Reichmann gives a more characteristic portrait of the cobbler master-singer of Nuremberg than Lassalle: one, too, much fuller of suggestive detail. . . . But in musical charm neither Gudehus nor Reichmann touched De Reszke and Lassalle, though at every other point they far surpassed them. I wish some man of science would provide critics with a psychology capable of explaining how the same man may sing through an opera like a genius and act through it like a country gentleman; or, conversely, why he may interpret the book like a student and philosopher, and sing through the score like an improved foghorn.[34]

The explanation for this phenomenon is that the two pairs of singers were participating in two different kinds of theatres; De Reszke played in a theatre of convention, where the interest of the audience was not in the informational content of the performance but in some sort of mysterious symbolism of style that Shaw calls "beauty"; the Wagner singers played to an international audience of Wagner devotees, many of whom were interested in no music except Wagner's, for as Shaw observed, "it is possible to cultivate a taste for Wagner without cultivating a taste for music. . . ."[35] In this theatre the values of the modern theatre predominated.

Most of Shaw's energies as a critic of operatic singing are directed toward getting each side to embrace the virtues of the other: that is to say, to get the *bel canto* singers to import informational values into their singing and to get the Wagner singers to sing beautifully. But any such effort must be doomed to frustration since, to some extent at least, the two ways of singing are mutually exclusive. The theatre of convention demands the perfect conformity to acknowledged stereotypes, to the ideals accepted by performers and audience; the modern theatre demands new information which is conveyed by breaking down stereotypes, by showing the individual reality instead of the ideal. Thus, the Wagner singers could not sing perfectly "beautifully" as Shaw demanded and at the same time achieve the fresh insight into the dramatic situation Wagner demanded. The devices a singer uses to be "dramatic"—emotional inflections, word-colouring, speech rhythms—conflict with the perfect legato and inhuman tone demanded by the *bel canto* aesthetic. If it seems to us today that a singer can be both "dramatic" and "beautiful" at the same time, it is because we no longer share the standard of beauty of Shaw and the *bel canto* singers.

It is necessary then to choose between one kind of theatre and the other, and this was a choice Shaw found difficult to make. His critical dilemma in this respect reached a kind of climax near the end of his period as a music critic, when it happened that, at her Albert Hall concerts, Patti chose to sing first a song by Wagner and then the prayer from *Tannhäuser*, startling innovations in her repertoire that indicate how strong the Wagner movement was becoming in England. At the same time, there was another season of Wagner in London, again with imported German artists. Shaw's comparison of the two events is enlightening:

It is a great mistake to assume, as these German artists evidently do, that their rough, violent, and inaccurate singing does not matter.

A very striking proof of this was forthcoming at the last concert at the Albert Hall, where Patti continued her new departure into Wagnerland by singing Elisabeth's prayer from Tannhäuser. Now, if I express some scepticism as to whether Patti cares a snap of her fingers for Elisabeth or Wagner, I may, after all these years of Una voce and Bel raggio, very well be pardoned. But it is beyond all doubt that Patti cares most intensely for the beauty of her own voice and the perfection of her singing. What is the result? She attacks the prayer with the single aim of making it sound as beautiful as possible; and this being precisely what Wagner's own musical aim was, she goes straight to the right phrasing, the right vocal touch, and the right turn of every musical figure, thus making her German rivals not only appear in comparison clumsy as singers, but actually obtuse as to Wagner's meaning.

He goes on to praise Katharina Klafsky, the leading soprano of the German company, for the dramatic power of her singing of Isolde's *Liebestode*, but he adds that

she completely perverted the music by making it express the most poignant grief for the loss of Tristan—the very sort of stage commonplace to which Isolde's sacred joy in the death towards which the whole work is an inspiration, ought to be the most complete rebuke.
If the song were beautifully sung, it simply could not take the wrong expression; and if Patti were to return to the stage and play Isolde, though she might very possibly stop the drama half a dozen times in

each act to acknowledge applause and work in an encore—though she might introduce Home, Sweet Home, in the ship scene, and The Last Rose in the garden scene—though nobody would be in the least surprised to see her jump up out of her trance in the last act to run to the foot-lights for a basket of flowers, yet the public might learn a good deal about Isolde from her which they will never learn from any of the illustrious band of German Wagner heroines who are queens at Bayreuth, but who cannot sing a gruppetto for all that.[36]

This is a highly interesting passage; it suggests, I think, that we have been simplistic in our distinction between "beauty" as the prime quality of the theatre of convention, and "information" as the prime quality of the modern theatre; the implication up to now has been, and I think it is an implication that Shaw himself sometimes deliberately conveys, that "beauty" is something empty, purely formal, purely sensuous, purely decorative, purely escapist. But when forced to compare the same music sung by the two kinds of artist, Shaw cannot deny that there is in some sense more *meaning* in the singing of Patti than in that of the Wagner artists, even though it is devoid of the kind of information we have been talking about—intellectual understanding, psychological insight, dramatic intensity. Patti understands Wagner's "musical meaning", which is something quite apart from his philosophical or literary meaning; this meaning must be expressed in formal terms, and yet it is clearly more than just the making of pretty patterns or the exhibition of virtuosity. It is a kind of meaning scarcely comprehensible to the twentieth century, which, with its objective, scientific bias, can understand by the term "meaning" only informational content.

It was this special kind of meaning that was, I believe, at the heart of the old theatre. It is not something that is captured in the documentary evidence of the eighteenth-century theatres; the spectators themselves rarely separated it from other aspects of their experience. Little can be said about it, except that it seemed highly valuable to many people, valuable enough to compensate them for the lack of many other values that are now the basis of our theatrical aesthetic. This special meaning that Shaw calls "beauty" can be understood only through experience, and this is why the operatic analogy seems to me so useful. The recordings of the "golden age" of singing provide us with an opportunity to experience something that has otherwise almost vanished from the theatrical scene, after centuries during which it was, I suspect, the theatre's *raison d'etre*. These recordings are thus more than a useful touchstone for the theatrical historian; to me they reveal how much the "progress" that has taken place in the theatre is like the progress that has taken place in other aspects of our civilization. It has been progress at the expense of something valuable, but something so intangible that most people do not notice its disappearance even though their lives have been impoverished as a result. And for me the only possible progress that could take place in the theatre now would be in the direction of recapturing some equivalent of this lost value.

NOTES

1. *The London Stage 1660-1800, Part 4: 1747-1776*, ed. George Winchester Stone, Jr. (Carbondale and Edwardsville: Southern Illinois University Press, 1968), p. cxc.

2. Bernard Shaw, "Palmy Days at the Opera", *How to Become a Musical Critic*, ed. Dan H. Laurence (London: Rupert Hart-Davis, 1960), pp. 112-13.

3. Bernard Shaw, "My Way with a Play", *Shaw on Theatre*, ed. E. J. West (London: MacGibbon and Kee, 1959), p. 271.

4. See Harry William Pedicord, *The Theatrical Public in the Time of Garrick* (Carbondale and Edwardsville: Southern Illinois University Press, 1954), p. 16.

5. Bernard Shaw, *London Music in 1888-89 as Heard by Corno di Bassetto (Later Known as Bernard Shaw) with Some Further Autobiographical Particulars* (New York: Vienna House, 1973), p. 179.

6. Bernard Shaw, *Music in London 1890-94*, vol. 1 (London: Constable, 1932), p. 28.

7. Harley Granville Barker, "Coriolanus", *Prefaces to Shakespeare*, vol. 2 (London: Batsford, 1958), p. 297.

8. See Thomas Campbell, *Life of Mrs. Siddons*, vol. 2 (London: Effingham Wilson, 1834), p. 38.

9. See Ernest Bradlee Watson, *Sheridan to Robertson: A Study of the Nineteenth-Century Stage* (Cambridge, Mass.: Harvard University Press, 1926), p. 3.

10. William Archer, *The Old Drama and the New: An Essay in Re-Valuation* (London: Heinemann, 1923), p. 167.

11. Harley Granville Barker, *On Dramatic Method, Being the Clark Lectures for 1930* (London: Sidgwick and Jackson, 1931), p.155.

12. Shaw, "An Aside", *Shaw on Theatre*, p. 224.

13. Desmond Shawe-Taylor, *Covent Garden* (London: Max Parrish, 1948), p. 36.

14. Shaw, "Palmy Days at the Opera", *How to Become a Musical Critic*, p. 115.

15. Shaw, *Music in London*, vol. 3, p. 230.

16. Ibid., vol. 1, p. 97.

17. Ibid., pp. 246-47.

18. Shaw, *London Music in 1888-89*, pp. 102-03.

19. Shaw, *Music in London*, vol. 1, p. 77.

20. Ibid., p. 72.

21. Bernard Shaw, *Our Theatres in the Nineties*, vol. 1 (London: Constable, 1932), p. 184.

22. Ibid., p. 162.

23. Ibid., pp. 212-13.

24. Bernard Shaw, Letter to Ellen Terry (June 24, 1892) in *Collected Letters 1874-1897*, ed. Dan H. Laurence (New York: Dodd, Mead and Company, 1965), p. 344.

25. Bernard Shaw, Letter to Janet Achurch (April 21, 1892), ibid., p. 338.

26. Ibid.

27. Shaw, *Music in London*, vol. 3, pp. 3-4.

28. Shaw, *London Music in 1888-89*, p. 270.

29. Shaw, *Music in London*, vol. 3, pp. 242-43.

30. Ibid., vol. 1, p. 173.

31. Shaw, *London Music in 1888-89*, pp. 148-49.

32. Harold David Rosenthal, *Two Centuries of Opera at Covent Garden* (London: Putnam, 1958), p. 247.

33. John Hetherington, *Melba: A Biography* (London: Faber, 1967), p. 198.

34. Shaw, *London Music in 1888-89*, pp. 191-92.

35. Shaw, *Music in London*, vol. 2, p. 266.

36. Ibid., vol. 3, pp. 267-68.

2

The Stage Techniques of Sarah Bernhardt

Robert Horville
(translated by Eric Salmon)

Admiration always tends to have a purifying effect. Posthumous fame scours those whom it touches of the imperfections which ordinary life showed up in broad daylight. The image of Sarah Bernhardt which has gradually emerged has been especially subject to this rather mystifying kind of distortion. Crowned with the halo of her legend, she has become a veritable myth. Hidden under eulogy, often of a retrospective kind, her stage technique is represented as perfect, proclaimed as incomparable, and is seen only as a part of this general myth, which does not allow the examining and savouring of details. The purpose of this chapter is to contribute toward the restoring of a detailed understanding of the dramatic technique of this great actress, to bring it back to a reality from which the mystique has been stripped by emphasising, certainly, the positive elements which characterise that technique but in no way ignoring the negative aspects. To achieve this, I have carefully avoided second-hand evidence and have referred exclusively to documents of the period, to actual responses recollected the day after the performance, or to considered commentary, actual recollections, reports of actual experiences.

A WOMAN OF THE THEATRE

Before going on to analyse the playing of Sarah Bernhardt, it is necessary to emphasise the link which will over and over again be noticed between her private life and her professional practice. I will not labour the theatricality of her behaviour—the many stories, many times repeated: those are part of the legend. They certainly demonstrate the extent of her commitment, but they are subjects to be treated with a measure of caution. The sincerity of her motivation may appear doubtful: what is the right place to give to the publicity for which she was so avid? Similarly, we will quickly pass over her *fondness* for performance. Suffice it to say that she continued to appear after her amputation and practically to the end of her life, when she was almost eighty years old and gravely ill. And yet, as to the real motive for continuing to act, she gave a purely materialistic reason—the obligations of her way of life rapidly exhausted her means, which made the continuing of her profession essential.

What seems to me more important is the enduring interest she had in every aspect of life in the theatre. All her life she wanted to have the right to supervise everything that went into the presentation of a play. In 1890, on becoming the director of the *Théâtre de l'Ambigu*, then in 1893 as the director of the *Théâtre de la Renaissance* and finally in 1898 as the director of the theatre which bore her name, she showed her determination to make herself mistress of the entire instrument of production and of administration. The part she played in that connection was not an imaginary or fictitious one. It was she herself who recruited the actors of the company; it was she herself who organised the tours. And Béatrix Dussane, on the day of Sarah's death, said with good reason " . . . we have lost a unique producer, a powerhouse of energy. . . ".

An indefatigable organiser, she was determined to have the right to supervise the choice of plays to be performed. This is one of the most important influences on the course of her career and on her technique. She was reproached often, during her lifetime, for her controversial choices. Her taste for melodrama is evident and it is certain that her talents were sometimes misapplied, a misapplication that was disguised by ephemeral acclaim for a work of no great merit. Thus, in his review of the first performance of *Médée* by Catulle Mendès, J. Gascogne wrote on October 29, 1898, in *La Libre parole*: "I imagine that if Mme. Bernhardt, instead of the mediocre love scene which she has played twenty times in twenty different plays, had spoken one page of Euripides, she would have given herself the greater challenge and given us the greater artistic satisfaction." Similarly, on March 27, 1923, the day after her death, Claude Farrère, in *Le Gaulois*, expressed the following opinion of *La Dame aux camélias*: "And the genius of the interpreter made up for the feebleness of the work interpreted", while Edmond Sée, in *L'Oeuvre*, confirms in a more general way: "She deceived us as to the value of a text and often immersed herself in the fleeting fame of mediocre works, as well as matching her talent to the great masterpieces." And one could, indeed, draw up a long list of mediocre plays—obviously, frankly, bad plays—in which she appeared. Her lack of judgment, it seems, did not stop there. She often made errors of casting. In *L'Eclair* of December 17, 1897, an anonymous critic notes after the dress rehearsal of Octavius Mirabeau's *Mauvais Bergers*: "Mme. Sarah Bernhardt, whose great talent we admire, is never at ease in her part: the great tragic actress wears the peplum better than the modest dress of the working woman". Apparently, the simplicity of the character she was representing hardly suited her. Referring to her interpretation of *L'Aiglon*, Maurice Ordoneau remarks rather cruelly in *La Libre parole* of March 16, 1900: "In spite of her success, it is impossible not to be struck by the difference between the age of the actress and that of the character. There is no reason why Mme. Sarah Bernhardt should not next play the part of Louis XVII".[1] Clearly, in spite of the flattering assertions concerning her eternal youthfulness, to play, at the age of fifty-six, the part of a young man, showed a certain insensitivity. This absence of artistic taste Sarah Bernhardt herself draws attention to—in spite of herself—elsewhere, when she declares in 1912 to an English journalist: "For myself, with the exception of Hamlet and L'Aiglon, I have no preference for one rôle in my repertoire above another": thus much is evident; the two exceptions to which she chooses to draw attention show that she put on the same plane major works and minor creations.

These notions of Sarah Bernhardt's had, furthermore, disastrous consequences on the building-up of her repertoire. To be played by her was the measure of success. Consequently, authors strained their wits to write for her, conforming in every possible way to her tastes, as if she herself had written the work in her own handwriting. She altered entire passages, as is demonstrated by a story told by Yvonne Lanco. After reading a manuscript of Edmond Rostand's, she impulsively said to him: "My dear, your play pleases me greatly but it is absolutely essential that you change some of the verse. You must understand that it is I, Sarah Bernhardt, who have to speak these lines."

Attentive to the text, she was equally so to the details of production. She took active part in the scene designing. Joseph Galtier, after watching a rehearsal of *Varennes*, remarked on March 2, 1892 in *Le Temps*: "The designers listen to her opinions, her comments which show incomparable experience of stagecraft. Sarah Bernhardt notices everything, controls everything." If she had not always time to take note of the experiments of other companies, she nevertheless favoured the rethinking and renewal of theatrical ideas. Alberty, a reporter for *Le Figaro*, put this question to her in October 1890: "With regard to stage presentation, what do you think about the Théâtre Libre?", to which she replied "I do not think anything about it. I confess that I have never set foot in it. But anything that can be done by way of reacting against the routine in which our theatre is engulfed seems to me laudable and deserving of encouragement." And, on occasion, she made her own contribution, either in original ideas or in putting into practice some useful, if not essential, modifications. In 1893, for the production of *Les Rois* at the Théâtre de la Renaissance, she suppressed the claque and removed the prompter's box. In an interview given on August 17, 1894, to *Théâtre et la critique*, she spoke out against the custom of the open dress rehearsal, which she considered humiliating, declaring unequivocally: "I'll tell you this, in any other country in the world one would see nothing like this. The critics are there among the audience at this first performance. They judge with that audience, condemn with that audience or forgive with that audience. Any theft can be committed—for I cannot find any other name for the indiscretions of which we are too often the victims. I am, therefore, in favour of the total suppression of the open dress rehearsal."

Only one sphere of activity really defeated Sarah Bernhardt—the training of actors. Certainly she taught several times at the Conservatoire but this teaching was temporary only and did not, it seems, bear much fruit. It is true that she promised to write an instruction manual for young actors, but she did not carry out this project. Certainly, her playing exercised some influence on her contemporaries and Francisque Sarcey commented, significantly, in *Le Temps* of August 2, 1888, in regard to the interpretation by Melle Sisos in *L'Aveu*: "The great artist has taught her the secret of her postures, her gestures and her cries . . . "; but numerous critics frequently noted the mediocrity of members of her company. It must be acknowledged: it seems that the thankless task of teaching did not much interest her.

BERNHARDT'S ACTING STYLE

Having thus shown Sarah Bernhardt's place in theatre organisation, let us define in depth the nature of her style of acting. Her attitude with regard to tradition constitutes a particularly important element at a time when to respect the intentions of the dramatists of the past was considered an essential. Now Sarah Bernhardt repudiated tradition with a constancy which she never went back on in the whole of her career. On June 16, 1899, in a letter addressed to the editor of the *Daily Telegraph*, replying to criticisms of her interpretation of Hamlet in London, she wrote: "But where is tradition? Each actor brings his own tradition with him." Later, in 1907, the year in which she became a teacher of elocution at the Conservatoire, she reiterated: "In the first place, I will fight what is called 'Tradition'. A teacher of elocution should, in my view, develop the character of her student and if she tries to suppress or change him she makes a dangerous blunder, for she deprives this student of his personality, that is to say, the essential motive-power of his future talent. . . . Similarly in a classical play, I have a horror of tradition, of a tradition narrow and outworn. Every actor assumes the character of the rôle he is playing and lives it, then interprets it in accordance with his own experience and his own talents".

And, in fact, the responses which she elicited fully proved the originality which she tried to give to her parts. Her revivals of the great classics did not always command universal admiration. The British public disapproved of her interpretation of Hamlet, and the catcalls which marked the *première* of *Andromaque* are equally significant, as are the words of the writer Gabriel Boissy, expressing his disapprobation: "Now a Hermione as frivolous, capricious, decadent as she is . . . is a character from de Musset, or perhaps Marivaux; never from Racine. It is a boudoir Hermione."

Such innovations had, it seems, their limits. They are interesting mainly so far as they affect the actual purposes of the acting itself which, according to witnesses, had little of the revolutionary in them. Sarah Bernhardt's contribution in this sphere was, in fact, on the one hand, to bring plays back to life by the use of new details in technique and, on the other hand, to develop to perfection a style already well-tried, the direct descendant of Romanticism, which will make Robert de Souza say, on the day after her death: "Neither in speech nor in movement was she a great innovator, nor did she seek to dominate fashion, to impose a new concept on the public. . . . Her decorative methods, moreover, were out-of-date thirty years ago, facile methods of a broadly romantic kind."

If Sarah Bernhardt did not, as it seems, introduce anything essentially new into her acting style, she did, on the other hand, marvellously diversify existing techniques. At the cost of ceaseless work, she tried always to discover the device which would most faithfully render the sense of the text; and of her real objective Tristan Bernard said, on the day after her death: "She searched ceaselessly, she made her début over and over again." She always did her utmost to avoid falling into stereotype. Often finding herself, by the very nature of her rôles, in identical dramatic situations, she varied almost infinitely the ways of handling them. A specialist in theatrical deaths, she died each time in a different way, to the great admiration of the audience, as Emmanuel Arène, at the end of a performance of *Adrienne Lecouvreur*, wrote ecstatically, though a little naïvely, in *Le Figaro* on April 4, 1907: "And it is remarkable that after being 'dead' so often and in so great a number of parts, Madame Sarah Bernhardt, at this stage in her artistic career, can still find new devices in herself and show us a way of dying that we did not know before." Moreover, she succeeded in offering two different versions of the same passage, thus demonstrating the strength of her imagination. Martin Gale, after having attended two successive performances of *La Dame aux camélias*, confirms this when he writes, on April 15, 1899: "What an admirable artist, this Sarah, who makes us weep thus, two evenings in succession, with the same words, the same phrases and yet gives me the sensation that she is a different woman the second day from the one I saw the first! . . . When the dying Marguerite lets the mirror fall, it breaks. The first evening, Sarah, leaning on the table, without gathering up the pieces, looked at it with terror and spoke to it as if from far away, leaving the world. This evening, kneeling down slowly, she goes right up to it, her outstretched hand trembling, and collects the pieces with infinite care."

This kind of stage practice raises a problem regarding the commitment of Sarah Bernhardt to the characters she plays. What is the proper place, according to her, for spontaneity and for restraint, for instinct and for deliberation? If one directs one's attention to certain of her pronouncements, one gets the impression of a fanatical actress, of a *monstre sacré* totally possessed by the characters she creates. In an interview given to the *Petit journal* on October 9, 1921, she states: "Our tears flow freely and are sincere and often the last sob still weighs on us when the play is over. Our laughter is real and sometimes has sorrow to soften its clamour". In *Le Figaro* of March 30, 1923, Robert de Flers reports the following words in the same strain: "I am still active, but I have almost died in all my stage deaths [see Plate 5]. Sometimes, at the end of a performance, it has taken me more than an hour to return to life. My heart was hardly beating at all; I was scarcely breathing. . . . But I had preserved that element of will that was needed for me to take hold of life again". This must have been an exhausting procedure, a sort of semiconscious state which enabled Sarah Bernhardt to live in actuality that which was only a fiction. This sense of being "carried away" she confirms elsewhere, as a matter of fact, when she tells this amusing story in which she crosses swords with Mounet-Sully: " 'In *Hernani*, when I throw myself on you, crying "You are my superb and noble lion", make up your mind to catch me and keep me: you know how violent I am on stage; you hold me so slackly that one day you will let me fall.' Well, I was right! I throw out my arms before me and Mounet, who is thinking of nothing but his own appearance, catches me so badly that I chuck myself on the ground"—an actress driven by an uncontrollable violence which led to thoughtless, unconsidered actions.

This confusing of real life with fictional life seems to be corroborated by Félicien Champsaur in a story, published in *Le Figaro* of November 26, 1887, about a rehearsal of a play by Victorien Sardou: "She enters, for example, raging: 'Wretch, you have deceived me!' . . . It is quite a scene; she scorns the script and plays from memory, sometimes finding words more precise, clearer, recalling the details of an old love-affair of yesterday. Often, she discovers in this way a particularly felicitous gesture, sprung from her own experience, or a particularly admirable phrasing." It seems, therefore, that she employed the technique of improvisation, giving her imagination full rein, submerging the character to be played in her own personality. She had a tendency to repeat her rôles endlessly, blending them with each other or blending them with herself. It is this that Gabriel Boissy reproaches her with when, in regard to *Andromaque*, he complains: "The basic fault of Madame Sarah Bernhardt is in never adapting herself to a rôle but adapting the rôles to herself and playing herself all the time. Her interpretation is of value only if there is some point of correspondence between her own experience and that of the character."

It is not surprising, in these circumstances, that personal ties grew up between the actress and her audience. Sarah Bernhardt felt an almost bodily passion towards what she called this "Beloved Monster". She was sensitive to the atmosphere of the house, modifying her performance, almost unconsciously, according to its reactions, according to the state of mind which she instinctively perceived. Thus, she discloses in 1899 in *La Vie illustrée*: "When I sense that the audience is benevolent and kind, ready with its applause, I surrender myself entirely, with tenderness, with love, with recognition, finding that even then I do not give enough of myself. On the other hand, when I feel them to be hostile . . . I act defiantly which, personally, does not displease me; however, if my playing gains in power from this, it loses in grace and above all in consistency". As for the audience, they joined in, they identified themselves with her. This is a far cry from what will much later be known as Brechtian "alienation": the audience vibrates with the actress, to whose magic they surrender, feeling in themselves the sentiments which she gives to the characters she is playing. The expression of personal opinions many times repeated leaves no doubt on the subject: Reynaldo Hahn, concerning her Phèdre, writes "In watching it, one felt penetrated by a coldness which numbed the whole body"; in 1896, an anonymous critic, speaking of her interpretation of Lorenzaccio, finds it "wonderful from beginning to end"; Emmanuel Arène, in *Le Figaro* of April 4, 1907, notes, in describing her Adrienne Lecouvreur, "The death of Adrienne, in Maurice's arms, surrounded by his friends and hers and her repentant sister, was a scene of extreme emotion . . . which made the whole of an agonised house shudder as if in very truth a dying creature really lay before it"; Madeleine Zilhardt, in *Le Jour* of March 24, 1931, recalling the performance of *Rome vaincue*, remarks " . . . her accent and her gestures were truly touching"; it is Colette who, in the *Paris-soir* of October 24, 1938, relates how the performances of Sarah Bernhardt, when she created them for the first time, "inhibited both judgment and, almost, the sense of hearing".

But, and such is the paradox of the actor, this exaltation did not prevent Sarah Bernhardt from mastering her craft. She was trained to be a conscious artist. And the critics insist with enthusiasm on the control which accompanied the passionate outbursts. This coherent frenzy La Bargy described well when, in *Le Gaulois* of March 29, 1923, he emphasises: "Though intoxicated, she remains lucid in her intoxication. She is frenzied, but yet within the bounds of logic, style and clarity." Robert de Souza confirms this: "She designed and worked on her rôles within the scope of the text, without losing the intensity of life", while an anonymous critic in *L'Intransigeant* of November 8,

1893, points out, in his account of the first performance of *Les Rois* "her methods and her theatrical skill". An anecdote told by Sarah Bernhardt herself witnesses elsewhere to this presence of mind which was hers during a performance. Playing in Voltaire's *Zaïre*, she was sufficiently lucid to notice that the false nose of the actor Martel was about to melt and to whisper in his ear: "Look out, your nose is running and it's dropping on me!"

Incontestably, Sarah Bernhardt was in control of her technique. The reproach that she always played herself seems a little excessive. In actual fact, she studied her rôles with great care and it was her gift to be able to know how to adapt her own powerful personality to the psychological demands of those rôles. Ludovic Fert makes clear this complex aspect of her style when he writes, in 1912, in *Le Gaulois du dimanche:* "What characterises Sarah Bernhardt's art is its diversity, the range of her shades of meaning, the extraordinary strength of her slightest accentuation, gesture or glance, her inspired understanding of all characters, all psychologies, the dramatic strength and the seductive force . . . which makes her always herself while being the character." She immersed herself in a profound study of the script she was to play and in the author's intentions. The realisation of her rôles was preceded by a thorough analysis which was most detailed, as is shown by the following letter which she wrote to the editor of the *Daily Telegraph* on June 16, 1899, replying to criticisms which had followed her playing of Hamlet: "I am reproached for being too lively, too manly. . . . I know that Hamlet is a scholar. . . . I am reproached for not being stunned and frightened enough when I see the ghost; but Hamlet went expressly to see the ghost, he went looking for it. . . . I am reproached for not being courteous enough to Polonius; but Shakespeare makes Hamlet say all sorts of stupidities to Polonius. . . . I am reproached for coming too close to the king in the chapel scene; but, if Hamlet wishes to kill the king, it would be necessary for him to get close to him." These are obviously common-sense comments which underline the interest which the actress took in the exact meanings of texts to which she had every intention of being faithful—to which she intended, with precision, to devote her playing.

APPEARANCE, GESTURE, POSTURE AND BEHAVIOUR

Having defined the general aspects of Sarah Bernhardt's playing, having underlined, to some extent, her basic principles, we pass on now to examine more precisely her actual technique, all those details which make it possible to construct a picture of the great actress's behaviour on the stage.

Her physical appearance exercised a not inconsiderable influence on her manner of playing and on her choice of repertoire. Her demeanour, on stage as well as off, was at one and the same time majestic and statuesque. But rather than sketch a portrait of her which is only more or less accurate, it would be better to quote Théodore de Banville who, in *La Lanterne magique*, describes her in these terms: "She is the only actress that the Sculptor has made expressly to practice the art of acting, for she is as tall as Rosalind and thin enough to wear any costume! Moreover, she is so well-equipped to give expression to poetry that, even when she is immobile and silent, one feels that her movement, like her voice, obeys a lyrical rhythm. A Greek statue, wishing to symbolise Poetry, would choose her for a model. A real actress should be able to play Juliet and Lady Macbeth, Iphigenia and Eriphile, Chimène and Pauline, and consequently should be neither blonde nor brunette. So Sarah Bernhardt, with her beautiful Dutch colouring, is neither blonde nor brunette; for her hair is blonde if she moistens it and brunette if she pomades it! And, moreover, it is so naturally curly, wavy and frizzy, a perfect mop and a goddess's sublime mane, like the hair of Diana of Poitiers entangled by Jean Goujon,[2] in which there is no room to poke a finger or plant a pin for the purpose of imposing the most elegant and complicated of coiffures. What a pity that Heinrich Heine did not know her when, in *Atta Troll*,[3] he painted his Herodias! With what love he would have copied her face for the Queen of Cappadocia or a Nereid who dreams of sea-pearls, her tiny face with its soft and shining skin, her eyebrows rather close together and bushy towards the bridge of the nose, her dark blue eyes very widely set and open a little, usually langorous but, when she is excited, alert and darting like black diamonds; and the pupil unusually small which, when the actress speaks in irony, seems to shoot from her eye and pierce you; the nose Jewish but nevertheless very charming because of a narrowing of the nostril which looks as if it were suspended from the little boss which is in the middle of the nose and which indicates both a poetic and combative nature; not forgetting the determined, resolute chin, the charming mouth with the thin red lips which allow a glimpse of a magnificent and terrible dazzle of white teeth! And to the end of time the image of Sarah Bernhardt will be evoked when Ruy Blas says 'She wore a little crown of silver lace!' " This is a very long quotation, but it does give us a good starting-point for our study of the acting style of Sarah Bernhardt and draws attention, in fact, to the most significant aspects of that style. Granted, it idealises them; but closer analysis will enable us to strip from them the veneer with which it covers them.

Théodore de Banville emphasises, in the first place, the slimness of the actress. He takes note only of the positive aspects of this. They are incontestable: elegance, a distinction the results of which constitute, theatrically speaking, trump cards which cannot be ignored. This physical characteristic also allowed the actress to be comfortable in every kind of costume. Continuing the same even into old age, this slenderness of body explains also the continued appearance of youth that never ceased to astonish her contemporaries and which enabled her for a long time to create characters in the prime of life. But, unfortunately, this slenderness verged on emaciation, as is shown by the numerous more or less cruel anecdotes about her which were circulated. It is Aurélien Scholl who tells this one: "An empty carriage draws up in front of the Théâtre Francais—and Sarah Bernhardt gets out." In *Le Trombinoscope* of September 1874, there appeared this rather witty sally: "Since Mlle. Bernhardt went to consult her doctor . . . her friends no longer call her the sculptured bone"; or again, the remark according to which she was no more substantial than the shadows of the other actors. It seems clear that this attitude to her was often hurtful. Particularly at the beginning of her career, it prevented her from asserting herself. Her bearing on stage must have been affected by it and there was no lack of those who criticised this extreme thinness. Félix Duquesnel, in *Le Gaulois* of March 2, 1911, confirms definitely that this physical trait constituted for a long time a real handicap for the actress: at the time of her engagement at the Odéon in 1866, Chilly had found "that she was thin with a tiresome thinness"; in February 1868 on the occasion of the first performance of Alexander Dumas's *Kean*, it was similarly noted "It is a pity that she isn't more plump", while the author of the play writes, not without humour, "It is like a virgin's head on top of a broomstick"; and the critic himself comments, in the same way, "I would add that she was adorably pretty but with arms so thin ('arms of a skeleton' she herself said) that her sleeves had to be made in a special way so as to hide them as much as possible." And one may assume that this lack of substance was one of the factors which influenced this adverse comment of Francïsque Sarcey in *Le Temps* on one of her first rôles, in Scribe's *Valérie:* "That Mlle. Bernhardt is inadequate is no great matter. She is making her début and it is natural that among those presented to us for the first time there should be some who turn out poorly." To be sure, Sarah Bernhardt, gaining confidence on the stage, gradually forgot this deficiency, but she never erased it entirely. On May 22, 1899, after the first performance of *Hamlet*, a critic noted again: "Slender and sinewy in her black costume, Sarah Bernhardt gives the impression of a Hamlet in miniature. In vain she tries to make us forget that her body is too frail for the violence of her gestures and the power of her voice. She only succeeds by such exasperating measures in creating misunderstanding"; apparently in this instance she did not "give it enough weight"—in the literal sense of that phrase. And we will have occasion to notice that this slimness was not without unfortunate consequences even on her voice.

Of her slimness she nevertheless learned by experience to make an essential element of her acting. Théodore de Banville emphasises that her technique owed a good deal to the art of the sculptor. She excelled, in the playing of a character, in giving her a faultless beauty of physical form, in introducing into the theatre an aesthetic dimension. It was not by accident that Edmond Rostand called her "the queen of posture". She exploited marvellously the effects of the draping of costumes to freeze a single moment in a pose marked by harmony and nobility. The stock examples which we hear about witness eloquently to this aspect of her playing. In *Phèdre* (see Plate 2), the folds of her gown cunningly arranged, she kept her body turned to the right, tall and slim, with her two hands stretched to the front. In *Adrienne Lecouvreur*, thrown down on a sofa, she held her arms wide apart, like a cross. In *Judas*, dressed once again in a long robe, a staff in her left hand, she held an ample gesture to the right with the other hand. The critics, the same ones who had regarded her with little favour, were unanimous in discovering her mastery of physical postures. And the frequent reference to statuary shows that this habit of basing her rôles on the perfection of physical form was, with her, an invariable practice (see Plate 8). Reynaldo Hahn comments thus on her creation of Phèdre: "Her entrance, alone, is one of the most beautiful things in the world that it is possible to see; for all that which is purest and most elegant in sculpture is combined here with the bodily ravages which the torments of love can inflict on a human being: it is Beauty beautified by Suffering"; or, again, Robert Kemp, in the newspaper *Liberté* of March 28, 1923, recalls, with reference to the same play, "You remember how she entered, drooping, in the arms of her women? The white veils about the pliable body arranged themselves in beautiful folds, that body of which every posture was expressive, every gesture harmonious and of a grace to ravish a sculptor." The same year, Robert de Souza expressed this sense of beauty in another way when he wrote " . . . she had a unique understanding of her rôles, without which they never come to life and she had at her command all the physical gifts, combining the strange with the remarkable in a way that made physical attractiveness express personality. This beauty asserted itself by the authority of gesture and posture, by precision combined with amplitude."

As Théodore de Banville explains, her appearance was imposing and regal. She used this freely, which explains her predilection for royal characters. Formal clothes suited her and she heightened her various rôles with a sumptuous figure in ceremonial dress. In *La Fronde* of March 16, 1900, Jane Misme notes, in relation to her rôle in *L'Aiglon*: "At one moment, posed in her white uniform, arms towards the clear night sky at Wagram, she makes an unforgettably beautiful impression." In a more general way, René Doumie, in *Les Débats* of October 3, 1896, says "in her manner of wearing costume, a very lively sense of the artistic." The anonymous critic of *L'Intransigeant* of November 8, 1893, emphasizes the same point when he writes, after the performance of *Les Rois*: "Wilhelmina is the personification of the ideal queen, chaste, courageous, beautiful. . . . Wilhelmina—that is, Sarah Bernhardt—is beauty, honour, distinguished appearance, vigour and passion: a great tragic actress . . . with a grandeur of presence."

Sarah Bernhardt, through this stylized approach, sometimes introduced a religious dimension, gave the performance an aspect of solemn observance. She herself, moreover, recognized this influence when, in an interview given to *Le Figaro* in October 1890, she states: "It is to the church and only the church that I owe my being in the theatre. Even as a child, my imagination was struck by ecclesiastical chants, the contemplative attitudes of the congregation, the mystical quality of the ceremonies, the solemn silence with which one listened to the priest." She unconsciously gave to her stage pictures a religious significance; in *Le Journal* of March 21, 1923, an anonymous critic recalls "her taste for hieratic postures"; commenting on the performance of *Vitrail*, Pierre Varenne notes on January 15, 1921, "She seems motionless, revered, a Byzantine saint laden with jewels, surrounded by incense." But she did not always manage to avoid *l'imagerie d'Epinal*.[4] Paradoxically, her asceticism was sometimes accompanied by over-elaborations of form which gave a baroque connotation to the work. Nobility a little encrusted with tinsel, perfection of form hidden beneath surface appearance, which did not, however, much weaken the imaginative strength of the whole. Colette, in the *Paris-Soir* of October 24, 1938, emphasises this apparent contradiction when she reminds us: "She played one of those plays which owed its continued existence to her. A play with cuirasses, with plumes, with torches, a play in which Sarah was girdled in Gallic-Roman jewellery, gold embroidery, opals, or covered in Renaissance brocade, wreathed in Merovingian cabochons;[5] she was resplendently anachronistic. I saw her, her tallness, the gold of her upper lip, the upward glance—

ecstatic and of the colour of azure water, her leonine nose, the red waves of her hair, inhibited in me both judgment and, almost, the sense of hearing."

Religious intensity did not exclude, to any extent, a very human sensitivity. Pierre Varenne concludes his analysis of her playing in *Vitrail* by giving himself up to this significant reflection: "Divine? Oh no: much better—human. . . . " The lyric tone borders on the epic tone. She rouses admiration; she also provokes pity. If pomp is a mode of which she often made use, she equally used the many-shaded colourings of melancholy, of complaint. She excelled in poetic evocations done in half-tones. Speaking of her performance in *Ruy Blas*, Jules Truffier wrote in 1881 in *Conferencia*: "Moreover, the whole rôle of Maria de Neubourg, like that of Doña Sol, seemed hewn out of the lyrical talent of the blonde fairy which was Sarah in 1872. What a bewitching sight was this melancholy queen with her limpid eyes awakened, by the lightning-flash of love, from the sombre torpor into which they had been plunged! What plaintive dignity in Sarah's noble and harmonious movements—making all the stronger the passionate and violent outbursts which followed!" On March 29, 1893, after a performance of *Phèdre*, Bertin confirms: "In all the scenes in which the rôle is gentle, melancholy, plaintive, or touched with an ardour which one feels but which does not break forth, Mme. Sarah Bernhardt is, as on former occasions, exquisite." On January 28, 1894, Henri Fouquier went one better in *Le Figaro* in regard to *Izéil*: "What makes the greatness of this artist, and which I have never more clearly seen than this evening, is the mixture in her of the poetry of an impersonal, mythical being with an almost frightening precision of movement" (see Plate 9). In *Les Débats* of October 3, 1896, René Doumie similarly notes this synthesis of "passion and poetry" which characterizes her playing, while J. Gascogne expresses the opinion, in his notice of *Médée* in *La Libre parole* of October 29, 1898: "Mme. Sarah Bernhardt was incomparable in her charm, her passion and her voluptuous tenderness." The subtle amalgam of the metaphysical with the human, of the brilliant declaration with the oblique innuendo, explains this actress in tragedy. And one can without hesitation subscribe to Nozière's eulogistic evaluation in *L'Avenir*: "But if the tragedy of Racine is a penetrating study of love, if it demands the engaging murmur, the adorable lapses, the calculated reticence, all the secret powers of woman, Sarah Bernhardt was the first of our tragediennes, the unique, the only one."

But the stage bearing of Sarah Bernhardt was obviously not limited to the striking of theatrical postures. It was demonstrated more clearly and in a more precise way by movement. Rostand, already flattering when he remarked on her bodily posturing, is downright dithyrambic, not hesitating to proclaim her "the princess of stage movement". The actress herself stresses the importance of this aspect of technique, declaring in a lecture which *L'Exelsior* quoted on January 25, 1914: "Gesture should always precede speech." Joseph Galtier who reports in *Le Temps* of March 2, 1892 on the rehearsal of *Varennes* confirms this order of priority when he relates: "Script in hand—not just a single rôle but an entire act—she reads her lines, paying more attention, it seems, to finding posture, movement and gesture rather than intonations."

She was content at that stage with a rough outline. Precise technique was not essential: she did not want a slavish copying. She acted with her whole body. And the critics were not slow to comment upon this physical exaltation, presented only just within the limits of decency. In 1893, Anatole France evokes in the following words her interpretation of *Les Rois*: "She did what no one had dared to do before her—she acted with her entire body. She put into her rôles not only her whole soul, all her mind and her physical grace, but also all her sexuality." Similarly, Henri Fouquier, in *Le Figaro* of January 28, 1894, remarks with regard to a performance of *Izéil*: "In the third act, Sarah Bernhardt wears a costume which clings to her figure so that she seems to be naked. She struggles against a rapist and her terror is translated into a gesture of the whole body."

Using her whole body did not hinder Sarah Bernhardt from entertaining a decided preference for certain gestures, particular bits of mimicry. She made great use of her hands, to which she permitted effects at once restrained and eloquent. If Gabriel Boissy laments that, in the Hermione of *Andromaque*, "anger, with Sarah, is a flapping with the hands", how many flattering remarks there are which proclaim, to the contrary, the expressive use to which she put them! In *La France* of April 18, 1889, P. Bertin, in his account of the first performance of *Léna*, alludes to "the sorrow with which the hands are wrung"; Emmanuel Arène, in *Le Figaro* of April 4, 1907, says of her interpretation of Adrienne Lecouvreur, "movements of her fingers striking the flesh of her arms"; on January 15, 1921, Pierre Varenne, after having seen René Fauchois's *Vitrail*, wrote "the sensitive hands emphasize only what is most important"; in *Liberté* of March 28, 1923, Robert Kemp, reporting on her performance in *Phèdre*, questioned: "You remember her admirable hands . . . ?"

She made use also, in a manner peculiarly her own, of all the resources of a very mobile face. Photographs taken during performances carry the suggestion of an expressionist play before its time, with an accentuation of the mimetic element and a voluntary acceptance of the limits imposed by those facial expressions which freeze in a moment into an emotion thus underlined, thus boldly rendered by the actress. Clearly, it is a matter of adapting for the stage the methods used in the silent film. Moreover, one realizes that Sarah Bernhardt played in seven films of which one, *La Voyante*, was completed just before her death. It is naturally the eyes which are most called upon (see Plates 1 and 4). The actress knew, in making use of such theatrical devices, that the critics would never tire of reporting them. P. Bertin, in *La France* of April 18, 1889, speaks of "terrors in which the glance was filled with fear"—this with reference to *Léna*. On December 14, 1896, Félix Duquesnel describes Lorenzaccio, the "clean-shaven face lit up by the restless eyes". On May 20, 1899, he describes Hamlet "'watching with uneasy eye for the effect which the playing of the murder of Gonzago will have upon the king." On January 22, 1898, Catulle Mendès, in *Le Journal* expresses the view that "She was, with her beautiful, useless eyes, the steadfast and uncomplaining reflection of all tragedy"—she played the part of a blind woman in D'Annunzio's *La Città Morta*. In *Le Gaulois* of March 16, 1900, Félix Duquesnel says of *L'Aiglon*: "One sees in his eyes the reflection of the tempest of his soul." Emmanuel Arène, in *Le Figaro* of April 4, 1907, remarks that her characterizing of Adrienne Lecouvreur "had distraught eyes". The anonymous critic of *Le Temps* of April 5, 1920 describes thus her playing of Athalie: "In the anxious look shot through now and then with fierce gleams, one follows the struggle of an instinctive superstition against the will. . . . Then, the eyes fixed, she pursues." One could multiply quotations which demonstrate this mobility of glance, able to show the infinite range of human feeling.

If the eye had, indisputably, a special function to perform, Sarah Bernhardt did not neglect on that account the other parts of the face. The lips are capable of varied effects. She could emphasize despair by their spasmodic twitching: "Then comes an agony which makes her lips shrink", says P. Bertin in *La France* on April 18, 1889, when he comments on the performance of *Léna*. She could portray resignation in a melancholy smile: "Her marvellous and moving smile underlines the verse; to make reparation for the years of irreparable outrage", says Antoine in *L'Information* of April 12, 1920, where he reports on her interpretation of Athalie. The ability to command all possible changes of facial expression permits, after all, the conveying of a more diverse range of feelings and of situations. "The queen relates, with a kind of dream-like amazement, her nightmare of the astonishing way in which she comes to search for the key in the Temple", notes Antoine, again in relation to *Athalie*; the debauchery "in the first scene has a startling effect—pale, sickly, the body of a youth, stooping slightly . . . all this has a terrifying reality" states Félix Duquesnel on December 4, 1896, after the first performance of *Lorenzaccio*; and, particularly, death, which produces "livid and distorted features", as P. Bertin says in regard to *Léna*, compels the whole face to undergo dramatic changes. Francïsque Sarcey calls attention to it in the following terms, in *Le Temps* of October 27, 1890, in relation to her interpretation of Victorien Sardou's *Cléopâtre*: "What is interesting to follow is the dissipation of the face and the succession of lamentings by which the actress outwardly conveys the feelings which the scene contains."

The skill with which she conveyed the background of a scene seems often to have been perfect. Sarah Bernhardt had the gift of making things real and it is indisputable that her ideas were sometimes very apt. Adhering to the characteristics of her rôles, she had the knack of finding the gesture and posture which would reflect the situation or the action with precision. On October 21, 1944, Robert Kemp, in *Le Figaro*, described her thus in the part of Phèdre: "An audacious posture, almost indecent, made the profane, soiled verses unforgettable: 'It is Venus herself, in all her power, clutching at her prey'. The word 'prey' had suggested it. With both hands clenched like the talons of an eagle on a captured animal, Sarah grabbed at her body at the precise place which doctors press to calm a sick person who is seized with 'the furies of Eros'." This faculty for adaptation showed itself most particularly in the diversity of her rôles. Brilliant in tragedy and in serious plays, she also tackled comedy felicitously, succeeding in reviving the part of Dorine in *Tartuffe*, as Jules Delini emphasises in 1911: "We must", he wrote, "congratulate Mme. Sarah Bernhardt for having helped to resolve the problem of type-casting in the theatre and for having not hesitated, after being the ideal interpreter of our great tragedies, to appear on the stage of her theatre in the rôle of one of Molière's 'soubrettes'. Dorine, in *Tartuffe*, is what is known in the theatre as a 'character part'. . . . As much as she detests Tartuffe, so much does she care for the union of Marianne and Valère. Her laughter is more excitable than sincere; her freedom, moreover, conceals a purpose; she is the faithful maid attached to an honorable family. Mme. Sarah Bernhardt renders in a very natural way the different sides of this complex character. Without sacrificing her own personality, which knows so well the value of the subtleties of Molière's text. . .she proves that the study of the great tragic rôles usefully serves the comic actress." Her perfect knowledge of dramatic technique enabled her to surmount the handicap which very soon would result from the illness which would culminate in her amputation. By playing skilfully with scenic elements, she was able to overcome and to disguise her disability: "In December", remarked one of her friends, "we repeat *Les Bouffons* in Paris. It is no longer, without the freedom of movement, the Sarah of *L'Aiglon*, nor yet, alas, that of *Bohémos*. She is no longer prodigal in the matter of stage setting; she economises in it. . . . And then, she subordinates the details of the *mise en scène*, so far as possible, to the convenience of her own moves and positions. The armchairs and the tables are placed in such a way as to serve her eventually as points of support. As one crosses a ford by stepping from stone to stone, she is able to go, if she wants to, from chair-back to sideboard, from balustrade to bank in a garden. Of course, no one in the audience will be aware, between these supports, of the subterfuges which her skill makes use of, for her talent as a speaker is without equal." After her operation, she naturally increased the number of her resources so far as positions of sitting and lying down were concerned; not, however, in order to keep herself permanently immobile, as she particularly emphasised in an interview given to *Comoedia* on April 1, 1920 before a run of performances of *Athalie*: "It is, therefore, in a chair that I shall make my entrance. But I shall not remain immobile for a moment."

If a kind of instinct usually guided Sarah Bernhardt and made sure, most of the time, that she aimed straight, it is inappropriate, nevertheless, to pass over in silence those errors of taste which, if they were unusual, were still there. She undoubtedly ruined her effects in several of her revivals by an excess of realistic detail, seriously distorting the spirit of the texts she was playing. On her interpretation of Hamlet, opinions have been much divided. I have already remarked on the criticisms made by the London audiences. One of her pieces of stage business, moreover, provoked contradictory responses. Approved by Félix Duquesnel, who wrote on May 20, 1899: ". . . she was supremely effective in the Players Scene, which she played uncut, with great mastery . . . holding, terrifyingly, the gleam of the torch to the face of the king, the better to see him betray himself . . ."; it is condemned by another critic, who considers: "It is thus that in this very impressive scene, while the play-within-a-play is being acted, Hamlet looks, with a shrewd misgiving, for the least trace of remorse on the face of the king. Sarah Bernhardt throws herself on him, menacing him with the torch with which she illuminates his face. It is a wild, frenzied movement, but it is not in character for Hamlet." In 1877, Gabriel Boissy was already bearing witness to the inconsistencies of her acting and to her anachronisms, when he noted after she had been booed in *Andromaque*: "She arranges her cushions with drawing-room gestures and threatens Pyrrhus as a Montmartoise threatens her lover with a catty remark. Her poses are sometimes pretty in themselves but 'pretty' is not an epithet suitable to tragedy. Sarah plays lying down, with the posture of a concubine in a harem ['avec des poses d'odalisque']. She is sitting or lying down for an hour and a half or two hours". The humorous tone adopted by Francïsque Sarcey, in *Le Temps* of October 27, 1890, after having seen the first performance of Victorien Sardou's *Cléopâtre*, amounts in fact to disapproval of a needless realism: "The actress", he reports, "is making for a little basket which we have seen brought in at the beginning of the act. Well, well! She has delicately put her hand into the opening and she has taken out a real snake, a wriggling snake . . . Mme. Sarah Bernhardt has put the little creature in her bosom."

Critics should remember these contradictory views before passing judgment upon the obviousness of her acting. There is no lack of comment underlining the austere nature of her approach, approving her sobriety, appreciating the moderation of the devices she used. In 1896, an anonymous journalist wrote, after seeing a performance of *Lorenzaccio:* " . . . without ceremonies and without over-exaggeration of purple passages, without excess and without cries, she moves us to the very depths of our souls". On January 22, 1898, Catulle Mendès remarks, about her performance in *La Città Morta*: "No violent effects. In the same way, she has disdained the wandering vacuity of the eyes of the blind." On April 4, 1907, in *Le Figaro*, Emmanuel Arène, speaking of her creation of Adrienne Lecouvreur, notes: "The great tragic actress portrayed this slow agony with a simplicity and a truth which are the highest points of art, the noblest and the greatest." In 1911, Jules Delini expresses the following view of her playing of Dorine in *Tartuffe*: "With the simplest means she made the voice of reason heard. She distinguished herself by the exactitude of her performance." On April 5, 1920, the critic of *Le Temps* emphasizes, in relation to her performance of Athalie: "On the contrary, Sarah devotes herself to not overacting the terrifying scene"; Antoine goes further in *L'Information* of April 12, 1920: "In the dream, no melodramatic underlining". And she herself, in *Comoedia* of April 1, 1920, warning the lovers of sensation, declared: "One does not expect the onset of an epileptic fit nor an eccentricity of gesture, which would be too facile a method. The effect should be obtained more discreetly and that is what I set out to prove."

But this is only a partial view of Sarah Bernhardt's behaviour. It seems that her playing was often characterised by an excess, which was, however, moderated toward the end of her career by the obvious effects of her disability. Her manner was marked by a certain edginess, by a certain abruptness of gesture. These noticeable twitchings are frequently commented upon by the critic. In 1877, at the time of the *première* of *Andromaque*, Gabriel Boissy criticized her: "The gestures are cramped, jerky, broken. She has sick nerves; it is a characteristic of our age." On October 3, 1896, René Doumie confirms, in *Les Débats*: "There was in her manner something too harsh, too excessively nervy. Feverish? Sickly? It matters little." On March 28, 1923, Robert Kemp, in *Liberté*, recalls: "And Hamlet, frail, black silhouette under cap and short hair, shaken by nerves, agitated, crushed by a task too onerous?" The critic of *Le Journal*, on March 21, 1923, expands the argument by speaking of this method of acting as if it were a habitual one: "One found it strange . . . her brusque gestures . . . a kind of feverishness and hyperaesthesia shocked the audience who, even while she flew into a passion, submitted to the ascendancy of this exceptional personality."

She did not always avoid, either, a certain affectation which led to over-emphasis of a gesture or the prolongation of a posture. In *Gil Blas* on October 25, 1890, Léon Bernard Derosne names amongst her common faults "her affectation, her mannerisms". More particularly, on December 27, 1884, Auguste Vitu, in his report in *Le Figaro* about *Théodora*, notes: "Madame Sarah Bernhardt, moreover, shows considerable spiritual grace, but not without a certain affectation." She did not always resist her taste for spectacular effects, which then led to a regrettable over-simplification. In 1877, Gabriel Boissy criticized her playing of *Andromaque*: "Besides, Sarah clears the ground: she clears away Racine. And, instead of Racine, she searches for theatrical effects." Similarly, on October 3, 1896 René Doumie, in *Les Débats*, censures: "She overdid all the stage effects . . . she replaced the utterance, the gesture, the postures by an incensed mimic."

Examples abound of her propensity for tumbling into the theatrical. She had, in particular, a genius for entrances of which the apparent ease belied the careful skill. Thus, on January 22, 1899, Maxime Gray describes in these terms, in *Le Petit bleu*, her entrance in *La Tosca*: "Sarah's entry. A smile all round, discreet and charming, a greeting to the audience, who replied with a sudden burst of applause." She took care over her exits, too, holding a pose after it had triggered off the cherished applause. Jean Labusquière, reporting in *Comoedia* of May 8, 1914, on the performance of *La Samaritaine* which she gave at St. Denis University, finishes with these words: "She stretched out her arms in the gesture of Jesus, as if to open them to the delirious audience which applauded and threw flowers." And this posture was so natural to her that she retained it, by her own choice, to announce at the end of the performance the names of those who had contributed to the production! "Similarly", it is recalled in the report on *La Samaritaine* in *L'Eclair* of April 16, 1897, "she was so carried away that she tossed the name of the author to us in the dithyrambic tone in which she had been declaiming the play: this was, perhaps, a little extravagant".

Her tendency toward melodrama has already been demonstrated by a number of examples which serve to illustrate her stage postures and gestures (see especially Plate 15). This was particularly apparent in her death scenes. Her representation of death always proved to be spectacular (see Plate 5). Madeleine Zilhardt, in *Le Jour* of March 24, 1931, describes in the following way a scene in *Rome vaincue*: "At this point in the play, pressing her daughter to her bosom, she asked her 'Where does your heart beat, my child?' and groped with a trembling hand seeking to drive home her dagger; her tone of voice and her gestures were most moving." But bathos burst out, in all its intensity, from the deaths which she suffered. We have seen that she made dying a specialty. We have examined several instances and have emphasized the variety with which she played them. A certain sensuality was often present; Le Bargy, in *Le Gaulois* of March 27, 1923, recalled: "With Sarah Bernhardt, grief and death have an air of intoxicating exaltation", while on October 27, 1890, Francïsque Sarcey, in his report on *Cléopâtre* in *Le Temps*, furnished this particular example: "The actress has rehearsed and has curiously delivered a new kind of death, a gentle death which seems to be nothing but a voluptuous slowing-down of life." But spasmodic movement was also involved; P. Bertin, in *La France* of April 18, 1889, characterizes thus the death which marks the end of *Léna*: " . . . and at last the agony, that inevitable agony in which one sees so clearly . . . the invasion of death, when all at once the body tumbles and falls into its final rigor. No one knows how to die like Mme. Sarah Bernhardt." The excess which crept in, however, did not escape her contemporaries; imagining the repertory of an ideal theatre, Maurice Curnonsky writes, with humour, in *Le Supplément* of January 12, 1897: "The final Friday, Mme. Sarah Bernhardt will demonstrate the violent death, with cries, death rattles, sudden starts, falls, overturnings and magnificent recoveries."

This theatricality seems ultimately to explain, in part, Bernhardt's predilection for male rôles. She played a great number during her career. One may cite, notably, in 1868, Chérubin in *Le Mariage de Figaro* by Beaumarchais; in 1869, Zanetto in Francois Coppée's *Le Passant*; a production which cast her, in 1874, as the page in *La Belle Paule*, by Louis Denagrousse; in 1896, Lorenzo in de Musset's *Lorenzaccio*; in 1899, the prince in Shakespeare's *Hamlet*; in 1900, the duke in Rostand's *L'Aiglon*; in 1916, Marc Bertrand in *Du Théâtre au champ d'honneur* by Louis Payen; in 1921, the hero in *Daniel* by Louis Verneuil. She herself explained this preference, however, in a lecture which she gave on February 7, 1914: "I do not prefer men's rôles", she declared, "but I do prefer men's brains. Hamlet, L'Aiglon, Lorenzaccio . . . I maintain that these rôles will gain in being played by an intellectual woman. But on the other hand there are some parts that a woman could not play—Nero, Faust, Romeo, Napoleon and some others. The intellectuality of the woman is no substitute for the virility of the man." We have here an interesting proposition: Sarah Bernhardt saw in the masculine mental processes a particular theatrical manifestation for which her theatrical style was especially apt.

VOICE AND DICTION

It remains now to analyse Sarah Bernhardt's voice. It is a study at once important and difficult: important because the Bernhardt myth owes much to her phrasing and to her skill in verse speaking; difficult because the subjective view occupies a large place in those testimonies to which we have been able to call attention. It is useless to insist on the explanation which recurs like a *leitmotif* in the writings of the critics—this actress had a golden voice. It was Victor Hugo who, at a banquet celebrating the hundredth performance of *Ruy Blas*, used for the first time this pretty but thoroughly vague phrase. A little more precise is the notion of harmony: in listening to Sarah Bernhardt, what apparently struck one at the onset was the pleasant quality in the tone of her voice. And the eulogistic comparisons certainly make this clear. Appeal is frequently made to music. Remembering the performance of *L'Aiglon* in 1872, Jules Truffier writes: "she drew from the verse a harmony beyond interpretative meaning by matchlessly lingering, at intervals, on some musical phrase, highly involuted, where the poet had indicated a pause. She found, to mark these pauses and these resumptions, intonations of incomparable simplicity, of charming sweetness." On December 21, 1874, the critic of *Théâtres* speaks, for his part, of "the flute of Mlle. Sarah Bernhardt". In a report of a rehearsal of *Varennes* appearing in *Le Temps* of March 2, 1892, the journalist notes: "when the moment comes she is certain, by the music of her voice, to convey all the nuances of her feeling." On March 15, 1933, Henri Bordeaux, recalling a performance of *Cathédrales* that she gave during the 1914 war to an audience of soldiers, points out, "The voice is somewhat 'broken', like the moaning of a 'cello." In a more general way, René Doumie, in *Les Débats* of October 3,, 1896, admires "this famous golden voice which makes the verse sing". Pierre Wolff, in *Le Journal* of March 21, 1923, recalls: "She was a musician so far as her voice was concerned, that voice of gold which was a song, a lullaby and a melody...". Robert Kemp, in *Le Figaro* of October 21, 1944, is enraptured: " . . . it was phrased as if by Mozart, the violin of Fritz Kreisler when each note of the andante is a sonorous thought, a pearl that dreams". Nature is also pressed into service to report this incomparable fluidity. Théodore de Banville marvels: "She speaks verse as the nightingale sings, as the wind sighs, as the stream murmurs." In *L'Echo de Paris* of March 21, 1923, André Beaumier compares her voice to a "resonant crystal". Robert Kemp adds: "The words seemed to be of suffering flesh; and then of the breaking sea, of the ardent rays of the sun."

This sweetness had, it would seem, its counterpart. Allied to her bodily slimness there was undoubtedly a thinness of voice which compelled Sarah Bernhardt to play in a minor key, which grated when it needed to go into the upper register. She suffered seriously because of this insufficiency at the start of her career. In 1866, at the end of a performance of *Le Jeu de l'amour et du hasard*, Chilly passed this severe judgment: "She did not make a good first appearance; she speaks badly, she has a bad voice." In 1868, he said again, at the opening of *Kean*: "It is a pity . . . that her voice is so weak." By dint of hard work she succeeded in reducing this defect somewhat. But it did not totally disappear. Constrained to force her voice, she produced a raucous and disagreeable sound. On December 21, 1874, the reporter of the review *Théâtres* deplores in the following terms her playing of Phèdre: "The performance was quite painful. The more she tried to force the tone, the more strangled her voice became, raucous and altogether ineffectual." On March 29, 1893, still on the subject of *Phèdre*, L. Bertin notes in *Le Journal*: "In return, in the forceful passages, the actress's outbursts made her go beyond the accepted limits of manners. The voice, forced to yield to a delivery too violent and jerky, became dry and hoarse. The harmonious inflections disappeared and the charm gave place to a painful sensation." On March 16, 1900, Richard O'Mon Roy says the same in *Gil Blas*: "her strident voice which cracked in the outbursts of rage", effects which she used in the rôle of L'Aiglon.

These difficulties explain in part, perhaps, the modulated character which she gave to her diction. Able only with difficulty to make use of differences of range, she skilfully exploited flexibility and variations of tone. By this means she was able to give her phrasing smoothness and a flowing quality. Francisque Sarcey draws attention to this essential aspect of her voice: "And as she follows the rise and fall of a sentence without ever breaking it, she protects the harmony of the flexible lines." Pierre Wolff, on March 21, 1923, spoke of her voice "which she could modulate infinitely". In *L'Ami du peuple* of March 8, 1931, Jules

Truffier states: "What an example of lyric diction, teaching us to follow properly the cadences of the sentence without fracturing it!" But, once again, Sarah Bernhardt had defects which sprang from her good qualities. Apt at bringing out the lyricism of the verse, her delivery could easily become monotonous, falling into a tedious chanting. She did not always avoid this pitfall. In his account of *Cléopâtre* in *Gil Blas* of October 25, 1890, Léon Bernard Derosne regrets "her indolent diction". On April 7, 1895, referring to Rostand's *La Princesse lointaine*, he says again in the same journal: "Creating a creature of dreams, she doubtless thought that it would be impossible to over-use the drawling singsong as a way of lazily indulging her admirable voice."

But there is no need to exaggerate this weakness and end with a boring uniformity. Her diction was equally strongly rhythmical. She had a habit of laying stress on certain words or certain syllables. This custom of scansion, of introducing strongly accented words by any means whatever, is noticed by numerous critics. Francïsque Sarcey says: "And with what subtle and searching intonations she emphasizes certain words, to which she thus gives an extraordinary value!" In 1911, Jules Delini wrote of her playing of Dorine, "hammering with her admirable voice all the verses which are needed to produce the effect, stressing all the tirades in which Dorine sets forth her claims and unveils Tartuffe's evil schemes". Michel Georges Michel, in *La France* for March 27, 1923, reiterates: "She sang, she hammered, she accelerated the cadence into a gallop which suddenly rolled, mounted, pranced, tumbled into a silence which nothing broke but a repeated sob." Perhaps this technique bordered on cliché, degenerated into bad habits? Léon Bernard Derosne thought so when he complained, on October 25, 1890, of "hammered diction", and above all when he remarked, in his review of Jules Barbier's *Jeanne d'Arc* published in *Gil Blas* on January 5, 1890: "I have been surprised more than once by this curious habit of hitting the first syllable of words which Mme. Sarah Bernhardt appears, I do not know why, determined not to be deprived of."

Be that as it may, the effects which she got from her voice completed the effects created by her posture and gestures. Moreover, the same melodramatic tendency made itself felt, exemplified in the intensity of contrasts and the frequency of pauses. There were innumerable plays which produced this same range of inflections to express all kinds of sentiments and situations. It is Anatole France who, in 1893, notes in *Le Courrier de la semaine* that, in *Les Rois*, "she has attempted to make her diction more artificial than has ever before been risked in the theatre". In 1896, concerning *Lorenzaccio*, Félix Duquesnel wrote, " . . . this voice of which the words are sometimes drawling, sometimes coaxing, sometimes strident, according to the feeling to be expressed, all of a terrifying truthfulness", while the critic of the *Monde et le théâtre* points out: "Sarah Bernhardt plays triumphantly the complex rôle of Lorenzaccio. As this is a transvestite part, she even modifies the sound of her golden voice to give more completely the illusion of the character she is playing." On April 5, 1920, the reporter of *Le Temps*, in his account of *Athalie*, bears witness to the same thing: "She begins with a voice which is white and distant. The first lines flow smoothly; a smiling, ironic inflection delays the second half of the celebrated alexandrine:

> *Pour répare des ans . . . l'irréparable outrage*

The narrative is enveloped in the atmosphere of a dream. When, finally, the blood-drenched vision appears:

> *Mais je n'ai plus trouvé qu'un horrible mélange. . . .*

the tone of voice is exalted and excited, only to fall again immediately into a mournful, fatalistic stillness."

It is only fair to point out, finally, that a clarity and a perfection of diction came to characterize all her vocal expression. We need not labour the point, sufficiently obvious, sufficiently emphasized by the critics. A reporter in *L'Intransigeant* of November 8, 1893, proclaims "the sovereign authority of her diction"; Pierre Varenne, on January 15, 1921, admires "the diction so clear"; Claude Farrère, in *Le Gaulois* of March 27, 1923, recalls "the marvellous articulation which saved the listener any effort of attention or nervous strain and doubled his pleasure"; Jules Truffier writes in *L'Ami du peuple* on March 8, 1931: "What smooth and perfect diction! One did not miss a syllable, even though the words seemed to leave her lips with no more force than that of a caress." Only one reservation arises, out of tune with the general praise: on October 3, 1896, René Doumie, in *Les Débats*, laments ". . . she spoke some speeches, some scenes, some entire acts in a manner altogether unintelligible". What is there to say? If one puts this opinion alongside some of the criticisms made of her jerky and exasperated tone, it only confirms what we have said earlier, that Sarah Bernhardt, when she forced her voice too much, produced an unharmonious tone which made her words practically incomprehensible. But it seems that this fault was intermittent, accidental.

To sum up this analysis of Sarah Bernhardt's acting: the things that strike one above all are the diversity of her technique, the imaginative power which was able to discover the right stage devices for interpreting feelings and situations, the confidence of a craft honed to a fine edge by many peformances in which she created many characters, the intellectual honesty which caused her to question herself and to repeat the question ceaselessly. In brief, it seems to me that what constituted her greatness was her professional conscience, her craftsman's skill. These are what we shall remember and they are, in fact, much more fascinating than the myth of a *monstre sacré*, inspired and infallible.

NOTES

(The notes on this chapter are notes made by the translator, not by the original author.)

1. Louis XVII, the second son of Louis XVI and Marie Antoinette, was a boy of ten when he died in 1795.

2. Jean Goujon was a sixteenth-century sculptor who was murdered in the massacre of the Hugenots on St. Bartholomew's Day (August 24), 1572. One of his masterpieces was a nude statue of Diana of Poitiers, duchess of Valentinois, done for the Château d'Anet; the figure is shown lying down and is remarkable for its coiffure, masses of flowing, twisted, tangled hair. The statue is now in the Louvre.

3. A long, epic, partly-satirical poem written by Heinrich Heine (1797-1856) in 1843 and published in 1847.

4. *L'imagerie d' Epinal* is untranslatable in any direct way. Epinal is a small town on the river Moselle in eastern France, noted in the eigh-

teenth century for its ceramics and later as the centre of the Vosges textile industry. It is best known now, however, for its popular, inexpensive coloured prints, which are known as "images d'Epinal": they are often rather crude and naïve and the phrase "image d'Epinal" has, in general conversation, come to mean naïve, artistically embarrassing.

5. That is, uncut jewels in the style of the Merovingian or Frankish kings who ruled Gaul and Germany from A.D. 500 to A.D. 752. The line was founded by Clovis.

3

Sarah and Coq: Contrast in Acting Styles

Marguerite Coe

Sarah Bernhardt and Coquelin the elder were friends for nearly fifty years—a friendship that ended only with his death. More than a decade later, in her *The Art of the Theatre*, Sarah praised and disagreed with her old friend like a bereaved widow. She had good cause. There is no record that they were ever lovers, but they supported each other, quarrelled with each other as if they, indeed, shared a single harness. The harness, of course, was art. When Sarah returned to Paris from her first international tour in 1882, she opened at the Gaîté, a theatre owned by Coquelin. For one of his many benefits, Sarah played—for the first time in her career—*La Dame aux camélias*, and thus discovered the most popular rôle of her repertoire. When Coquelin returned to Paris in 1895, in the middle of a contractual dispute with the Comédie Française over his own international tours, he opened at the Renaissance. Its manager was Bernhardt, and immediately Coquelin proved, to the consternation of the sociétaires, that he was still a master of Molière.

It seems worthwhile to examine in some detail the similarities and differences in the performances of this illustrious pair, giving consideration to the uses of the voice, pantomime, spectacle, stage presence, characterization, repertoire and acting theory.

To begin, let us consider their nicknames. Bernhardt was often called "the divine Sarah", indicating a creature from another world. To his many friends, Coquelin was simply "Coq"—the rooster—a commonplace fowl, perhaps, but one with decidedly aggressive tendencies: a male. We find that both Sarah and Coq considered the voice an actor's chief asset. But where Sarah stressed quality—a "beautiful voice", Coq stressed diction—making oneself understood.[1] This was no accident, although both had superior voice quality. Sarah's was high and light, a "silver" or lyric soprano. It is true that Victor Hugo described her voice as "golden" in 1878 but others used terms like "crystalline", "silvery", or "argentine". After careful study of re-recorded cylinders of Sarah's voice, Gerda Taranow concluded, as she reports in her book *Sarah Bernhardt, The Art within the Legend*, that Bernhardt was, indeed, a "silver soprano" who used deep chest notes sparingly, even in *travesti* rôles. In fact, Sarah admitted in *Ma Double vie* that to offset the limitations of a high, light voice, Regnier had suggested that she play Phèdre with pathos rather than passion.[2] The lady only partly followed Regnier's advice, for she added shouts ("cris sauvages") to express passion from 1874 (*Phèdre*) up to 1908. In later years, Sarah's sweet pathos would help to assure her divinity. Coq's voice was essentially deep, with a biting, nasal edge that reminded one of a bugle. Yet he learned to add the mellow tones of a lute and, as Sarah recalled, could produce "every possible note and every shade of resonance".[3] As Robert de Flers wrote in 1909, Coq was a man of many voices, who adjusted his quality to the character he played.[4] I once had a chance to hear Coq's recording of the duelling scene in *Cyrano de Bergerac*. For a moment, I thought I was hearing Franklin D. Roosevelt: the pitch, the slightly nasal resonance, the bursts of force on key words—all were there. I wondered if Coq's other voices were as distinctive as that.

Neither Coq nor Sarah approved of the trilled, theatrical "r" taught at the Conservatoire, but they eschewed pure *verité*, or prosy delivery, taught at the school after 1885.[5] Even in that, however, they differed. Until 1895, Sarah tended toward *chant*, the tragic sing-song dominating the boulevards, and critics often complained of, or parodied, her "chopped" and "hammered" sounds, the rapid rate which distorted her diction.[6] Coq's diction was never faulted, even when he whipped through a long narrative passage in a single breath.[7] But he slowed his rate a little after his first foreign tour, even as Bernhardt speeded up hers.[8] And Coquelin always used a blend of *verité* and *chant*, a technique combining music with meaning, as taught by Samson and Regnier. As a result, wrote a Mexican critic, Coq differed from all his French contemporaries on tour. Where they clicked through their alexandrines like an "English horse on a wooden pavement", Coq spoke and "there was music in the air".[9] Bernhardt joined Coquelin in blending *verité* and *chant* in 1896, and Taranow has verified this fact by studying the actress's recordings.[10] In later years, Sarah claimed to have discovered a personal technique.[11] The facts are: between January and April of 1896, Sarah played beside Coquelin on a public stage for the first time in nearly twenty years, and was playing his beloved Molière.[12] Was he, then, as demanding as the harsh young Benoît, the director whom Sarah scolded in *The Art of the Theatre?*[13] His first name *was* Benoît and he *did* have a reputation for being tough as a coach and *semainier*. Three of the ladies he reduced to tears were Jane Hading, Gabrielle Tholer, and Geraldine Ferrar. I doubt that Sarah escaped their fate, but whatever the cause, she could subsequently share in De Flers's tribute to Coquelin in an obituary. He was the last man (said De Flers) who "excelled in pieces where there are words, not furniture".[14] Despite Coq's efforts, dating from 1886, and Sarah's dating from 1907 or 1908, they were eventually almost alone among French actors who married music to meaning.[15]

The two performers were equally adept in managing silence. Sarah was particularly skilled in listening, and after 1882, some critics thought her listening skills more notable than her speaking.[16] In 1882, Lillie Langtry wrote of Coq: "He says more in a pause than most actors can say in hundreds of words."[17] Pantomime was another facet of the pair's adeptness in using silence. Sarah's technique reflected the fashions of the boulevards, while Coquelin's pantomime was largely individual—a result of his independent nature as well as his success in improvisation.

Sarah learned—through Talma and Sardou—to mime a climactic scene in the following order: glance, gesture, speech.[18] Sardou's element of "glance", wrote Sarah, was important in forestalling unwanted laughter in a melodrama like *Tosca*.[19] On her own, apparently, Bernhardt early learned effectively to pantomime death scenes. Between 1868 and 1922, her lingering deaths invariably brought shouts of approval. The most popular was the ending of *La Dame aux camélias*.[20] Another effective bit of mime was turning her back to the audience—long fashionable on the boulevards and, as one recalls from *The Art of the Actor*,[21] anathema to Coq.

We find that, a few months before Coquelin wrote the first draft of this essay, he had tried the back effect in Amsterdam, coupling it with a clear passing of his hand over his eyes during the prison scene of *Don César de Bazin*. Traditionalists were shocked. The effect "humbled" and "humanised" Don César— it was too realistic for an old Frédérick Lemaître vehicle, they said.[22] Thus, for good cause, Coq warned: "it is not your back that the audience wishes to see. . . . You will never be able to create on your back all those shades of feeling your eye can muster. . . ".[23] We also find that Coquelin was especially noted for facial play centering on the eyes. As early as 1862, Sarcey had noted the "bold eye" and the "singularly expressive and mobile face".[24] More than forty years later, at the dawn of motion pictures, critics were urging spectators to bring lorgnettes the better to study Coq's facial mime, especially the subtle changes around the eyes.[25] Yet this was far from all in Coq's silent acting. As a youngster of twenty-one, he stunned Théophile Gautier and other critics by the naturalness and spontaneity of his movements as Figaro. He was said to have dispensed with the traditional poses and bits of business, as well as the usual intonations, to display the "*sang-froid* of a diplomat, the spirit of a demon, and the suppleness of a clown".[26] Two years later, at twenty-three, he was elected a *sociétaire*, and was portrayed among his elders in the Pierrot costume of Deburau, another innovative mime. For Sarcey, he would never display the "cold perfection" traditional to the House of Molière, and for many years the vigour and spontaneity of his movements would alarm the traditionalists among his critics.[27] Only in dramatic rôles, begun in 1875, would Coquelin display the reserve described by Lillie Langtry in 1882: "He drops a hand, he raises an eyebrow, and one feels the controlled power of his gestures."[28]

After returning from Russia in 1889, Coquelin surprised Parisians by using broader, more specific gestures than he had formerly. This soon passed as he returned to the informal, instinctive gestures inspired by his understanding of the character.[29] Like Regnier, Coquelin insisted that if one would "think the thought" and adjust to the playing of other actors, the right movements and bits of business would naturally follow.[30] The problem, as he knew, was to remember those bits and conserve them for subsequent performances.[31]

In terms of general spectacle, we find striking disparities between Sarah and Coq. The lady sought to please, even seduce, her audience with famous smiles, serpentine movements, flowing gowns (see Plate 11) and a face painted in enthralling shades of crimson, pink, and white.[32] As in pantomime, Sarah's spectacular effects—increased after leaving the Comédie—were a blend of opposing traditions: classical and melodramatic. She was especially famous for what may be called "appropriately costumed attitudes" animated by an "S" curve resulting from turning her shoulders in one direction while turning her hips in the other. This infuriated an American critic, William Winter.[33] But we should not believe that Sarah's poses were as contorted as cartoons or adverse criticism would maintain. Part of the effect was achieved through costuming and through a hand "property" such as a cane. This latter was adopted long before the leg injury. Although often parodied, Sarah's visual style became so effective that, during climactic scenes, words were often unnecessary: a real boon to her foreign audiences. And the picturesque poses had another advantage: they suggested paintings by old masters such as Gainsborough, thus reinforcing the blend of classicism and romanticism obtained in movement (see Plates 9, 10, and 11).

Both at the Comédie Française and on the boulevard, Sarah often used postures of supplication which intensified her pathos. To indicate penitence, pleading, prayer, or anguish, she would kneel or lie prostrate on stage (see Plate 7) in rôles as diverse as the classic Phèdre, the romantic Marian de Lorme or the melodramatic Jeanne Doré. These spectacular effects were usually prolonged by vigorous admiration from the audience.[34]

Coquelin did not condemn picturesque poses or costuming

out of hand; he questioned their use as a substitute for detailed character study.[35] As might be expected, it was Coq's interpretation of the play—not his costume, poses, or specific gestures—that drew comment. The very absence of striking visual effects annoyed William Winter intensely.[36] Thus, to visualize Coq in terms of spectacle, we must depend primarily upon paintings or photographs. We will often note the soldierly bearing that struck Sarcey in 1871, after Coq's service in the Franco-Prussian war, and will always see little attempt to suggest a distinctly theatrical personage. The man is clearly middle class, as Winter said, and his most notable characteristics are the face and, if shown, a pair of well-formed athletic legs, well suited to period rôles. In later life, the silver hair and the laugh-lines around his eyes will suggest the kindliness of a popular bishop. In those final years, he may even seem dashing by adding a trim silver goatee and jaunty hat. He was determined to project a plebian attitude, and in costume he often slouched in a decidedly casual manner. Coq's attitudes differ from Bernhardt's, even in classical rôles, as impressionistic or expressionistic paintings differ from the serene formality of old masters. Coupled with the candid informality is the diversity of Coq in costume. I once showed some photographs of him in costume to an agent experienced in hiring actors. His first remark was: "Who are all those men?" His second was: "I'd like to hire them."

In 1900, in New York, Coquelin dared to expose his bare face as Scarpia. As he explained to Brander Matthews, he wanted to create a more "subtle" and "suave" portrayal than the usual melodramatic villain with huge mustachios and bristling brows. To many New Yorkers this face—with a powdered wig above—was not sufficiently evil to invite boos as he menaced the divine Sarah. Yet this face belongs to a politico, diplomat and millionaire businessman. It is Coquelin at sixty—and who does not now believe that politicos, diplomats, and millionaires can be sinister? Coq believed so, even then, but he was ahead of his time.[37]

Scarpia was by no means Coq's first rôle without makeup. As early as 1864 he had learned that he did not need greasepaint, wigs, or costuming to portray such characters as an English tourist, a bereaved mother, a drowning dog or a plate of soup at salons or in benefits. Gradually he added these dramatic monologues to his touring repertoire, appearing without sets or props between one-act plays. Even foreign critics found these one-man shows convincing and hilarious or touching.[38] Then, in 1903, Coq appeared before the court of Kaiser Wilhelm in Molière, using only a table and two chairs for stage dressing. He was heartily congratulated for this seeming innovation.[39] Yet, two years earlier, New Yorkers stormed at seeing *Tosca* with curtains filling in fragmented sets.[40]

As a rule, both Sarah and Coq spared no effort or expense in coordinating sets and costumes for a lavish effect (see illustrations, especially Plates 5, 12, and 13). For example, in 1905, Coq transported twenty-five sets and six hundred costumes for a repertory of twenty plays presented throughout South America.[41] And while Sarah's costuming was exquisite, it tended to follow the same design whatever the period of locale of the play, to enhance her pantomime and picturesque poses.[42] Coq's costumes, on the other hand, were as diverse as his repertoire. We know that even at the Comédie, he designed his own wearing apparel, paying special attention to color (drab or bright) and the degree of neatness to be achieved. He made these decisions about midway in his analysis of the rôle—sometimes months or years before the play reached the boards.[43] And while Sarah's costume designs were dictated by desired movements, Coquelin's seemed to function in the reverse. A. B. Walkley of the London *Times* noted that Coq was restrained in modern dress, but as a romantic swashbuckler, in boots and plumes, "what a fine, blustering, swaggering manner is his! Alone he fills the stage!"[44]

In the nineteenth century, audiences loved to cry, and both Sarah and Coq were expert in extracting tears. Bernhardt played upon emotions largely through pantomime.[45] Coquelin stirred tears with vocal inflections—a wise choice, offsetting the encroachments of age and fat.[46] No wonder he wrote that "all the picturesque exteriors in the world will not move an audience like one cry given with the right intonation. . . . "[47] One almost wishes they had had a "cry-off", to see who could garner the most salt!

Each artist had a characteristic presence that set them apart from their predecessors and lent much to their acting styles. Sarah's presence is easy to describe, since critics dwelt upon it so frequently. She was feminine—the very archetype of nineteenth-century femininity (see, for example, Plate 3). In 1879, Tom Taylor described Sarah as a typical Victorian heroine: pale, soft-spoken, clinging, and very much in need of protection.[48] Earlier, as Phèdre (see Plate 2), she was deemed more feminine than Rachel because she appeared more vulnerable with her high, light voice and slim, fragile figure.[49] Jules Lemaître thought that Sarah's thin frame and noble bearing saved her from seeming vulgar and wanton in the seductiveness of her pantomime.[50] Sarcey summed up the effect as a "chaste sensuality".[51] Following her first appearance in London, Sarah increased her seductive mannerisms and by 1888, Boucicault accused her of using "Zolaisms". Coq leaped to Sarah's defence, suggesting that she was too lady-like to mix the grossness of naturalism with her realistic allure.[52] What he meant was, at the Comédie Française, under *semainiers* like Coquelin, the lady had learned to mix her voluptuousness with classical decorum.[53]

Coquelin's presence is rather difficult to describe, since it varied from rôle to rôle. Yet always, underneath, lay a warm, vibrant personality and a bubbling humour. "He has only to appear on stage to bring laughter", wrote Sarcey in 1871.[54] By 1876, Coq could also appear menacing—the agility, the aggressiveness and the strong, athletic build was used to good effect as the evil Duc de Septmonts.[55] As he grew older, Coquelin continued to project the image of a hard-driving nineteenth-century male. We must remember that Cyrano de Bergerac was created when Coquelin was fifty-seven and was played until the eve of his death at sixty-eight. Yet no one ever suggested that he was too feeble or too fat to portray a deadly swordsman. Even William Winter was nonplussed by his speed and strength as the Mascarille of *L'Étourdi*.[56]

In their repertoires, we again find a disparity between Sarah and Coq. He excelled in comedy or modern drama, while she excelled as tragic heroines. He was afforded a greater acting range through his repertoire, but he never essayed classical tragedy and, as a romantic hero, he was best equipped for swashbuckling rôles or men whose pathos stemmed from physical deformities. The brisk movements, bold eye, stocky build and military bearing would forestall his suggestion of poetic nobility for many years, and kindly priests—so popular between 1905 and his death—did not emerge until he was in his sixties. Yet he could always express tenderness, and his love scenes as Gringoire (in the 1866 play by Théodore de Banville) at twenty-five were as poignant as those of Cyrano more than thirty years later.[57] "Warmth" describes a Coquelin performance: an infectious warmth that made even the cavernous Porte St. Martin seem intimate.

By contrast, Sarah was "cool"—a fragile, delicate coolness that offset the seductive passion of her performances. By 1890, Sarah discovered that audiences despised her in rôles unleavened by a tender idealism. Hampered by age and increasing girth in her rôles as "soiled doves", she turned increasingly to *travesti* rôles. Here again, we find her most successful as young men who are essentially fragile and delicate, and, as always, she succeeded most memorably in poignant, prolonged death scenes. In contrast to Coq, whose vigour and rugged appearance denied him a "tragic" aura according to nineteenth century tastes, Sarah seldom had trouble at all in stirring an audience's pity. She was exalted, an untouchable type that the nineteenth century still cherished. Her image, in play after play, reminds one of Talma's description of the ideal tragedian who "must quit the accustomed circle and plunge into idealism . . . preserve grand proportions while subjecting elevated language to natural accents and true expression. . . produce grandeur without pomp and nature without triviality".[58]

Now, let us illustrate these last generalizations. Both artists' repertoires fall conveniently into three periods: the early years, dominated by their service at the Comédie Française; the middle years, encompassing their first foreign tours and their returns to Paris; and the final years, when each managed a Paris theatre and continued tours of major cities on four continents.

While Sarah's repertoire in the early years was dictated by government directors at the Odéon and Comédie Française or the administrators of the Comédie, Coquelin had more latitude. Shortly after becoming a *sociétaire* at twenty-three, he was appointed to the powerful reading committee, which selected new plays; and in 1871, at thirty, he was a member of the still more powerful administrative committee, replacing Regnier. Sarah did not become a *sociétaire* until 1875, when she was thirty-one, and, as a woman, could not function as an administrator. Nor, for all her noise, was she as aggressive as Coquelin, who—from the beginning—demanded and usually got his own way. Thus, at twenty-one, he played the "great Figaro" of *Le Mariage de Figaro*, a man supposedly thirty-five years of age. His smashing success led to Coq's precocious election as *sociétaire*. By contrast, Sarah did not play the pivotal rôle of Phèdre until she was thirty, although most tragediennes have essayed the rôle by the age of twenty-four.[59] The next year, she was elected *sociétaire*, but until her departure from the Comédie at thirty-five, Bernhardt continued to specialize in "virginal" rôles.[60]

During these early years, Coq and Sarah often played together, sometimes as husband and wife in new comedies as curtain-raisers. Sarah's aptitude for comedy—classic or modern—may be measured by the fact that in the *première* of *Chez l'Avocat*, in 1873, Coq drew all the attention for playing in total silence, although Sarah stormed and screamed from curtain to curtain in the best Bernhardt tradition.[61] Her luck changed only in 1895, when she played the lovely, wronged Alcmène in Molière's *Amphitryon*, while Coq—previously the mischievous Mercury—undertook the rôle of her poor, duped husband.[62]

Both artists played villains in Dumas fils' curious new drama, *L'Etrangère* (1875). She played an American mulatto in the title rôle—a rich, sirenish man-eater, while he played her lover, the wicked Duc de Septmonts, killed in a duel by her irate husband. Both played their rôles in Belgian engagements with great success, but it was Coquelin who offered the greater surprise. The duke was his first rôle without comic relief, and not only did he surprise Paris with his sinister, aristocratic gravity, but also he inspired Henry James to paragraphs of praise.[63] One calls to mind James's description: an unfolding portrayal worthy of the best efforts of a psychological novelist.[64]

Sarah would try other thesis plays, most notably two staged long after her break with the Comédie. Mirbeau's *Les Mauvais bergers* (1890) was a qualified success since the theme of the play in no way interfered with Sarah's love scenes, picturesque postures and concluding death agony.[65] Less fortunate was her appearance in Ibsen's *The Lady from the Sea* played for one performance only in Geneva, in 1906. After studying the play, Taranow concluded that neither the psychology nor the restraint that the character demanded was suited to Bernhardt's techniques.[66]

While Sarah pursued most successfully *ingénue* or *jeune princesse* rôles in tragedy or romantic drama at the Comédie Française, Coq continued largely as *première comique* or *jeune première* in both classical and modern repertoires. He had become a kind of "switch hitter" by 1878, performing in nearly every play in the classical repertoire of comedy, and creating rôles in new productions that his elders, for one reason or another, considered unsuitable for their own talents. Coquelin's enormous adaptability was considered so valuable that he was denied the right to tour America with Bernhardt in 1880. Lawyers and critics declared that, of all the *sociétaires*, he represented the "heart" of the Comédie Française repertoire.[67]

By 1886, Coquelin had played over 160 rôles at the House of Molière, 110 of which had first been played between 1860 and 1874.[68] During the next twelve years, he maintained only eighteen of his original creations, but added eighteen new ones to the repertoire and dominated fifteen important revivals. He was not happy. Critics said he was tempted by American gold, like Sarah.[69] Coq said he was tired of youthful rôles; he wished to attempt great leading rôles like Molière's Alceste and Arnolphe, but others insisted that his nose was too short to convey the dignity or maturity required.[70]

Obviously Coq hated losing by a nose, but it would be many years before he could remedy the situation on the stages of Paris. Meanwhile, Coq had to content himself with his one tragedy, *Jean Dacier*, written especially for him by a youngster, Charles Lomon, who died soon after. The play opened in April of 1877, when Coq was thirty-six, and received glowing reviews, as well as a lengthy tribute by Henry James, who claimed to have been moved to the point of sleeplessness by Coquelin's sensitive portrayal.[71] In a month, the work was closed for good by the notorious *seize mai* affair, which hurt the business of every theatre in Paris. Over twenty years later, *Cyrano de Bergerac* would confront the Dreyfus affair and play to standing room only for a year and three months, when its star was forced by exhaustion to close the play.[72] What was the difference? If we only compare the characters, we find that Jean Dacier, like Cyrano, is a soldier—but a soldier whose only handicap is peasant birth. In a republican France, peasant birth was hardly a tragedy. On the other hand, Cyrano's big nose is the sort of handicap known to every social class. It reminds us of the starvation suffered by Gringoire (1866) and the hunchback of *Luthier de Cremone* (1876), two one-act creations in which Coq enjoyed enormous success as a pathetic hero, albeit aggressive, argumentative heroes. I would suggest that nineteenth-century audiences knew what they were about: the sight of a physically and emotionally sound Coquelin suffering the slings and arrows of outrageous fortune makes about as much sense as John Wayne losing a fist fight. There must be an additional problem—preferably a physical one.

In the six years following Sarah's departure from the Comédie, Coquelin created several rôles in the modern repertoire that foreshadowed today's vogue for anti-heroes. Not that they were *written* to convey complexity—Coq did not have Ibsen or Strindberg at his command—but they were *played* with a complexity that increasingly confounded the critics. One example is Brichanteau, *Un Parisien*, who emerged in 1886 as the hero of a situation later developed by George Bernard Shaw for *Pygmalion*. Did Brichanteau saunter suavely through his predicament? Yes, and more. Through silent acting, Coq conveyed far more than critics believed the author intended: a selfish, cynical, lazy man whose indifference to his ward's attractions was considered "an affront to French manhood".[73] Needless to say, foreigners would love it. Within months, Coq would be off on the first leg of a tour ending in the Americas, and would not be seen in Paris for three years.

Sarah's return to Paris after her first American tour was in 1882. She had triumphed, especially in death scenes. Six of the eight plays had ended in her prolonged demise and for the remainder of her career a final agony was practically mandatory for a Bernhardt vehicle.[74] With *La Dame aux camélias* (1882), Sarah found not only her finest death scene, but also the type of rôle that dominated her middle period. This was the "soiled dove", the paradoxical creature demanded by Hugo in his Preface to *Cromwell*. During the middle period, Sarah played ten different soiled doves, most of them tailored to her talents by Sardou, and of the four plays she herself wrote, three offered such heroines.[75] Between 1890 and 1902, Sarah attempted four heroines in whom sensuality was leavened by little or no chastity. In varying degrees (depending upon the ratio of sensuality to chastity), audiences rejected these characters: the last (Francesca da Rimini) with incredible harshness.[76]

Faced with a dwindling supply of suitable rôles, Sarah relied increasingly upon *travesti*. In the first thirty-two years of her career she played nine rôles in masculine dress. In the last twenty-seven years, she played eighteen. Unlike English "breeches parts", French *travesti* never involves a discovery of the character's true sexual identity. Thus, Barrie's *Peter Pan* is a typical *travesti*, whether played by Maude Adams or a neighborhood child. In fact, Peter Pan represents the sort of *travesti* made famous by Virginie Dejazet of the mid-nineteenth century. Dejazet was so successful as "sexless" supernatural creatures like Puck and Ariel that she gave her name to the rôles, and "dejazets" were often imitated by others.[77] Bernhardt picked up the Dejazet *travesti* and gave it tragic overtones. Her most popular, by far, was Rostand's *L'Aiglon*, which Sarah described as a "white Hamlet".[78] Critics scoffed at the play itself, and the tedium of the piece tempered their praise of Sarah's performance. Nevertheless, *L'Aiglon* had nationalistic overtones, plus a tenderly fragile Sarah, that assured its popular success in Paris.[79]

During the final period, Sarah's rôles were either repetitions or imitations of rôles performed during the middle years. Too often, they were unworthy exaggerations of her previous taste and talent.[80]

Coquelin's middle period began in 1886 with two lecture-essays on acting published in American magazines, which may be viewed as types of publicity for his approach to art. He did not pretend that they were full statements of either his theories or his performance. Of the ninety-nine rôles listed on available touring programmes during the middle and late periods, twenty-seven were listed most frequently, although the exact number of performances is not known. Of these twenty-seven, nine were

first played before foreign audiences. Of these nine, only four—
Tartuffe, Don César de Bazin, L'Abbé Constantin and *Le Bourgeois Gentilhomme*—were eventually performed in Paris. Of the remaining rôles, three—the old servant Noel, the stuffy bourgeois M. Poirier and the Alsatian murderer, Matthias—were exclusive properties of the Comédie Française and were banned from other Parisian theatres. The other two rôles—the famous tourist, M. Perrichon, and the divorced husband, Henri Duval—represent the sort of light farce Parisians considered beneath the dignity of their ex-*sociétaire*.

These twenty-seven rôles are representative of Coquelin's touring repertoire, since we find that, of the ninety-nine rôles listed, thirty-four were first played on tour. Furthermore, the twenty-seven most frequently-played rôles give a good idea of Coquelin's versatility as an actor. Ten belong to classical comedy or are adaptations of the classics. Four are heroes of romantic or neo-romantic drama. Three belong to realistic melodrama, or thesis plays. Two are elderly heroes of sentimental comedy. By devoting so much time and effort to French classical comedy, Coquelin gambled heavily with his financial success and international popularity. Schreck has noted that French classical comedy represents manners and mores too remote for today's actors and audiences to grasp with conviction.[81]

It would seem that Coquelin was the only celebrated comedian of the nineteenth century who dared to cross so many linguistic and cultural barriers. He acknowledged his daring himself, in a New York speech on opening night in 1888. He then discussed the purpose of comedy: "to reveal ourselves as our neighbours see us, through a window, in our underwear".[82] Certainly no segment of society escaped Coquelin's ridicule for the next twenty-one years, in either classical or modern rôles, in romanticism or realism. Now gentle, now brash, he depicted the foibles of man in his own characters. But the character lurking behind Coquelin's choices in touring rôles seems to be Gringoire, whom he once described as the character most like himself.[83] Gringoire has been described by a textbook editor as a "peaceable hero, capable of great things, despite his apparent uselessness . . . (pleading) before the great ones of the world the cause of those who toil and suffer".[84] Going to a less exalted level, we find Gringoire to be a ragged young lout of a troubadour worthy of the company of François Villon and the original Gringoire of the *Basôchiens*. He is brazen enough to confront politicians, but he is shy and self-conscious before an infatuated young lady. Between 1866 and 1890, Gringoire was Coq's most popular rôle outside of the stage of the Comédie Française. Then he hung up his troubadour's suit, and Sarah wore it in *travesti* for her tour of 1891-1893. A few years later, she whispered to Rostand that Coq needed a play. The result was *Cyrano de Bergerac*.

Before 1890, Gringoire and the Mascarille of *Les Precieuses Ridicules* were often presented on the same bill, separated by an hour of dramatic monologues. Not only did this bill give a sampling of Coquelin's versatility, but also it offered a sampling of the socio-political history of his homeland. Between Gringoire and Mascarille, Coq gave his audience good reasons for the emergence of a republican France.

If one reads carefully the critical accounts of Coquelin's most controversial performances, one easily finds strong comments about contemporary society. For example, he showed no mercy toward Matthias, the Alsatian patriarch who ruthlessly kills a Jewish peddler and awaits the outcome for the balance of the play. If Irving brought to Matthias "the tortured sensitivity of a Hamlet",[85] Coq gave his character the hard-nosed pride and bigotry that would soon lead to the Dreyfus affair and eventually to Hitler's concentration camps.

Coquelin's Figaro was equally astonishing. From 1862 to 1908, he presented a character that was only incidentally the family butler, but very much the embittered, witty pamphleteer who strode with dignity and seemed grieved by his station in life. Parisians always adored this Figaro, who was dusted off frequently for national celebrations, and Coq would still be called *"le grand* Figaro" a generation after his death.[86] Foreigners would only accept it gradually, as in Holland, where the only Figaro known was that of Mozart's and Rossini's operas.[87]

Tartuffe was another frequently played rôle on tour. In 1876, Brussels critics wrote that Coquelin's Tartuffe was the epitome of the earthy churchmen of Rabelais—as astonishingly funny as he was devious.[88] When the "grand tours" began in 1886, Coquelin's Tartuffe either stirred the joys of recognition—as in

Belgium, Spain, Mexico and South America—or caused a profound shock, as in New York in 1888. Dithmar of the *Times* was still stunned while writing his first review of the play, noting that the audience remained fixed in its seats until Coq returned with a dramatic monologue.[89] During the New York engagement of 1894, Coquelin performed Tartuffe five times in a week, but each time he took care to end the evening with the hilarious Mascarille of *Les Precieuses Ridicules*. William Winter tells us that, in the Coquelin tradition, there was no hint of the character's sinister qualities in the opening moments of the play.[90] Dithmar found the "charming suavity" uncommonly attractive.[91] To Brander Matthews, the "consistent geniality" was a wholly satisfactory approach, although he, too, responded to the horror of the end, realizing that this charming scoundrel was only too likely to escape his just deserts.[92]

After Coquelin's second departure from the Comédie Française in 1893, Petruchio joined his list of frequently-played characters on tour. In Paul Delair's adaptation of Shakespeare's *Shrew*, Coq had thrilled Parisians and Belgians with his jaunty, Molièresque touches. But in Chicago soon after, audiences were disappointed. The character was too frankly down-at-the-heels, too obviously a fortune hunter, to satisfy their romantic tastes.[93]

If Americans were annoyed by Petruchio and shocked by Tartuffe, they adored Coquelin's sweet old rabbi of *L'Ami Fritz*. The *Mirror* reported that "Coquelin does not play the rôle of the rabbi, he *is* the rabbi", showing that some progress had been made between 1888 and 1893—at least on the part of the specators.[94]

Whenever we find critics disagreeing about a Coquelin performance, it is—as Puck of Mexico City pointed out—only about the nature of the character, not the quality of the techniques. "When is Coquelin Coquelin?" asked Puck. "To judge this actor, one must judge his character."[95]

In the late period of Coquelin's career, from 1895 to his death, we find increased acceptance of the famous comedian's aproach to his rôles. Even William Winter mellowed, preferring Coq's old sergeant to Sarah's young duke in *L'Aiglon*, and finding Scarpia so vicious that "when Tosca inserted the carving knife into his gizzard, the public heart experienced intense gratification".[96] Norman Hapgood agreed about Coq's merits, but heard some spectators sigh with disappointment when Coq's Scarpia was done in.[97]

From December 28, 1897, the most frequently played rôle in Coq's repertoire was Cyrano de Bergerac. He played the part over 900 times in Paris alone, and heaven knows how often while on tour. By 1908, the wispy black of his goatee changed to a trim, bushy silver, but he was forever Cyrano to his public— a kind of national hero.[98]

Hapgood gives the best description of Coq's portrayal, since he saw it only after attending English, German and American productions. Mansfield's Cyrano was more flamboyant, the German portrayal more sentimental. The American version was so inept that the player's identity has been mercifully forgotten. Coquelin's version had a special "unity" and an atmosphere that was "strangely haunting", wrote Hapgood, and, as usual, Coq's performance amplified "one's understanding of the script". Overall, Coq's Cyrano was more gentle than one might expect, his gaiety and sadness tempered by the poetic and philosophic elements of his nature.[99] After forty years onstage, Coq had finally made his point. No longer was a poetic or noble appearance essential to moving portrayals of stalwart heroes or tender lovers. Nor could Frédérick Lemaître or Mounet-Sully challenge him now. Jules Lemaître wrote after the Parisian *première*: "He is without possible comparison the great classical actor of swashbuckling rôles."[100]

While Sarah's last period was haunted by inferior imitations of her earlier self, Coq moved on to the great leading rôles he had been denied, even as a "youngster" of fifty. An adorable old priest, L'Abbé Constantin, became the toast of Paris even as France moved toward the separation of Church and State.[101] In 1908, Coq offered his last creation: a brilliant Jesuit more tactful than Cyrano in fighting his battles, and therefore more successful.[102] In February of 1909, Coq was to *première* as Rostand's Chantecler, but a sudden and fatal heart attack forestalled a probable success.

In general, we may conclude that Coquelin's personal convictions were as important as his physique and his technical mastery in portraying a character, yet—like Bernhardt—he did not portray his private self in any rôle, even those for which he was most admired. To Parisians, he would always be *"le grand Figaro"*, striding with dignity and denouncing injustice at every turn. Offsetting this grave image, wrote Sarah, was a riotous humour and a unique laugh that could overwhelm the deepest despondency in others.[103] He was universally declared the most versatile actor of his day, and would still be a candidate for that title, but now he might be allowed to essay classical tragedy, especially Corneille. In naturalist, realist or even absurdist characters, he would feel right at home. But he wouldn't mumble.

Where Coquelin's art looked foward, bringing realist, naturalist and symbolist touches that "modernized" romantic and classic rôles that paved the way for public acceptance of Ibsen, Shaw, Chekhov, Strindberg and the dark comedies of recent years, Sarah's art looked backward, linking romanticism and classicism. Through their works on acting, each fostered a legend. She stressed a spontaneity approaching the exotic recklessness of her publicity pranks in the 1870s and 1880s. He stressed a studied approach consonant with the traditions of the Conservatoire and the Comédie Française. Neither discussed the special qualities apparent to spectators of a Bernhardt or Coquelin production. She was studied and mannered at her best, while he was vigorous and instinctive at his best. Spontaneity or carelessness damaged her art. Too much subtle complexity in a characterization confounded or confused his audiences. In sum, Coquelin strove to achieve a quality he had observed in Shakespeare: his characters *became*, gradually revealing themselves as the play progressed.[104] Sarah attained a perfection identified with Molière: her characters *were*, remaining a special, identifiable type from the first scene to the last, from play to play. Sarah hypnotized her audiences with idealism. Coquelin could also hypnotize his audiences, with fresh glimpses of reality. Together, they could work magic, creating a tension between reality and idealism that French aestheticians of the eighteenth century considered the fountainhead of art. One may say what a pity they could not perform together more often. Yet they chose their *métiers* wisely, according to their natural gifts. And while he was the comedian and she the tragedienne, a strange alternation occurred that provides a clue to their greatness: the ''being'' of great comedy and the ''becoming'' of great tragedy. And if some New Yorkers smiled as Coquelin prepared to rape Bernhardt in *Tosca* in 1900, it only proves that the world was emerging from romance. There will always be those who root for the rooster, no matter how divine his victim.

NOTES

1. Sarah Bernhardt, *L'Art du théâtre* (Paris, 1928), p. 48; Benoît-Constant Coquelin, *L'Art du comédien* (Paris: Paul Ollendorff, 1894), pp. 17-18.

2. Sarah Bernhardt, *Ma Double vie* (Paris, 1907), pp. 348-49; Gerda Taranow, *Sarah Bernhardt: The Art within the Legend* (Princeton, N.J.: Princeton University Press, 1972), p. 25.

3. Bernhardt, *L'Art du théâtre*, p. 48.

4. Robert de Flers, *Le Figaro*, January 28, 1909.

5. A. Strobel, ''A Visit to the Paris Conservatory'', *The Theatre*, vol. 4 (1888), p. 449; May Agate, *Madame Sarah*, 2d ed. (London: Home & Van Thal, 1946), p. 29; Benoît-Constant Coquelin, *L'Art de dire le monologue*, 10th ed. (Paris: Paul Ollendorff, 1904), p. 15; *L'Art du comédien*, p. 18.

6. Jerome A. Hart, *Sardou and the Sardou Plays* (Philadelphia and London: J. B. Lippincott, 1913), p. 130; Taranow, *Sarah Bernhardt*, pp. 62-63.

7. Francïsque Sarcey, *Quarante ans de théâtre*, vol. 2 (Paris: Bibliotheque des annales, 1900), p. 53.

8. ''A. B.'', *Le Figaro*, April 6, 1889; Edouard Noël and Edmond Stoullig, *Les Annales du théâtre et de la musique*, vol. 15 (1889), p. 23.

9. Puck, *El Universel* (Mexico City), April 19, 1894; cited by Luis Reyes de la Maza, *El Teatro en Mexico durante el Porforismo*, vol. 2 (1888-1899) (Mexico: Imprenta Universitaria, 1965), p. 260.

10. Taranow, *Sarah Bernhardt*, pp. 62-63, 69-70.

11. Bernhardt, *L'Art du théâtre*, p. 125.

12. Noël and Stoullig, *Les Annales*, vol. 21 (1895), pp. 171-72, 176-77, 215-19.

13. Bernhardt, *L'Art du théâtre*, pp. 22-23.

14. *Le Figaro*, January 28, 1909.

15. *Le Figaro*, January 28, 1909; Bernhardt, *L'Art du théâtre*, p. 69; Coquelin, *L'Art du comédien*, p. 18.

16. Taranow, *Sarah Bernhardt*, p. 96.

17. Lillie Langtry quoted by Noel B. Gerson in *Because I Loved Him* (New York: William Morrow, 1971), p. 353.

18. Bernhardt, *Ma Double vie*, pp. 101-2; Bernhardt, *L'Art du théâtre*, p. 115; Taranow, *Sarah Bernhardt*, pp. 86-87.

19. Agate, *Madame Sarah*, p. 185.

20. Taranow, *Sarah Bernhardt*, p. 92.

21. Ibid., p. 99; Coquelin, *L'Art du comédien*, p. 29.

22. J. N. Hall, "M. Coquelin à Amsterdam," *Revue d'Art dramatique* (January 1, 1887), p. 122.

23. Benoît-Constant Coquelin, "Acting and Actors," *Harper's Magazine*, vol. 74 (1887), pp. 900-01.

24. Francïsque Sarcey, *Le Temps*, June 16, 1862.

25. Noël and Stoullig, *Les Annales*, vol. 28 (1902), p. 279; ibid., vol. 31 (1905), pp. 320-21.

26. Theophile Gautier, *Moniteur*, June 16, 1862.

27. Sarcey, *Quarante ans de théâtre*, vol. 2, p. 53; Georges D'Heylli (E. A. Poinsot), *Journal Intime de la Comédie-Francaise*, 1852-1871 (Paris: E. Dentu, 1879), pp. 345-46; Felix Jahyer, "Coquelin," *Paris-Théâtre* (17-23 December 1874), p. 2; Noëll and Stoullig, *Les Annales*, vol. 1 (1875), pp. 66, 150-51.

28. Gerson, *Because I Loved Him*, p. 353. For a summary of the vigour, speed and imaginative complexity of Coquelin's movements in classical comedy, see Jules Lemaître, *Journal des debats*, January 3, 1885, cited by André Antoine, *Le Théâtre* (Paris: Les Editions de France, 1932), p. 173.

29. Brander Matthews, "Diary of a Playgoer", *The Theatre*, vol. 26 (May 1917), pp. 263-65; Félicien Champsaur, "Coquelin", *Les Contemporains*, no. 34 (July 28, 1879).

30. Coquelin, *L'Art du comédien*, pp. 16, 23. Regnier, Coquelin's early mentor at the Conservatoire and Comédie-Française, also coached Samuel Silas Curry of "think the thought" fame in America. Compare Curry's comments in *The Province of Expression* (Boston: The Expression Company, 1891), with those of Coquelin above. Regnier wrote of gesture not at all, and is said to have taught neither set gestures nor mannerisms. See Henry Lyonnet, *Dictionnaire des comédiens français*, vol. 2 (Paris, 1908), p. 591.

31. Coquelin, *L'Art du comédien*, p. 16; Champsaur, "Coquelin", p. 3.

32. Taranow, *Sarah Bernhardt*, pp. 102-4; Bernard Shaw, "Duse and Bernhardt" (June 15, 1895), in *Dramatic Opinions*, vol. 1 (New York, 1922), pp. 135-36.

33. William Winter, *Shadows of the Stage*, vol. 2 (New York and London, 1893), p. 319.

34. Taranow, *Sarah Bernhardt*, pp. 133-34.

35. Coquelin, *L'Art du comédien*, pp. 30-31.

36. William Winter, *New York Daily Tribune*, October 9, 1888.

37. Letter to Brander Matthews, December 1900, in Brander Matthews Collection, Columbia University; Letters to Miss Marcia H. Dehon, 1894-1908, Yale University; Marguerite Coe, "Benoît-Constant Coquelin: The Art of a Rhetorical Actor", 2 vols. (unpublished dissertation, University of Southern California, 1974).

38. *New York Times*, October 9 and 30, 1888, April 5 and 7, 1889; Reyes, *El Teatro*, pp. 31, 260, 263; *Times* (London), June 4, 1889.

39. "Coq à Berlin", January 20, 1903; unidentified clipping in the files of the Bibliothéque de l'Arsenal (Rt. 6623).

40. Bettina Knapp, "Les Tournées de Coquelin aux États-unis", *Revue d'Histoire du Théâtre*, vol. 13 (July-September 1961), p. 235.

41. "Tournée Coquelin", June 3, 1905; unidentified clipping in the files of the Bibliothèque de l'Arsenal (Rt. 6620-1), p. 85.

42. Reynaldo Hahn in Taranow, *Sarah Bernhardt*, p. 106.

43. Félicien Champsaur, *Les Hommes d'aujourd'hui* (Paris, 1878), p. 3.

44. Arthur Walkley, *Times* (London), November 1, 1887.

45. Taranow, *Sarah Bernhardt*, pp. 136-37.

46. E. A. Poinsot, *La Comédie-Française à Londres* (Paris: Paul Ollendorff, 1880), p. 143; Adolphe Brisson, press clipping May 16, 1889, in the files of the Bibliothéque de l'Arsenal (Rt. 6623).

47. Benoît-Constantin Coquelin, "Acting and Actors", *Harper's Magazine*, vol. 74 (1887), p. 898; Coquelin, *L'Art du comédien*, p. 17.

48. Tom Taylor, *Times* (London), June 11, 1879.

49. Taranow, *Sarah Bernhardt*, p. 111.

50. Jules Lemaître, *Journal des debats*, November 5, 1885.

51. Francïsque Sarcey, *Le Temps*, September 27, 1869.

52. Benoît-Constantin Coquelin, "Reply to Boucicault" in Brander Matthews, ed., *Papers on Acting* (New York: Hill and Wang, 1958), p. 91.

53. Taranow, *Sarah Bernhardt*, p. 120.

54. Sarcey, *Quarante ans de théâtre*, vol. 2, p. 53.

55. August Vitu, cited by Noël and Stoullig, *Les Annales*, vol. 2 (1876), p. 87; Henry James, *The Scenic Art* (New York: Hill and Wang, 1957), p. 216; Brander Matthews, *Diary of a Playgoer*, p. 265.

56. William Winter, *New York Daily Tribune*, October 11, 1888.

57. E. A. Poinsot, *Journal intime de la Comédie Française*, pp. 358-60; Noël and Stoullig, *Les Annales*, vol. 23 (1897), p. 257; René Peter, *Le Théâtre et la vie sous la Troisiéme République*, 2d ed. (Paris: Marchot, 1947), pp. 96, 106-9.

58. François Joseph Talma, "Reflections" in Brander Matthews, *Papers on Acting*, pp. 25-26.

59. Beatrix Dussane, *Reines de théâtre* (Lyon: 1944), p. 174.

60. Taranow, *Sarah Bernhardt*, p. 109.

61. *Paris-Théâtre*, no. 11 (July 1873), p. 7.

62. Noël and Stoullig, *Les Annales*, vol. 21 (1895), pp. 171-72.

63. Noël and Stoullig, *Les Annales*, vol. 2 (1896), p. 87.

64. James, *Scenic Art*, p. 216.

65. Taranow, *Sarah Bernhardt*, p. 209.

66. Ibid., p. 210.

67. Noël and Stoullig, *Les Annales*, vol. 6 (1880), pp. 118-20.

68. Poinsot, *Journál intime de la Comédie-Française*; Jahyer, "Coquelin", p. 2.

69. Frédéric Loliée, *La Comédie Française: histoire de la maison de Molière de 1658 à 1907* (Paris: Lavour, 1907), p. 305.

70. Benoît-Constant Coquelin, *L'Arnolphe de Moliére* (Paris: Paul Ollendorff, 1880), p. 2.

71. Noël and Stoullig, *Les Annales*, vol. 3 (1877), p. 86; James, *Scenic Art*, pp. 209-13, 214.

72. Noël and Stoullig, *Les Annales*, vol. 25 (1889), p. 266; Coquelin, letters to Miss Marcia H. Dehon, February (?) 1899; June 26, 1899; letter to Fernand Labori, February (?) 1899.

73. Noël and Stoullig, *Les Annales*, vol. 12, (1886), pp. 44-45.

74. Taranow, *Sarah Bernhardt*, p. 204.

75. Ibid., p. 197.

76. Ibid., pp. 200-01.

77. Georges Duval, *Virginie Déjazet* (Paris, 1876), p. 215.

78. Bernhardt, *L'Art du théâtre*, p. 141.

79. Maurice Baring, *Sarah Bernhardt* (Edinburgh: 1933), pp. 139-41.

80. Taranow, *Sarah Bernhardt*, pp. 180-81.

81. Everett M. Schreck (Richard Morrill), *Principles and Styles of Acting* (Reading, Mass.: Addison-Wesley, 1970), p. 312.

82. Benoît-Constant Coquelin, unpublished address delivered at Palmer's Theatre, New York, N.Y., October 8, 1888, from Brander Matthews Collection, Columbia University.

83. Benoît-Constant Coquelin, *L'Art et le comédien* (Paris: Paul Ollendorff, 1880), pp. 43-44.

84. Léon Séror, "Notes sur Gringoire", in Theodore de Banville, *Gringoire* (Paris: Librairie Hachette, 1935), p. 9.

85. Arthur Walkley, *Times* (London), November 8, 1887.

86. Noël and Stoullig, *Les Annales*, vol. 13 (1887), p. 57; *Paris Soir*, November 21, 1930; *Midi* (Paris), February 23, 1931; *L'Oeuvre* (Paris), March 3, April 1, September 3, 1941.

87. Hall, "M. Coquelin à Amsterdam", pp. 125-26.

88. Antoine, *Le Théâtre*, p. 67; Noël and Stoullig, *Les Annales*, vol. 2 (1876), p. 136.

89. *New York Times*, October 17 and 18, 1888.

90. Knapp, "Tournées de Coquelin", pp. 236-37; William Winter, *The Wallet of Time* (New York: Moffat, Yard and Company, 1913), p. 405.

91. *New York Times*, October 18, 1888.

92. Brander Matthews, *These Many Years* (New York: Charles Scribner's Sons, 1917), p. 198.

93. Knapp, "Tournées de Coquelin", p. 228.

94. *New York Mirror*, January 27, 1894.

95. Puck, *El Universel* (Mexico City), April 18, 1894, in Reyes, *El Teatro*, p. 259.

96. Winter, *Wallet of Time*, p. 401.

97. Norman Hapgood, *The Stage in America, 1897-1900* (New York: Macmillan, 1901), p. 366.

98. Peter, *Le Théâtre et la vie sous la Troisiéme Republique*, p. 96.

99. Hapgood, *Stage in America*, pp. 260-64.

100. Jules Lemaître, *Revue des deux mondes*, vol. 145 (February 1, 1898), p. 701.

101. Noël and Stoullig, *Les Annales*, vol. 31 (1905), p. 31.

102. Jean Aicard, quoted by Gaston Sorbets, "L'Affaire des Poisons' à la theatre de la Porte Saint-Martin", *L'Illustration theatrale*, no. 84 (March 14, 1908), inside back cover.

103. Sarah Bernhardt, *The Art of the Theatre*, trans. H. J. Stenning (London: G. Bles, 1924), p. 66.

104. Benoît-Constant Coquelin, "Molière and Shakespeare", in Brander Matthews, *Papers on Playmaking* (New York: Hill and Wang, 1958), p. 241.

4

Bernhardt and the British Player Queens: A Venture into Comparative Theatrical Mythology

Richard Findlater

I begin with a personal note. I particularly welcome the opportunity to write this chapter not only because of its subject's intrinsic interest for me but also because it compels me to face up to a ghost who has been shadowing me for the past eight years—the ghost of Sarah Bernhardt. While I was writing my book about the leading British actresses of the past three hundred years I felt, very often, that the Great Sarah was looking over my shoulder. There I was, battling with a book rashly called *The Player Queens*, and I had left out of it the actress who was probably the greatest player queen of them all—just because she wasn't British. The omission was inevitable but unfortunate, as Sarah's spectre has not infrequently reminded me. So I now have a very welcome opportunity to start exorcising that ghost—or, at any rate, placating it.

Let me begin with a well-known voice from the opposition—what one might call, in English terms, her majesty's opposition: "Sarah Bernhardt's art is out of date and her drama is dead." That was what Bernard Shaw said, over eighty years ago, while she was still very much alive. Now over half a century has passed since her death. Most of her repertory died with her—or, indeed, predeceased her. She left no school of acting behind her. If she could be said to have any successors, they have been seen not so much on the stage but rather in the cinema—among the vamps and sirens of the silent screen and some outsized soloists of the talking pictures—and they followed her in the accessories of her behaviour, rather than in the practice of her art. In the theatre, the Great Sarah has still not yet been rediscovered as a fashionable model for serious young actresses—those who still believe that acting is an art, a vocation and a mystery (in the old sense of that word). Serious young actresses don't seem to be turned on by monsters of showmanship and egotism, for those who can't see more in her than that. And if you believe in the theatrical gospel according to Brecht or Grotowski or Brook (whatever Brook's gospel *is* these days), if you believe in group creation and backstage industrial democracy and conspicuous socio-political relevance—well then, you are likely to find the Bernhardt legend not only theatrically dead but somewhat immoral—for rather different reasons from those that conscientious objectors to Sarah found in her own time. There are, of course, other grounds for dissent: dissent from putting performing egos first; choosing vehicles rather than works of art—and fancy-dress vehicles at that, ignoring the world beyond the stage doors; disregarding the rights of players and characters below star level. There have always been objectors to Bernhardt and there always will be. But for latter-day theatrical Puritans especially, I suspect, she is still a handy symbol for the era of glamour, staginess, illusion, melodrama and theatricalism—the era that seems to them a part of the dark ages and appears to many of us to be not beyond the pale but beyond recall, except in other people's prose.

And yet, and yet . . . Sarah Bernhardt herself isn't really dead, in reputation and allure. In the past few years two new books about her have been published, bringing the total devoted to her alone to over a score. Her own memoirs have just been reissued in Britain, after seventy years. In Canada, CBC fairly recently screened a special documentary about her, with Zoe Caldwell playing the part of Sarah. A large capital investment has been made in a film about her, with Glenda Jackson. *Memoir*, a new play about her by John Murrell, directed by Eric Salmon with Siobhan McKenna as Sarah, was performed at the 1977

Guelph Spring Festival for the first time anywhere, and was later repeated in London. Whatever else people may say about Sarah, it seems fairly clear that she is still going strong in the immortality stakes. I can't help remembering something that Maurice Rostand said about her: "The mysterious thing about her is that her most lasting radiance began when the curtain fell."

I am not here proposing to discuss in any detail Sarah's acting style, the quality of her repertory or the aesthetics of her productions. My colleagues on other pages are far better qualified to do that. What I'm going to do is to take a look at Bernhardt from the other side of the English Channel, in comparison with some leading British actresses of her time, in the context of being a player queen in Britain, and suggest some of the things that the comparison tells us about queenship in the theatre.

As everybody knows, it was just over a century ago, in 1879, that Bernhardt was first seen outside France, when she came to London with a company from the Comédie Française. She was then thirty-four. Her astonishing, instant success in that season changed the course of her life, the kind of actress that she was to be. Already, at the end of that brief season, Henry James could write about Sarah's ecstatic reception that she was "a sort of fantastically impertinent victrix poised upon a perfect pyramid of ruins—the ruins of a hundred British prejudices and proprieties". She was victrix, too, over the handful of actresses who then led the British stage. And she stayed victorious over them—and their successors—throughout her career: not necessarily in what they did, but in what she *was*. There were challenges elsewhere, of course: from Duse, most of all. But there were no real challenges to Bernhardt's supremacy from English actresses in 1879, or at any time during her life, or since: on the stage, at least.

What made Bernhardt so dazzlingly different—or *seem* so dazzlingly different—from British actresses, past and present? Before we look at some particular players, let us look at some of the general answers to that question: the question of the Great Sarah's great difference. And let us assume—as I am assuming here—that this difference lies primarily in the fact that she was a great theatrical artist, showing greatness in her intelligence, her imagination, her presence, the way she used her body on the stage, the way she died, her eyes and, above all, her voice. (I use the word "great" here advisedly, in the belief that it may safely be applied to no more than a dozen Western actresses in our theatrical history.) Prodigies like Bernhardt are very, very rare. That should be obvious, whether you approve of them or not, but it has seemed at times to be overlooked by commentators. Now I have to stress another platitude, at the risk of seeming facetious: the fact that she acted in French and that she came from Paris. Paris was, at that time, the source of some 90 percent of the acted English drama, after a great deal of neutering and deodorising. It was also, in middle-class myth, the pulsating source of sin and pleasure, out of bounds: the capital of theatre—and the capital of sex. Sarah was an exotic, *ipso facto*, and far more exotic than the rest, both on and off stage. Like many visiting exotics in Britain, at least until recent times, she throve on the amiable disposition of London playgoers to find actresses far more significant, oracular and disturbing if they were acting in a language that the majority of the audience didn't understand (a *spoken* language, as distinct from a language of the body). They were satisfied as long as there was something *going on*; and with Sarah Bernhardt there was usually *plenty* going on—blackmail, treason, torture, suicide, murder and *lots* of adultery.

Another manifest difference between Bernhardt and her English contemporaries in her prime time was her personal showmanship or, rather, show*woman*ship, because she didn't answer to any male ringmaster. Henry James said about her London début that she was an instant celebrity because she "desired with an intensity that has rarely been equalled to be a celebrity, and to this end all means were alike to her". He did not make the mistake of saying that this was the *only* reason; he admitted that she was a remarkable artist, as well as a remarkable publicist; but many people in the anti-Bernhardt camp—which looks like being a permanent settlement—have continued down the years to set most of Sarah's glory down to her Barnum side: her extravagance of behaviour and dress, her show business razzmatazz, her carefully managed exposure of parts of her off-stage lives. Certainly she had no real competition in this respect from any English actress. The gold rush of personality prospectors was well under way in Britain before Bernhardt made her last headlines; but she was—and still is—unequalled in the theatre as a self-promoter.

Another reason for Bernhardt's difference from the natives was that she was a loner: a liberated woman, in comparative terms. Most notably, she had no consort. Most leading British actresses acted in conjugal partnership. Their husbands were their managers, often their leading men, usually their main financial beneficiaries. In her hey-day Bernhardt was in business, effectively, on her own, as a star, for herself. Male partners met temporary needs, including the servicing of the publicity machine, but the contracts were not indissoluble. Unlike British actresses, Bernhardt could defy conventions and still keep her throne. The fact that some people thought of her as a scarlet empress did not matter: indeed, in box office terms, it helped— as it would never have helped a British actress on her home ground. She was, ultimately, her own mistress; and much of the time she was her own manager, with her own theatre as well as her own company.

If Bernhardt seemed so different in the 1880s, it was partly because she came at a time when in England the art of acting as *little* as possible was ousting the old addiction to the art of acting as *much* as possible. One could say, very roughly, that the mainstream of acting style was running closer to naturalism, under the influence of comedy. Tragedy was increasingly out of fashion. The school of Shakespeare was breaking up. What Sarah did—the effect she had—was closer to opera than to the contemporary drama of the spoken word that British audiences knew. If it *hadn't* been operatic, she would never have scored such a hit in so many countries where audiences had little idea of what she was saying. To them she was, among other things, a kind of singer. (It is worth recalling that a number of her rôles were translated into opera—Adrienne Lecouvreur, Fédora, Tosca, the Queen in *Ruy Blas*.) People came to see the prima donna rather than the play—how she sounded, how she looked, what she did and how she did it.

What's more, at this time, British actresses were becoming increasingly lady-like—and that meant exalting good behaviour, self-restraint, and not "making a scene". Being violent, over-emotional, gesticulatory and passionately demonstrative had come to be thought of as *common* and *foreign* among the respectable middle class in America as well as Britain. That Ibsenite pioneer Elizabeth Robins tells us that Shaw rebuked her for her gentility. "You'd be a better actress," he said, "if you were less taken up with being a lady." This was partly because she didn't want there to be any misunderstanding about her profession, which was still, even in the 1890s, she said, "liable to be confused with the oldest profession". And it was partly, one supposes, because she was reacting against staginess of behaviour among old-guard actresses. Yet if British actresses were getting more lady-like, it was largely because more of them were actually ladies—recruits from the middle classes, often better educated (though less theatrically experienced) than their predecessors. They were the new generation of amateurs, among the old pros. Sarah Bernhardt didn't worry about being a lady. She was a queen. And in queenship as in nearly everything else she was an immensely professional technician.

There is, I believe, a further difference between Bernhardt and British actresses, which has to do with Shakespeare. Until some eighty years ago the greatest rôles that Englishwomen could act in English were written by Shakespeare, although by no means all were available to the Victorians and those that they did play were often trimmed and bowdlerised. These characters include creations of genius: in romantic lyrical comedy there is nothing to touch them, perhaps, in any national repertoire. Yet in other kinds of rôles, beyond the Rosalinds and Beatrices and Juliets, the opportunities open to an ambitious English actress were more restricted than those that could, with luck, be seized by a French actress—in Racine, for example. Compared with Racine's more notable women, many of Shakespeare's—as seen on the Victorian stage in Victorian versions of the texts—lacked a full sexuality; and one may well remember that Racine wrote his rôles for women, some of them women he knew intimately, while Shakespeare wrote his for boys and men to play. The classic drama of antiquity appears to have had comparatively stronger roots in France, through the French classic drama of the seventeenth and eighteenth centuries, and the models set aspiringly by the Comédie Française and the Conservatoire. This repertoire, combined with the Romantic drama and the boule-vard theatre, gave French actresses a wider range than most of their English contemporaries in the Victorian age. This was especially true in plays other than comedies, no matter how Parisian fashions ebbed and flowed. The American critic Brander Matthews, talking about the French nineteenth-century drama, observed that "Only half of life gets into our literature." I think one might say that only half of woman got into the Victorian theatrical repertory in Britain—at least until the end of the century.

One reason for this was, of course, the difference between France and England in attitudes to sexual morality and sexual practices. This was an England, remember, in which Dumas's sentimental war-horse, *La Dame aux camélias*, could not be staged in English for years after its first production in Paris, although the story could be sung in Italian, in *La Traviata*. When an English version was staged, under the title of *Heartsease*, Dumas was given no credit for its original authorship: in polite circles he had the reputation of being little better than a pornographer. In *Heartsease*, Marguerite and Armand were presented for propriety's sake as being in some way *engaged*; and Henry James tells us that Marguerite's occupation was "enveloped in the most bewildering and mystifying pruderies of illusion", passed off as a "flirt" or a "coquette". Another English version was indeed dubbed *Camille: or, The Fate of a Coquette*. It is odd to reflect that it was apparently *Heartsease* that led to the first performance of the French original in England; or so Helena Modjeska says in her autobiography. Edward VII, when he was Prince of Wales, came round to her dressing room to see her after she had appeared in *Heartsease*. Full of enthusiasm for her performance, he asked about the original play; and when Modjeska told him that it could not be staged in England, the Prince said that he would do something about it. Be that as it may, it was in the following season that *La Dame aux camélias* was staged in London for the first time, nearly thirty years after its Paris *première*, with Bernhardt at the Gaiety.

That delay—even in the untranslated drama—is one of the absurder signs of the times. The British stage desperately relied in the last century upon the French stage to supply its raw material; but the material was often, by Anglo-Saxon standards, so *very* raw—morally. To quote Henry James again (in youth): "The light drama in France is a tissue of fantastic indecencies, the serious drama is an agglomeration of horrors." In France there was, he said sternly, "A congenital want of perception of certain rudimentary differences between the possible, for decent people, and the impossible." So what ensued was "an extraordinary manipulation and readjustment of French immoralities which goes on in the interests of Anglo-Saxon virtue". There were at least 80,000 prostitutes of all kinds at work in London, many of them very obviously plying their trade near the theatres and in theatre bars and restaurants. Some of them were fairly celebrated characters, with celebrated male patrons and protectors. Yet until the 1890s a British dramatist could not acknowledge the existence of even the most refined and civilised courtesans. Across the Channel, however, the courtesan had not only been morally rehabilitated in the drama but sentimentalised and idealised; and this process had been going on at a great rate for some fifty years before Bernhardt first came to London.

The fact is that there was in Britain a persistent, even—in some quarters—obsessive, Puritanism, reflected in the official censorship of the Lord Chamberlain. This made it impossible for British actresses—even if they wanted to do so—to play many of the characters and say many of the things that were possible for French actresses. Victorian players were naturally influenced by the prudery and humbug of the time, by the double-think about sex and the double-feel—combining fear and fascination, envy and disgust. What is more, some were also fighting against the traditional view that all actresses were fair game and easy pickings. If they wanted to give their profession a new social status, it was clearly helpful if they kept themselves to characters who were irrefutably *pure*—close to that womanly condition, so admired by Victorian male moralists, of being an Angel in the House. To quote Fanny Kemble:

What knows the foreign artist of the inexorable element of Respectability—a power which, tyrannical as it is, and ludicrously tragical as are the sacrifices sometimes exacted by it, saves . . . the artistic class of England from those worst forms of irregularity which characterise the Bohemianism of foreign literary, artistic and dramatic life.

So much for generalities: now to some particulars. Let us start by looking at the lady who was the doyenne of British actresses when Bernhardt first came to London. It was in that year of 1879 that Helena Faucit made her last appearance—in *As You Like It*, at the age of sixty-two, as Rosalind. She was married to the biographer of the Prince Consort, Sir Theodore Martin, and was eminently eligible to be a guest at Windsor. In her time Helena Faucit had been highly praised by Dumas and Gautier when she had played in Paris with Macready. She had seen and admired Rachel. I do not know if she ever saw Bernhardt, who is not mentioned by Sir Theodore in his biography; but he tells a story about Rachel which is worth citing in this context as a pointer to the canyon between the world of Sarah and the world of her British contemporaries. Miss Faucit had found in 1841 that she and Rachel had what she called "a natural bond of sympathy". At that time Rachel had what Sir Theodore describes as a "spotless character", and was received by "some of the best families in the Quartier St. Germain". When Helena Faucit returned to Paris in 1844, Rachel's "bond of sympathy" had not snapped: on the contrary, she was among the warmest admirers of the British actress and tried hard to meet her again and renew their relationship. But Miss Faucit was told that Rachel's character was no longer spotless and that she was no longer received by those families in the Quartier St. Germain; so she refused to meet Rachel, and never saw her again.

Here is another pointer that concerns us. Some years later Helena Faucit appeared in one of Rachel's successes, *Adrienne Lecouvreur*—or, rather, in a version of the play by Sir Theodore. Even in a deodorised form, she found the piece too disturbing and dropped it from her repertoire after only a handful of performances. Her husband explained in his biography that she turned back to heroines with whom she was "in fuller sympathy"—in particular, "the healthful heroines of Shakespeare and our own dramatists". In the work of those dramatists, like Sheridan Knowles and Westland Marston, Helena Faucit appeared to be a major actress. The *Dictionary of National Biography* sums up her achievement revealingly: "In imaginative parts she had a species of poetical inspiration which was in its way unique. In fact, as a representative of wifely devotion, virginal grace and moral worth, it is difficult to know whom to oppose against her." Note the logic of that "in fact"—as if equating poetical inspiration with moral allegiance to the masculine codes of how women should behave and actresses should act. As Ellen Terry once said, "In our profession *behaviour* is everything."

The high-minded tradition of Helena Faucit was strikingly incarnated in one of the leading British actresses of Berhardt's golden days—Madge Kendal. Bernard Shaw didn't think much of the plays in which Mrs. Kendal appeared, but said that she was "supreme" in high comedy and praised her "mastery of her art and of herself". James Agate ranked her with Bernhardt, Duse and Réjane among the six greatest actresses in his experience (the other English contenders being Ellen Terry and Mrs. Patrick Campbell). Clearly, she was another major actress—even if Agate's estimate seems bizarre—and she exerted not only a theatrical but a moral influence. She and her husband worked together for nearly forty years without a breath of scandal about them, or about the plays they chose. Indeed, if artists who had worked for the Kendals later acted in a play that Madge Kendal thought was morally dubious, she would cross them off her visiting list. Mrs. Kendal once said that to be a great actress you required "the courage of a lion, the strength of an elephant and the hide of a rhinoceros". In that case, you may think, Bernhardt might qualify. But Mrs. Kendal gave no evidence of any real enthusiasm for Sarah's work. She told James Agate, in old age, that Ristori was a greater actress than Bernhardt because Ristori had no sex appeal; but that Rachel was greater than either. She wrote in her memoirs that Modjeska was a greater Marguerite than Bernhardt, because Bernhardt always gave her "the impression that her passion was temporary and could not endure till the end of her life". She makes scarcely any other reference to Bernhardt, although she lavishes praise on some other forgotten actresses, with a tendresse for those who died or retired early. But she was more explicit in talking to Margaret Webster, who in her autobiography quotes Mrs. Kendal as saying, "Yes, indeed, Sarah was a great actress—from the waist down."

The real English player queen of the day was Ellen Terry—of all artists, almost certainly, the one who least resented Sarah's glory. In the last decade of both their lives, when Bernhardt was honoured on the stage of the London Coliseum, Ellen presented her with a bouquet, saying, "Queen Sarah, you have no more devoted subject than Ellen Terry." And she *meant* it—allowing for a bit of Ellenish extravagance.

In some ways Sarah and Ellen were alike. Both were devoted to their sons. Both attracted passionate loyalty from women as well as men. Both were painters' actresses: superb makers of stage pictures. Both were original dressers. Both invented a new kind of beauty. For Ellen, as for Sarah, part of her unique power on the stage derived from the quality of her life off the stage. Both had a fierce appetite for life. Both were great charmers. But the differences between them were far more conspicuous than their similarities. To English audiences Ellen Terry seemed to be "immensely natural". By comparison, in Britain Bernhardt appeared "supreme in artifice". Ellen seemed ultra-English. Bernhardt's training was rooted in the French theatre, but she transcended time and place. Ellen has rightly been described as a liberating personality, yet the freedom she enjoyed outside the theatre was not sought by her inside it. She said, "I have always been more woman than artist"; and she put "a good heart" first of all requirements for being a good actress, closely followed by imagination, industry and intelligence. Ellen's range of rôles was surprisingly small, not only compared with Bernhardt's but also with that of some of her English contemporaries. In the prime of her acting life she was subordinate to an actor-manager, Henry Irving, as the leading lady of the Lyceum Company; and, although she was two years younger than Bernhardt, her career effectively stopped a dozen years before Sarah's.

Ellen Terry first saw Sarah Bernhardt act in 1866, when Sarah was at the Comédie Française. Ellen was there that Easter on her first visit to France. She couldn't speak a word of French but she was very impressed by Paris in the spring, and by Bernhardt. As thin as a harrow, Ellen called her. Later, when they got to know each other, Ellen admired Sarah even more. When she saw Bernhardt as Cleopatra in Sardou's version, Ellen thought her "the essence of Shakespeare". She wrote in her diary: "I went round and implored her to do Juliet. She said she was too old. She can *never* be old." When Ellen saw Sarah in *Frou-Frou* (which Ellen had played in a pasteurised version), she wrote: "I wondered that I had the presumption to meddle with it. No people in their right senses could have accepted my Frou-Frou instead of Sarah's." There is a justly celebrated passage in Ellen's memoirs describing Bernhardt in the 1880's: "She was as transparent as an azalea, only more so; like a cloud, only not so thick. Smoke from a burning paper describes her more nearly. She was hollow-eyed, thin, almost consumptive. Her body was not the prison of her soul, but its shadow." To Ellen, Bernhardt on the stage always seemed "more a symbol, an ideal, an epitome than a woman. It is this quality that makes her so easy in such lofty parts as Phèdre." We have to remember that one of the qualities for which Ellen Terry herself was most persistently praised by British critics was her *womanliness*—a quality that seemed detestable to one of her greatest admirers, Bernard Shaw. But Ellen went on to say, in this discerning passage, that it was "this extraordinary decorative and symbolic quality of Sarah's which made her transcend all personal and individual feeling on the stage. No one plays a love scene better, but it is a *picture* of love that she gives, a strange exotic picture rather than a suggestion of the ordinary human passion as felt by ordinary human people."

And what did Sarah think of Ellen? On the surviving evidence, not much. I can discover nothing of consequence in the Bernhardt biographies. All that Ellen herself says in her memoirs is that Sarah saw Ellen's Juliet, on the one hundredth performance at the Lyceum, and afterwards "said nice things to me". Mrs. Comyns Carr told a story about a supper party in the Beefsteak Room at the Lyceum in 1892 when the talk turned to the effect of old age on acting. Irving said mournfully that it would come to them all, but Sarah leaned over the table to Ellen and said, "My darling, there are two people who shall never be old—you and I." That is about all that we have on record. But we are told by Graham Robertson—who admired both Sarah and Ellen immoderately, and was a devoted friend of both actresses—that while Ellen "understood Sarah completely and, as a natural result, liked her greatly", Sarah "knew little or nothing about Ellen". There is no mention of Ellen in Sarah's memoirs, published in 1907, and the omission seems significant. Bernhardt praises only two British players—Henry Irving and Mrs. Patrick Campbell. In his book about Sarah, Maurice Baring confirms that she admired "hardly any actors and actresses on the English stage without great reservations". She admired the music hall performers Arthur Roberts and Little Tich without any reservations at all; and for her the really outstanding artist on the British stage was Marie Lloyd, who was, said Sarah, "a great genius". Mr. Baring explained that Bernhardt was "a severe critic of acting"—especially when it was done, perhaps, by actresses.

Stella Campbell—Mrs. Patrick Campbell, as she was always known—was sometimes compared with Bernhardt, and was even ranked with her (or above her) by some admirers who talked (as Bernard Shaw did) of her "genius". Of all English actresses in that time, Mrs. Pat was probably nearest to Sarah in temperament, if not in talent, and she maintained a long-standing friendship with Bernhardt, which survived the curious experiment—made at Bernhardt's insistence—of acting together in *Pelléas et Mélisande*, with Sarah (aged sixty) playing the young male lover. Mrs. Pat deployed an un-English capacity for passion on the stage, and a Mediterranean, voluptuous beauty (she was part-Italian by birth). Like Bernhardt, she was a beautiful mover, had lustrous eyes and a musically expressive voice, deep and throaty, and exuded immense charm and personal magnetism. Early in her career, Mrs. Pat was praised (by William Archer) for her "affectively undulant and Bernhardtesque languor"; and her supreme success——as Pinero's Paula Tanqueray in 1893— was achieved, significantly, in the rôle of a contemporary (though retired) courtesan: a break-through (scandalising as it seemed to many Victorians) to freedoms long enjoyed by French actresses and authors. Mrs. Pat attempted several Bernhardt rôles; and here the comparison begins to fail. For she had to give up Fédora after a few weeks because she could not cope vocally with the part; and her first Magda was dismissed almost contemptuously by Shaw (though years later she is said to have excelled in the rôle). Like Bernhardt she went into management on her own, with an imaginative programme of new European plays; but this venture, like many of her enthusiasms, was short-lived.

Although Mrs. Patrick Campbell had the makings of a great actress—the proof lies in the impact of her best performances on actors and critics of two generations, like James Agate, John Gielgud, Ralph Richardson and Maurice Baring—she was, it seems clear, far below the Bernhardt (or the Terry) class. In Graham Robertson's words, her life appears "a record of talent thrown away, wasted time, lost opportunities". Among the principal reasons for this protracted failure in self-realisation is that she lacked some of the requisites of greatness which Bernhardt exemplified: self-discipline, concentration, industry, stamina, and professionalism. "I choose to be an amateur", Mrs. Pat once said to Shaw; and he replied, "You don't want to be an amateur. You want to be a lady." She enjoyed the personality cult that grew up around her; she prized the social success that her acting brought; but, as her autobiography and her working life show, she never took that acting seriously enough or sufficiently valued the theatre itself. For Bernhardt, the stage was a devouring obsession; for Mrs. Patrick Campbell, it was a diversion that soon became boring, a way of making money and friends, a bit of a joke.

To find an English actress who may be considered as in any way really comparable with Bernhardt—as a woman, a phenomenon, an artist—I think we must go back beyond the Victorians, right back to Sarah Siddons. Mrs. Siddons still seems the greatest, certainly the grandest, and about the best-known name among the island player queens. She is almost the only one who appears to have combined Bernhardt's volcanic intensity and power with her impact on taste and her personal authority— allowing for differences in acting conventions, the climate of the time, and British *pudeur*. Mrs. Siddons was a paragon of the big bow-wow style. She could rage and weep with all the stops out. She put audiences in awe, even in fear and trembling, by her blazing contempt and fury. She could set them off crying by her torrential grief. There was no one to touch her in her hey-day, from about 1782 to 1812: no competitors on the scale of Duse. She was immensely regal: disdainful, imperious, majestic. She was also very feminine: capable, especially in her early career, of projecting great tenderness. But there was *steel* in Mrs. Siddons, as there is in all great players; and there must have been a strong masculine streak—something, again, indispensable to a great actress.

Mrs. Siddons had a great actress's voice: if not "golden", like Bernhardt's, bronze. It had a wide range, in anger, tenderness, pathos and terror; and she could shriek and scream in a way that seemed unparalleled. She had a great actress's eyes, too. You could see them from the back of the theatre, glaring or shining, large and liquid and *speaking*: they could tell you volumes before she spoke. Like all great actresses, she was a mistress of silences. She was also a mesmerist: holding in her eyes a crowded theatre—and those theatres were often much bigger than today's—just standing there, looking, without saying a word. "Her very body seemed to think", one admirer said. And she was a great listener. All this helped to make Sarah Siddons seem more than human, as Sarah Bernhardt sometimes seemed. She, too, was compared with prophetesses and goddesses. She, too, seemed to command a supernatural power.

So far, the two Sarahs may sound somewhat alike. But there were obvious and significant differences between them. Sarah Siddons was not, by most accounts, good in comedy. She never played outside Britain. She brought up a large family, was firmly married to one husband and, as far as we may tell, never took a lover. There were, in her late middle age, two scandals about supposed affairs or emotional embroilments with younger men. Yet it is a signal tribute to her reputation that both scandals soon died out and that she seems to have survived them, in public esteem, totally unscathed. The immense national authority that she enjoyed was, ultimately, *moral*. The goddesses to whom she was sometimes compared were Greek only in their outer aspect, as depicted chastely in classical marble. In Sarah Siddons there was nothing of the seductress, the siren, the witch or the vamp. Her passion and her violence were those of the doting mother, the loving sister, the faithful wife, the vengeful widow. About her queenliness there was something sexless—or at any rate supra-sexual. When she played a Fallen Woman or a Soiled Dove (in the idiom of Bernhardt's time), it was in deep penitential gloom. She did manage to present two such object lessons (taken from the German) who were *not* punished for their sins by being killed off in the last act, and these were among her most successful rôles. In those characters as in others, however, "Sex was out of the question", as William Robson said in *The Old Playgoer*. You can see why Byron might have remarked that he should as soon think of going to bed with the Archbishop of Canterbury as with Mrs. Siddons. Yet Byron thought she was "the beau ideal of acting". Nothing, he said, "ever was, or can be, like her".

So much, or rather, so briefly, for Sarah Siddons. For another parallel to Bernhardt, I think, we must go back yet another century, to a world where, for a time, not only actresses but a lot of other Englishwomen who didn't sell their labour or their bodies for a living enjoyed a degree of sexual freedom largely denied to women until the present century. It is also a world where theatrical freedoms were wider for British actresses than they were in the era of Madge Kendal and Ellen Terry.

The woman I have in mind is Elizabeth Barry, who flourished in the post-Restoration period. When she retired in 1710 at the age of fifty-two she had been on the stage for thirty-seven years, most of them at the top of her profession—which was still a brand new one. (The very first English actress to be seen on the London stage had appeared only fourteen years before Mrs. Barry made her début.) Now, Mrs. Barry did not have the least shred of moral authority, unlike Mrs. Siddons; and unlike Mrs. Siddons she never married (Mrs. was a courtesy title) and had a number of lovers. These apparently included a number of authors—Rochester, Otway and maybe Etherege. What's more, she was a fiercely independent loner who fought for her rights. She helped to lead a players' rebellion in 1695 and to organise a new company: not as a second-class citizen, not at the heels of a husband, but on level pegging with the male actors. That sounds more like Sarah Bernhardt. Like Sarah, Elizabeth Barry could rant and flame and frighten as exotic empresses, princesses and sinners from all parts of the Grub Street globe. Like Sarah, she could play in comedy as well as tragedy and heroic drama. She was a "mistress of tears" and had regal dignity— "born to excel and to command". She could excel in the nearest English equivalents to Racine and Corneille, as well as in Shakespeare and Otway. Unlike Mrs. Siddons, Mrs. Kendal and Miss Terry, she also successfully filled the off-stage rôle of Jezebel, *femme fatale*, Temptress, and Medusa. She was a scapegoat for male lust, frustration, hatred and guilt. And that is another point of comparison between Elizabeth Barry and Sarah Bernhardt, another link with an older British tradition. For part of the function of a star actress may be to serve as a scapegoat as well as an idol.

As we have seen, however, the main British tradition of player queenship—displayed primarily in Shakespeare—has come to be one of professional supremacy reinforced by moral authority: a tradition exemplified in the twentieth century by the work of Dame Sybil Thorndike and Dame Peggy Ashcroft, who have served the theatre not as prima donnas and virtuoso soloists but as collaborators in the realisation of great plays, and who have reigned with the supra-sexual authority of great technicians, great artists, great democrats and great ladies.

Ultimately, of course, no valid comparison may be made between Sarah Bernhardt and anyone else—if you consider her as a whole: she was, and is, unique. Yet she does illustrate, in an exceptional way, one aspect of human behaviour which is a meaningful ingredient in the history of the British theatre and the entertainment industry as a whole. A. B. Walkley described it when he was writing about Bernhardt. He said: "The mythopoeic instinct in human nature insists upon having its wicked way with celebrated actresses". And Bernhardt gave that mythopoeic instinct more scope in Britain than most celebrated actresses. You can see the instinct at work in the prose of some of the best British critics and essayists of the day, writing about her as "a heathen idol that one ought to worship" and "more of a myth than a human being". Here is part of what Maurice Baring said about her:

She was . . . an incarnation of the spirit that in all times and countries, whether she be called Lilith or Lamia or La Gioconda, in the semblance of a Belle Dame sans Merci, bewitches the heart and binds the brain of man with a spell, and makes the world seem a dark and empty place without her and Death for her sake and in her sight a joyous thing.

Bernhardt created a new kind of ikon woman. In some ways she was a precursor of the New Woman—but in others she was the quintessence of the Old, a sort of ageless She-Ancient. She was a bitch goddess, and her cult was partly fed by the adoration of the bitch goddess of success. There is usually a good deal of ambiguity in the idolatry that focuses on a female star: an emotional muddle reflected, for instance, in Charlotte Brontë's description (in *Villette*) of the impact made by Rachel: "It was a marvellous sight, a mighty revelation. It was a spectacle low, horrible, immoral." Worshippers may turn quite rapidly into vengeful iconoclasts, as the history of Hollywood has shown from time to time. And the violence is illustrated by some of the more preposterous anti-Bernhardt propaganda—how she had seduced the Czar, or had a child by the Pope; how she used to rehearse with the skeleton of a man who had killed himself for love of her. That ambivalence was demonstrated in a poem written to her by one of her most ardent fans, Arthur Symons, when he was twenty-seven and she was forty-eight:

> I would taste all her agonies, have her to spare not,
> Sin deep as she sinned. . . .
> To be, for a moment, the man of all men to her,
> All the world, for one measureless moment complete;
> To possess, be possessed! To be mockery then to her,
> Then to die at her feet.

That was a very ninetyish sentiment; with echoes of Swinburne and a good deal else. You can see what George Jean Nathan meant when he said that the theatre lives by emotional sadism. But the cult of Bernhardt does not belong any more exclusively to the 1880s and 1890s than it does to France. It is probably, indeed, a good deal more vigorous in Britain and North America today than it is in the land of her birth: just because she was so magnificently strange, disturbingly different, a great outsider. Bernhardt gave to British playgoers the experience of being mastered by a woman in complete authority, a mesmerist at work. The hypnosis worked all the better because the abracadabra invocations were in a language that many people could not understand. She gave them the experience of paying homage, in a way that had long been impossible to give to real queens; and in a way that British player queens could not quite evoke. She gave people the chance of worship, in an age of increasing unbelief. She satisfied the British idea of the Actress Incarnate—in her voice, her clothes, her personality, her scandals. She brought back the sexuality that was missing from the serious British stage. And, for those people who cared about the art of acting, she was a great artist.

What kind of artist? What kind of woman? There she is, after half a century, still tantalising and provoking, still making people write books about her, produce films about her, write plays about her, organise international conferences around her, although very few of these people ever saw her act. They are all guessing, as we are guessing. I think Maurice Baring was right when he said that Bernhardt "will always be one of the permanent and beautiful guesses of mankind".

Finally, let us bring in a very different kind of English witness—Virginia Woolf! I take her evidence from a piece she wrote not long before she died, a piece about Ellen Terry; but I am taking the liberty of substituting for Ellen's name the name of Sarah, although Sarah was not, I think, Mrs. Woolf's sort of actress:

There is, after all, a greater dramatist than Shakespeare, Ibsen or Shaw. There is nature. Now and again nature creates a new part, an original part. The actors who act that part always defy our attempts to name them. But when they come on, the stage falls like a pack of cards and the limelights are extinguished. That was [Sarah Bernhardt's] fate—to act a new part. And while other actors are remembered because they were Hamlet, Phèdre or Cleopatra, [Sarah Bernhardt] is remembered because she was [Sarah Bernhardt].

5

Bernhardt on the London Stage

J. C. Trewin

1

I would like to move selectively across Sarah's visits to a city that—in spite of Bernard Shaw—she loved; and midway, to unveil (for a moment only) a personal King Charles's Head.

May I begin by dropping into poetry?—not my own, but that of the nearly forgotten Stephen Phillips, dramatist of the golden shuttle and the violet wool, the dreaming keels of Greece, the souls that flashed together in one flame. The year was 1912. Sarah Bernhardt, aged sixty-five, was appearing at—of all theatres—the London Coliseum, today an opera house, then the most celebrated music-hall in Britain. Hardly, I would say, a citadel of the classical stage—though that may not have troubled Sarah, with her admiration for Marie Lloyd: two rather different splendours of the Theatre Theatrical (it is a phrase that, in such a book as this, the reader will surely forgive me for repeating).

A distant cousin of Frank Benson, and trained as an actor in Benson's touring university of the stage—the supreme company of what, in my part of England, we call "the pomping folk"— Stephen Phillips was the shooting-star of verse dramatists. At the turn of the century he had been ranked incautiously with Sophocles, Shakespeare, Dante, Marlowe, Webster and—according to that usually restrained Scot, William Archer—"the elder Dumas speaking with the voice of Milton". It was rather

a lot for one man. In spite of those early intimations of immortality, the critics soon regretted their rapture. After three ornate
productions—and the *Nero* which came a few years later—Phillips and his neo-Elizabethan verse (all revival, no begetting)
swiftly declined. Even so, twelve years after his first outbreak,
he was still about, still ready with the kind of glib ceremonial
verse he wrote for Sarah Bernhardt, the actress who had ruled
the world's stage, the rival of the Italian Duse. Phillips's ode,
zoological and ornithological, began like this:

> O myriad-minded child of France
> That still canst half the earth entrance!
> Now panther stealing on its prey,
> Now waking lark in breaking day,
> Now tigress crouching in her lair,
> Then dove afloat on summer air,
> Enchantress of the voice of gold. . . .

And so on, and so on, to the last invocation, presumably the
Phillippine voice of Milton:

> Temple with classic phantoms tread,
> Thou resurrection of the dead!
> Here we salute thee from a shore
> From France divided now no more;
> No longer sundered by the brine,
> But lightly, strongly, bound to thine.

Yes, dreadful . . . but the poem was printed in the old *Westminster Gazette*. And the *Gazette* did have a genuine literary reputation. We must suppose that Sarah's protean fame, lark,
panther, tigress, and dove, and the remembered fame of Phillips, echoing in a vault, had between them overpowered the
editor. The simple fact was that Sarah had overpowered everyone since she first landed from the sundering brine at Folkestone
pier. She was then, in the early summer of 1879, on the way to
London for the visit of the Comédie Française—forty-three performances, in eighteen of which she would appear—at the Gaiety
Theatre by the Strand. This was John Hollingshead's theatre,
devoted to extravaganza, burlesque, the "lighter lyric stage".

Not that Sarah minded: Gaiety, Adelphi, Coronet, Coliseum—through life she never troubled about her theatres; whatever they were she made them her own. She was thirty-four when she landed that May morning: looking taller than she was, very thin, neither fair nor dark, her eyes deep and dark brown, her face the "delicate features" that Matthew Arnold would see under a shower of hair and a cloud of lace.

As (if we may change again) this orchid of the French theatre appeared on the Folkestone landing-stage, she heard a cry of "Vive Sarah Bernhardt!" Next, a tall, pale young man "with the ideal face of Hamlet"—it was Johnston Forbes Robertson, not yet with a hyphen in his name—came up to present her with a tribute about which there is a slight difference of opinion. It could have been a bunch of violets. Sarah, typically, preferred to call it a gardenia. One of her companions and rivals said, with a certain spite: "They'll be making you a carpet of flowers next." And, on the word, the carpet arrived. A young man with long, flowing hair, who always doubled and redoubled any gesture—his name was Oscar Wilde—scattered at Sarah's feet an armful of lilies. Sarah had no wish to trample on them. But there they were. It was, on the whole, a complicated beginning, and it must have been something of an anti-climax to arrive later in a London drizzle at Charing Cross Station, with no noticeable welcome and no flowers, either in the hand or underfoot. Indeed, even the promising red carpet in the station was not for the French company but for the Prince and Princess of Wales, Edward and Alexandra. Tactlessly, they had left that afternoon for Paris: not in itself the most heartening news.

Never mind. Half an hour later Sarah was handed down from her carriage at the wide-open door of the house in Chester Square where she would lodge. Within she found an immense bouquet inscribed simply "Welcome! Henry Irving." It was a semi-regal salute from the English stage, though Ellen Terry would murmur, much later, that "of [Sarah's] superb powers as an actress, I don't believe Henry ever had a glimmering notion". One great idiosyncratic player unable to recognise another.

Sarah was to open at the Gaiety on June 2, 1879. This, in its various ways, was quite a year in international stage history: a major event, the appearance of Ibsen's *A Doll's House*; a minor

one (at the time), the inauguration of the Shakespeare Memorial
Theatre at Stratford-upon-Avon. We must decide for ourselves
where Sarah's début in London can be placed. Though Sarah
came to love London, that summer it depressed her. She wrote:

Those tall houses with sash windows uncurtained; ugly monuments in
mourning with dust and grime; flower-sellers at the street corners, faces
sad as the rain, bedraggled feathers in their hats, and lamentable cloth-
ing, the black mud of the streets; the low sky; the funereal mirth of
drunken women hanging on to men just as drunken; the wild dancing
of dishevelled children round the street organs as numerous as the
omnibuses—all this caused a curious indefinable suffering to a Parisian.

That was the London of a century ago. She would find that
it was, in fact, a special city; slowly its charms were revealed,
the "beauty of the aristocratic women", the "dizzying movement
of Hyde Park", the generous hospitality, the men's wit which
compared favourably with that of Frenchmen: "Their gallantry—
much more respectful and so much more flattering—does not
make me regret the gallantry of the French."

The first Gaiety programme was an ample triple bill, its centre-
piece (in which Sarah would appear) the second act of *Phèdre*
where Phèdre owns to Hippolyte her fierce and incestuous love.
London playgoers, excited by the news from Paris (a city regarded as a kind of blissful and perpetual orgy) waited for Sarah
as they had always waited for some mysterious and exotic for-
eigner. True, some—like the obstinate Yorkshireman in quite
another context—refused to yield to rumour. "*Show* me!" the
man had said; that night at the Gaiety many were saying "*Show
us!*" as they waited in the elaborate scarlet and gold theatre.
Outside were the six lamps that, ten months before, had lit the
Strand with electricity for the first time.

Sarah herself would electrify any doubters. A single night
established her in London. In effect, it would establish her there
through forty-two years. It was the more remarkable because
Rachel was still remembered, and comparison can be the dead-
liest form of criticism, something Dogberry said better and more
briefly. Moreover, Sarah was what the French know as a *tra-
queuse*, subject to stage fright. That evening, in her hot Gaiety
dressing-room, she was almost afraid to go on:

Three times over I put rouge on my cheeks and darkened my eyes. Three times I took it all off again with a sponge. I thought I looked ugly, and it seemed to me that I was thinner than ever, and not so tall.

Then she closed her eyes and listened to her voice, which sounded to her off-key. Distraught now, she was warned that the second act of *Phèdre* was about to begin. She had put on neither veil nor rings; her cameo belt was unfastened; she felt that the words were escaping her. The actress, Thénard, who was playing the Nurse, said soothingly: "Calm yourself, Sarah! All the English have gone to Paris. There are only Belgians in the house."

"How silly you are!" Sarah cried. "You know how frightened I was in Brussels."

"All for nothing", said Thénard, who gets more and more like someone out of *Alice in Wonderland*. "There were only *English* people in the theatre that day!"

With this, Sarah Bernhardt, pardonably bewildered, found herself for the first time on an English stage. In desperation she pitched her opening speech on too high, too hysterical a note. She suffered acutely, and the suffering intensified her performance. She herself described what happened:

I wept, I implored, I cried out; and it was all real. . . . My tears were flowing, burning and bitter. I implored Hippolyte for the love that was killing me, and the arms I stretched out to Mounet-Sully were the arms of Phèdre, tense with cruel longing for his embrace. The inspiration of "the god" had come.

The "god" never left her. At the end she fainted and was carried to her dressing room, though when the audience, in a prolonged standing ovation, insisted upon seeing her again, she did return to take a call, supported in the arms of Mounet-Sully. Always, Sarah Bernhardt was a child of the Theatre Theatrical; as London knew her first, so she went on. That second act of *Phèdre* had decided her future. She would be an actress-manageress.

2

The Gaiety season was astonishing, Sarah's success more than that of the great national company. On her nights the guinea stalls were often re-sold for five guineas. The critic Francisque Sarcey wrote back to Paris: "Nothing can give any idea of the craze Sarah is exciting. It's a mania." Undeniably it was, though on only her second night she had fainted three times as she dressed for the play, the *L'Etrangère* of Dumas *fils*, and managed in the third act to cut her big scene entirely. I may be forgiven for remembering an old actor in the West-Country city of Plymouth, who flourished at about the same time as Sarah (whom he would never have heard of) elsewhere. When his memory went, as it did frequently, he was accustomed to say to anyone on stage with him, in any play of any period at any time: "Hold! Thou weariest me! Take thou this purse of gold, furnish thyself with richer habiliments, and meet me at my lodging straight." Whereupon he would leave the stage and let the other actors get on with it. (They did: provincial "stock" was a training that fortified them against any disaster.)

During her second Gaiety performance Sarah should have told to her fellow-actress an interminable and important story—important, at least, to the plot. Instead, she said quite calmly: "The reason I sent for you here, Madame, is that I wished to tell you why I have acted as I have. I have thought it over and have decided *not* to tell you today." It seemed to her and to the rest of a startled company that she had ruined the piece, but apparently neither audience nor critics—they can behave like this even now—noticed anything wrong. An influential Frenchman, who later read the text, exclaimed to Sarah: "So much the better! Very dull, that story, and quite useless!"

Anyway, after this sub-editorial adventure, all was triumphantly well. Sarah completed a double event by exhibiting some of her pictures and pieces of sculpture in a Piccadilly shop. She made enough money to run up to Liverpool, on one of her days off, to buy a cheetah and a wolfhound, and to receive a present of six chameleons. "I would have liked", she sighed wistfully, "to have a dwarf elephant."

It had been a startling visit. During the following summer, 1880, she came back to London, but without cheetah, wolfhound, dwarf elephant or, for that matter, the support of the Comédie, with which she was at war and to which she would have to pay substantial damages for breaking her contract. Sarah was a permanent Declaration of Independence: she had to have her own company. A. B. Walkley, a young man then, who one day would be a principal drama critic, said long afterwards: "The extraordinary, the exaggerated, the unreasoning fuss that was made over her in London in 1879 suggested to her soul to become like a star and to dwell apart. It was the Gaiety French season of 1879 that turned Sarah Bernhardt into Sarah Barnum."

Extraordinary, exaggerated, unreasoning: those are harsh words. Agreed, London audiences lost control: a "mania", as Sarcey put it; but the mania would endure in varying degrees through four decades. As he showed when he became a drama critic, Walkley—quiet, fastidious and, with reservations, an admirer of Sarah—was not a man for the theatre's more tumultuous acclamation, today's fan-worship. Still, there seems to have been a certain mild discomfort among practising drama critics in the season for 1879. Joseph Knight of *The Athenaeum*, for one. He began with a ponderously-expressed cheer:

What in most members of the company is true and highly cultivated talent is in Mlle. Bernhardt genius. We are not disposed to plunge into the sea of troubles that awaits those who attempt a definition of the quality. We content ourselves with a bare assertion that the powers of dramatic exposition possessed by this lady reach this point.

And yet:

The present generation attests, maybe too warmly, certainly with something of fanaticism, its delight in a class of acting which seemed to have been lost to the stage, and in so doing contrives to spoil what it so profoundly admires and enjoys. Prudential considerations are not likely to weigh with the public, nor can they be expected to do so.

They seldom did. Thenceforward, Sarah would usually be a storm over London; a disciplined frenzy; on her night—for her performances could be a sierra—a technician who watched herself acutely through the whirlwind and the tempest of passion. As for the "seductive Sarah", *Punch* had hailed her as early as 1879:

Mistress of Hearts and Arts, all met in you!
The picturesque, informed by soul of passion!

> Say, doest thou feed on milk and honey-dew,
> Draining from goblets deep of classic fashion,
> Champagne and nectar, shandy-gaff sublime . . . ?

She brought back her champagne and nectar, and not a little shandy-gaff, sublime or not, when in 1880, again at the Gaiety Theatre, and within a few breaths of Irving and Ellen Terry at the Lyceum, she roused her audience with the death scene—death from poison—in *Adrienne Lecouvreur* (naturally, she collapsed in the dressing room afterwards: "I die quite well", she said). She was also the social butterfly in *Frou-Frou*, a part Ellen Terry acted later in the English provinces. Bernhardt had developed a true affection for London and Londoners, though she was never sure of the physical aspect. She once wrote:

> I prefer our pale mud to the London black mud, and our windows opening in the centre to the horrible sash windows. . . . Ours open wide: the sun enters the heart of the dwelling. . . . English windows open only half-way, either the top half or the bottom half. One may even have the pleasure of opening them a little at the top and a little at the bottom, but not at all in the middle. The sun cannot enter openly, nor the air. The window keeps its raffish and perfidious character. I hate the English window.

3

In spite of the "perfidious windows", she never failed to return on these flamboyant visits, the sun entering the heart of the dwelling, her London audiences carried through what Henry James called an "agglomeration of horrors" and John Gielgud, in a preface to Dr. William Emboden's *Sarah Bernhardt*, has summarised as "the great procession of queens, princesses, adventuresses, and courtesans, as well as some of her strange transvestite excursions". Through the years (and again Gielgud speaks) she would glow as Théodora, coquette as Tosca, yearn and swoop as Marguerite Gautier. Or, in the words of Bernard Shaw, who never liked her, she would come every season with a new play in which she killed someone with any weapon from a hatchet to a hammer.

In London she was married, during April 1882, to an actor, Ambroise Aristide Damala (the marriage lasted less than a year). One by one, through the seasons, she played all her parts, fierce, seductive, orchidaceous, not invariably with complete critical approval (William Archer, whatever he thought of Phillips, could be unsure of Sarah), but keeping throughout her tireless personal power and her life-long death-wish. No actress was happier in her dying, and her audiences expected it, at any length. The theatre would change about her. She cared nothing for that, nothing for the day's social and ethical variations. She went on being herself, through the 'nineties, through the Edwardian era, Sarah Bernhardt insulated in her own world. Her most fervent English admirer was Maurice Baring, who combined a passion for the romantic Theatre Theatrical with a milder homage to the Theatre of Ideas. Sarah had little to do with the second of these. It did not worry Baring, who would write of the actress's caressing voice in the first act of *La Tosca*, and of her foreshadowing glance when she caught sight of the knife on the supper table in the fourth act (see Plate 6); of Théodora, walking on like a Burne-Jones vision come to life in the glories of Byzantium; of La Samaritaine, evoking the spices, the fire, the vehemence, of the Song of Solomon; mediaeval Gismonda, with orchids in her hair. He remembered Sarah's movements and how a Frenchman, describing her descent of a hotel spiral staircase, said that, as she came down the steps, the staircase seemed to turn and she to be motionless. Baring remembered her voice, "so soft, so melting, so perfectly in tune and in time, with so sure a rhythm, and so perfectly clean-cut that one never lost a syllable, even when the words seemed to float from her lips like a sigh". We can add to this the memory of May Agate, whom Sarah taught, and who remembered her simile for final consonants. Sarah likened the actor to a fisherman casting his line. "It's all very well to throw it out, but you must bring it back again. Don't let your final sound go floating away, but be sure of a good, clean-cut finish."

In 1895, there was the unpremeditated "contest" between Bernhardt and Duse when Shaw insisted that they were playing

La Dame aux camélias and Sudermann's *Magda* against each other, one actress at Daly's Theatre, one (Duse) at Drury Lane. Shaw, of course, championed the quieter Duse; he insisted that Sarah, instead of first-class acting, offered only her reputation: "She does not enter into the leading character; she substitutes herself for it." Very well; but let me quote also a younger critic, James Agate (May was his sister), who, through life, was at Bernhardt's feet. He wrote in 1917: "Her art has been subject to a thousand comparisons: to a summer's day, to tropical lightning, to a wild beast ravening upon prey,* and by one gifted writer, C. E. Montague, to four such dissimilar things as the view of Florence from Fiesole, a pheasant's neck, Leonardo's Mona Lisa, and ripe corn with poppies in it. . . . Admittedly, it is a tedious and thankless task to translate fine acting into fine phrases. Those who have never seen Sarah will wonder at the tiresome excess of her critics' raptures; those who remember her acting at its best will marvel at the panegyrist's ineffectual poverty."

At the end of the 'nineties, for a while leaving Sardou and her usual repertory (now hardly from the quick forge and working-house of thought), Sarah played Hamlet. No half-measures: simply Hamlet. Baring was sure that she was the first to give to the French public an exact idea of the part, which she saw as a passionate, highly-coloured portrait of a young man of unclouded intellect. It was a less improbable choice than one might have imagined; after all, she had acted men before, Lorenzaccio for one, and she would come to L'Aiglon. In a previous *Hamlet*, several years earlier, she had cast herself as Ophelia without much success: not, I think, a Bernhardt rôle (death-scene off-stage). Now in 1899 she opened in Paris, in the Place du Chatelet by the river, her new theatre under her own name—the name, alas, has recently been changed—and during May of that year she put on *Hamlet* in a new and contentious prose version. Aged fifty-five, she went over to London during the following month to appear at the Adelphi in the Strand.

Female Hamlets were by no means rare. Sarah Siddons occasionally played the part in the provinces. During 1864, Shakespeare's tercentenary year, an actress named Alice Marriott, who

*This, not very happily, was the phrase of Arthur Symons. J.C.T.

(not that it mattered) would be Edgar Wallace's paternal grandmother, sought to make her audiences liegemen to the Dane at
Sadler's Wells, a theatre she had managed for six years. Apparently, it was quite a competent performance if (as with all
woman Hamlets) the onlooker could once suspend disbelief: not
altogether easy. There were other aspirants (according to the
Referee's critic, old Chance Newton) of "all shapes and sizes".
They included Clare Howard at the Pavilion in Whitechapel, an
actress "addicted to music cues": her Hamlet was presented in
the melodramatic fashion, with illustrative "chords" and
"crashes" when needed—and they were needed a great deal.
There was also Mrs. Bandmann-Palmer, who took the first half
of her name from her husband, a German Actor, Daniel Band-
mann. A short, squat woman, she did much of her playing on
the dark circuits of the manufacturing north of England during
the 'nineties and the early years of this century. Off-stage she
usually wore tweeds and hob-nailed boots, carried an oak walking stick, and had an insensate passion for watercress at all
times. She is said to have played Hamlet with some tragic force,
though because of rheumatism she had difficulty in rising from
her knees. Baliol Holloway, afterwards a renowned Shakes-
pearian, was in her company as a youth. One day, entering our
house in Hampstead like a gentle whirlwind—he was well over
seventy at the time—he exclaimed: "This is Mrs. Bandmann-
Palmer's doing. At my first rehearsal with her she said: 'Advance
boldly, young man, and do not lurk, I will not have lurkers in
my company.' "

This was the odd regiment of Hamlets that Sarah Berhardt
joined. No one would have called her a lurker. It was bad luck
that in that summer of 1899 she had in her audience Max Beerbohm, "the incomparable Max". Aged twenty-seven, he had
followed Shaw on *The Saturday Review* only twelve months earlier. Elsewhere he could admire Sarah—he called her "volcanic"—but on this occasion, Hamlet was a challenge he could
not resist. Heading his notice "Hamlet, Princess of Denmark"—
we assume that it was his own title and not a sub-editor's—he
began by marking the polite solemnity of the night. He objected
to the translation by Marcel Schwob: "The French language,
limpid and exquisite though it is, affords no scope for phrases

[that are] charged with a dim significance beyond their meaning, and with reverberations beyond their sound." Then he turned to Sarah:

Her friends ought to have restrained her. The native critics ought not to have encouraged her. The custom-house officials at Charing Cross ought to have confiscated her sable doublet and hose. I, a lover of her incomparable art, am even more distressed than amused when I think of her aberration at the Adelphi. Had she for one moment betrayed any faintest sense of Hamlet's character, the reminiscence were less painful. Alas! she betrayed nothing but herself, and revealed nothing but the unreasoning vanity which had compelled her to so preposterous an undertaking.

And he added:

One could not help being genuinely impressed by her dignity. One felt that Hamlet, as portrayed by her, was, albeit neither melancholy nor a dreamer, at least a person of consequence and unmistakably thoroughbred. Yes! the only compliment one can conscientiously pay her is that her Hamlet was, from first to last, *très grande dame*.

Mischievously amusing though he was, Max could be dangerous (thus, he did great harm to the Benson company by a silly and distorting notice of *Henry V*). Presumably Sarah had read his dismissal. No doubt she would have preferred Clement Scott, who thought that she was imaginative and poetical: though that does tell us little, at least he omitted "convincing" which, of all critical words, is the least helpful and should by this time have been ground into powder. Whatever Sarah felt, she appears to have kept it to herself. Certainly she was not prevented from making a journey to Stratford-upon-Avon as the only female Hamlet that had appeared, or ever would appear, in the first Memorial Theatre.

Nothing at all like the severe Royal Shakespeare Theatre that guards the Avon today, the Memorial was an eccentric, much-abused, much-loved building by the river: a "striped sugar-stick" built of brick with dressings of stone and some half-timbering, and with gables, turrets, a tall, fussy central tower and an assortment of sham-gothic decoration. Its architect, a Mr. Unsworth, protested that, on the whole, he had brought in everything pretty well. He had. Ultimately, his masterpiece was opened on the drenching night of April 23, 1879, Shakespeare's Birthday, with a *Much Ado About Nothing* in which Helen Faucit, once Macready's leading actress and the First Lady of the mid-Victorian stage, left her retirement to play Beatrice to Shaw's favourite, Barry Sullivan. This was just five weeks before Sarah's first appearance in London.

Presently, the Memorial grew into the home of the Frank Benson festivals. Benson was a remarkably winning man who could coax "great leviathans to dance on sands". Besides his own guests, heads of the London stage, there would frequently be extra-Festival visitors who wanted to play at Stratford simply because it was Shakespeare's parish. The American actress Ada Rehan came as both Rosalind and the Shrew (who seems now to leap from her portrait in the Picture Gallery); and about midday on June 29, 1899 Sarah Berhardt arrived at the town in state to end her visit to England with a flying matinée of *Hamlet*.

Certainly in state. Sarah's appearance caused intense excitement in what was still a secluded Warwickshire market-town. Its decorated streets were filled with people who waited to cheer the great actress on her way to Waterside. The High Steward of the borough met her special train—for Sarah could have no less—with the Mayor and the entire Corporation behind him; Marie Corelli, the novelist, not a retiring personage, and owner of the old house that today is the Shakespeare Institute (she would have liked this) presented Sarah with a bouquet tied in tricolour ribbon. Then—in the circumstances it was quite natural—Sarah drove down in the Corelli carriage through Wood Street and Bridge Street (but not by Shakespeare's Henley Street birthplace), and along by the river, to a theatre close-packed to the roof. (The members of Sarah's company managed to get there as well.) Stratford had never known higher-priced seats. People paid a guinea each, which was vastly expensive in those days, for either stalls or places in the front row of the circle. Even the gallery was five shillings. The reception was frenzied ("mania", Sarcey would have said). Bernhardt, dressed like pictures of the young Raphael, was called again and again. Years afterwards, Beerbohm forgotten, she was still saying: "I shall always remember my pilgrimage to Stratford. It is one of my heart's memories."

Critics less ironical than Max had spoken of this as an always-practical Hamlet who realised his task and his own danger in performing it. Maurice Baring, calling it the only intelligible Hamlet of the time except Forbes-Robertson's, put it among the finest achievements in Bernhardt's career:

What is perhaps the most poignant scene, if it is well played, is the conversation with Horatio just before the final duel when Hamlet says, "If it be not to come, it will be now." Sarah charged these words with a sense of doom, with the set courage that faces doom, and with the underlying certainty of doom in spite of courage that is there to meet it.

We can think also of Desmond MacCarthy. He remembered the moment when Hamlet ran his sword through the arras and heard the body of Polonius fall. "Sarah stood for a moment, tiptoe, like a great black exclamation mark—her sword glittering above her head." That was indeed Hamlet of the Theatre Theatrical. Max had not responded to it. Neither had *Punch* ,which unkindly suggested Irving for Ophelia.

4

Richard Findlater has named the other player queens of Sarah's time: none of them true rivals, and none likely for half a moment to consider a Hamlet. I have never been able to believe wholly in Mrs. Patrick Campbell—who seems to be a kind of theatrical folk-myth—but I once saw Madge Kendal, claimed by some critics to be the supreme English actress of her day. In later life, she seldom created any specially challenging part. (Who now remembers *The Likeness of the Night?*) Over eighty, and in retirement for nearly twenty years, Dame Madge had come down to the West of England to open a church bazaar. She looked like an angry Volumnia. The staff at the church hall shivered before her, and the chairman was in visible distress. She made her opening speech in tones that would have been heard across the estuary of the river Plym outside the doors, and the summer-heavy woods of Saltram beyond. When someone asked her what she thought of the city, she replied in a voice as steely as Dickens's Miss Murdstone: "It has changed greatly—for the worse". I disliked her intensely; but I could see, even then, that she must have been a remarkable actress—to Sarah as the Arctic to the tropics. They would never have understood each other. In life and art they were irrevocably sundered by the brine; and I cannot begin to imagine what Dame Madge would have made of the near-operatic Queen Elizabeth film Sarah made in her final years. Certainly I cannot imagine Baring writing of her as he did (before the preservative devices of our own period) in one of his most familiar tributes to Sarah:

She will always be one of the permanent and beautiful guesses of mankind, one of the lasting dreams of poets, one of the most magical speculations of artists, like the charm of Cleopatra, the beauty of Mary Stuart, the voice of the masters of the *bel canto*, the colours of Greek painting, and the melodies of Greek music. But it will be only a guess; because the actor's art dies almost wholly with the actor.

I said I would unveil my King Charles's Head. So much depended in Sarah's time, and indeed depends now, upon the drama critics of the period. It has been so since drama criticism began. In a sense, we might say that Edmund Kean (who, at his worst, must have been a really bad actor) was a superb romantic invention by Hazlitt. In the London of our own time Donald Wolfit's Lear, impressive but certainly not the best of its period (he was better as Kent in a Stratford production years before) entered history largely on the evidence of one man, James Agate. Fairly recently—a minor example—the British National Theatre has staged *Julius Caesar*. I happened to meet half-a-dozen people who had not seen the play, but who had read (between them) half-a-dozen reviews. Every reader had taken his or her opinion from his or her favourite critic and was prepared to defend it more or less to the death. Now, though (as it chanced) the reviews of John Gielgud's Caesar were unanimous, other opinions were sharply diverse. Those diverse opinions, read in various households over the country, will harden into fact. The fact will become legend; and that, in time, will become irrefutable. What will theatre historians do, a century on, when they seek to explain just what happened on the Olivier stage of the National Theatre on March 22, 1977?

Who, for that matter, can really say now what Sarah's Hamlet was like? We can guess, but it can be only a guess. Are we with Beerbohm or Baring?

We know a great many things about Sarah, yet it remains uncommonly difficult to see and hear her in the mind as she was in her prime. Every major artist was once the creation, for the public, of a single observer, or a small group of observers. Release the snowball of the written word, and presently, reinforced by narrative, rumour, interview, reminiscence, it swells to an avalanche. When, years ahead, the historian picks his way among the moraine of evidence, he can be alarmed—as this book may testify—by the conflicts of opinion, the contradictions, the repetitions: B borrowing from A, C from B and so on through the alphabet. Who was A? What was his authority? As the dying Alexander says in Rattigan's least typical play, "Where did it all begin?" Who is to be trusted, and why? Where would Sarah be if we had only the testimony of Bernard Shaw? There are hypnotic players. There have also been over-hypnotic drama critics. Over and over, in our mosaics, we return to the same names; and sometimes, I think, all credentials should be more closely examined. Minor critics have held major appointments. We examine the status of the player, but do we always examine the status of the witness?

5

Sarah seemed to flower again with the new century. When she wanted to take lessons to play Lady Macbeth in English, the teacher said: "I would gladly do it, but I can spare only half an hour a day." "Very well", Sarah replied, "You must try to let me have the half-hour from two to two-thirty a.m., for it is the only time I am not engaged." During each successive May and June she rarely failed to come to London. In 1905, when no West End theatre was empty, she went out to the semi-suburban Coronet (which is now a cinema) in Notting Hill, and in Maeterlinck's tragedy played Pelléas to the Mélisande of the comparably temperamental Mrs. Patrick Campbell. A Dublin critic said that they were both old enough to know better, but W. L. Courtney wrote in the *Daily Telegraph*, arguably, I think: "When criticism has nothing to say, one may be sure something has been seen rare and strange and beautiful." Courtney did not know—and it was lucky he did not—that at one of the performances Sarah took Mélisande's hand during a tender love scene and gently squeezed into it a raw egg.

Though she was unfaltering, her mid-Edwardian audiences and critics were a trifle less responsive. They were responding to her less as a sensation-drama in herself than as a guide showing them expertly round an ancient monument. Then, once more, there was fresh life. Some of the most tingling of her later appearances were on the immense prairie-stage of the Coliseum, the variety house where Sir Oswald Stoll booked her on five occasions, the first in 1910. Originally, she had cabled back the resolute refusal: "After monkeys, not", but she was persuaded to change her mind, and she arrived in St. Martin's Lane during the autumn of the year when she was sixty-six. That dignified figure, Sir Squire Bancroft, with the inevitable silk hat, morning coat, and dangling monacle, met her at Folkestone; this time the only lilies were from an unknown little girl who had bought them herself. Sarah first acted at the Coliseum in the second act of *L'Aiglon*, and during a further fortnight, as Tosca. She was paid a thousand pounds a week, the houses were reverent and rapt, and people stood five deep at the back of the circle. In 1912—thirty-three years after her English début—it was Arthur Bourchier, burly and authoritative, on the familiar damp pier at Folkestone. Sarah played some of Lucrezia Borgia, Phèdre, and Queen Elizabeth; and the Coliseum's publicity manager, Arthur Croxton, said: "In a great democratic house she got right into the heart of people to whom hitherto she had been a name." The management, over-awed, was not particularly democratic. From her dressing-room to an immaculately clean stage Sarah would walk for nearly eighty feet over a Turkey red carpet: it was laid so that her feet would not touch the boards that possibly performing elephants (even dwarf ones) had trod. Her manager would support her on her right and the leading man on her left; other members of the company would be in attendance. The passages Sarah chose were invariably the most florid; reeling, writhing, and fainting in coils, but always in the grand manner. If she felt the house was restless, she would cut as she went on (in the manner of *L'Etrangère* long before, but not for the same reason). There were occasional problems. I cannot resist mentioning the kind of triviality familiar in most stage autobiographies. On the first night, the Coliseum's official black cat, a little bored with the plate-spinners who had preceded *Phèdre*, had been washing herself in the wings; when the scene from *Phèdre* was ready to begin, the cat walked gravely across the stage—a long and arduous journey—inspected the audience, highly disliked what she saw and walked off by the opposite prompt entrance. Mercifully, a roar from the audience was obliterated at once by cheering for Sarah, who had seen nothing. Neither, we presume, had A. B. Walkley of the *Times*. "From the moment Phèdre tottered across the stage in the Nurse's arms, unpacking her heart, not so much with words as in a low, wailing melody, we were spellbound" (the customary phrase).

On this visit Sarah said to a London interviewer: "What you need is a real National Theatre with substantial aid from public funds. Every nation ought to have such a theatre." In its way, this might have been a gesture to the Comédie Française from an actress who, for British audiences, seemed to be herself the national theatre of France.

In 1913 she was back, now in scenes from Sardou's *Théodora*, Barbier's *Joan of Arc* (see Plate 7) and, inevitably, Marguerite Gautier. All, with their various arias and tirades, were from many years earlier or, as Agate said, the postscripts and codicils to masterpieces that were conceived and perfected long ago. Finally, in 1916, after her right leg had been amputated, she continued to act with an artificial limb: "I accept being maimed, but I refuse to remain powerless." She had to play everything seated; her most dramatic part was as the Cathedral of Strasbourg from a poem in which nun-like figures represented the cathedrals of France exhorting the country's youth to vengeance:

> Pleure, pleure, Allemagne,
> L'aigle, l'aigle allemand, est tombé dans le Rhin!

It was in a half-hour sketch she had written herself in a morning's work (though anonymous, most people knew it was hers) that John Gielgud saw her for the only time. He was thirteen years old, and, in his preface to Dr. William Emboden's book, he remembered the experience like this:

She played the part of a young French *poilu* lying mortally wounded on a bank in the wood near the battlefield. I remember so well how she looked in her short brown wig, her horizon-blue tunic open at the neck, and the lower half of her body covered with a rug. In her right hand she grasped a tattered flag, and during the course of the action she recited some patriotic verses, after which she fell back dead. I understood very few of the words she spoke, but there was a magical stillness in the big auditorium, and her voice rang out, throbbing with energy and varying modulations of rhythm and colour. The curtain fell, but rose again almost immediately to reveal her standing proudly upright on one leg, leaning her hand on the shoulder of one of her fellow-actors. I was spellbound.

(Hear how the word recurs.)

Gielgud wrote this in March 1974. I was curious enough to look up what his mother, the enchanting Kate Terry Gielgud, had written twenty-one years earlier about the same performance. Not much. "Sarah", she said, "played a most poignant death scene, and I saw her for the last time as the stretcher-bearers lifted her inanimate form." Kate Terry Gielgud had watched Sarah in the theatre for nearly forty years. She had seen her in 1880 as Adrienne Lecouvreur, and the description takes us back from the crippled tragedienne of the last brave years to a "tiny, pale face cut by scarlet lips, reddish-gold hair, a long thin neck swathed to the ears in soft white material, long thin arms and hands, and nails cut to sharp points and very much polished". One of the only parts Kate Gielgud (as good a critic as any professional) disliked, was Hamlet: "No sense of awe, no sense of humour, no fatalism, no self-pity."

6

We near the end. It was on April 6, 1921, when she was seventy-six, that Sarah Bernhardt began her last engagement in London, at the cavernous Princess Theatre (since re-named) at the top of Shaftesbury Avenue. Here she was "a noble-hearted gentleman aged about thirty, addicted to morphine" in *Daniel* by Louis Verneuil, shortly afterwards her grandson-in-law. It was the first full-length play she had given in London for many years. There had been mishaps on the journey from Paris two days before. She had been held up for a night; she had had a rough Channel crossing; her car broke down while they were travelling up from Dover; and she was suffering from a cold. But Sarah was set to keep faith with her English impresario, C. B. Cochran. The performance itself was uncanny. She appeared at the beginning of the third act, an unhappy lover dying of a broken heart. (Again, Sarah's Angel of Death.) We have the critic Archibald Haddon's picture of the night straight from the theatre: the picture of a young man in a high-backed chair, wearing a plum-coloured dressing-gown, his feet on a crimson footstool and a rug over his knees. He was deathly pale; there were black rims to his sunken eyes; he coughed distressingly. Sarah acted with her old command. May Agate recalled a small piece of miming when the man spoke of a rum omelette he had enjoyed, and the little sparkling flame that would light it up—something Sarah suggested with a slight quivering gesture of her fingers. At the end she died upon the stage, a fading away during the reading of a letter. The death took a full five minutes, Sarah's own theatre of silence: and the ultimate cheering, Haddon said, "swelled into a mighty roar as the curtain rose and fell a dozen times". That was the final first-night sound in London of what Sarcey called the "mania": a salute profoundly affectionate and admiring: a farewell to the supreme professional, the most formidable actress of her world. She never appeared in London again. Within two years she lay still in her Paris room, her bed covered in flowers—roses, lilacs and forget-me-nots. It was four decades since the bleak noon of Folkestone, the gardenia (or violets) and the lilies, the journey to a lost London, Henry Irving's flowers, the despair in that hot dressing-room before the scene from *Phèdre* and the night's thrust into an excitement sustained across the turbulent years.

We began with Stephen Phillips. We can end with a finer mind, that of Baring, who had adored Sarah from his playgoing childhood and who remembered her in the sonnet that begins: "Her gesture is the soaring of a hymn". It closes with these lines:

A sorceress, the victim of her snare;
A wounded eagle, struggling to be free,
Whose kingdom was the sunlight and the snows—
More queenly than all empresses is she,
Discrowned albeit, defeated and in despair;
The stricken lily puts to shame the rose.

6

Sarah Bernhardt's Influence on the Theatrical Life of Montreal

John Hare

The amazing career of Sarah Bernhardt was chronicled in thousands of articles in the many countries she visited during her sixty years of presence on the stage. The impact of that presence has hardly diminished even today, a half-century after her death, as can be witnessed by the proliferation of publications and albums devoted to Sarah in the last years alone. Our generation, brought up on a diet of visual experience through the cinema and the television screen, knows very well the phenomenon of the star and his or her impact on the multitude. Yet the international stars of the past half century can come to life once more on the screen. Thus, we have the illusion of coming to grips with their impact. What, then, of the stars who came of age before the audio-visual recording industry reached a certain level of perfection?

Yes, what then of Sarah Bernhardt? How many of her present-day devotees have seen her upon the stage? What remains of her more than 150 rôles? Of her more than 10,000 performances? Can we explain her impact from the thousands of still photographs, the few scratchy records, the half-dozen or so silent films? In fact, so little importance has been attached to her work upon the stage as such that it is impossible to discover in any biography just how many rôles she really performed. Cornelia

Otis Skinner and William Emboden both list 134 different rôles in their books, but not the same ones! Sarah herself stated in December 1896 that she had already performed 112 rôles[1] and there would be a further sixty or so according to the two sources just mentioned. Again, every biographer places much emphasis on her many tours; yet nowhere can one discover a complete list with dates, plays, names of the company and so on. How then can we explain, on the other hand, the intense interest in the star and, on the other, the almost total lack of basic research into her work?

Jean Duvignaud, in his most perceptive essay, *L'Acteur: Esquisse d'une sociologie du comédien* (Paris, 1965), sees the actor as the focus of the desire for personal freedom of choice in Western society, freedom of choice which is denied to most individuals through economic constraints. The biographies or pseudo-biographies of actors make them notorious and the public then crystallizes in the person of the star actor the possibility of attaining individual freedom of choice. Duvignaud contends that "Since the actor presents passions, he or she is seen to be endowed with all of them, as if the playing of imaginary rôles implied a greater capacity for living."[2] Duvignaud cites the examples of Rachel, Eleonora Duse and Sarah Bernhardt. Sarah must however remain the proof *par excellence* of this capacity for special individuals to condense and incarnate all the emotions, all the passions towards which man secretly aspires. How else can we explain the packed houses all over the United States? Night after night, during her nine tours, people came to see Sarah, even though they could not understand a word coming out of her golden throat.

Edmond Rostand tried to capture the essence of her impact in a sonnet he recited during the grandiose ceremonies in Paris, on December 9, 1896, celebrating her twenty-nine years in the theatre:

> En ce temps, sans beauté, seule encor tu nous restes
> Sachant descendre, pâle, un grand escalier clair,
> Ceindre un bandeau, porter un lys, brandir un fer.
> Reine de l'attitude et Princesse des gestes.

> En ce temps, sans folie, ardente, tu protestes!
> Tu dis des vers. Tu meurs d'amour. Ton vol se perd.
> Tu tends des bras de rêve, et puis des bras de chair.
> Et quand Phèdre parait, nous sommes tous incestes.
>
> Avide de souffrir, tu t'ajoutas des coeurs;
> Nous avons vu couler—car ils coulent tes pleurs!
> Toute les larmes de nos âmes sur tes joues.
>
> Mais aussi tu sais bien Sarah, que quelquefois
> Tu sens furtivement se poser, quand tu joues,
> Les lèvres de Shakespeare aux bagues de tes doigts.[3]

What deep impulsion led this actress, who could dominate the Parisian stage, to travel literally all over the world, from the late 1870s until a few months before her death in 1923? Her biographers have reduced the importance of her tours to a simple need for money, for gold, a desire for easy success. Of course, the monetary rewards made the tours worthwhile. Yet this alone cannot explain the almost compulsive necessity to travel into foreign lands. Who can tell to what extent a need for adulation drove her incessantly from country to country? However, we know that she felt the call of a more noble and patriotic mission. France had been profoundly humiliated in 1870. All those who loved that great nation suffered to see her defeat at the hands of the Prussians. Louis Fréchette, the most important man of letters in Quebec at that time, spoke eloquently of his anguish at the news of the war and his anger at the arrogance of those who exulted in the thought that France was finished:

> La voix du sang parla; la sainte idolâtrie,
> Que dans tout noble coeur Dieu mit pour la patrie,
> Se réveilla chez tous; dans chacun des logis,
> Un flot de pleurs brûlants coula des yeux rougis;
> Et, parmi les sanglots d'une douleur immense,
> Un million de voix cria—Vive la France![4]

Sarah felt instinctively the need to flaunt the greatness of French culture as an antidote to the feeling of defeat, and for many years she refused to perform in Germany. In December

1896, she explained her feelings to Jules Huret in a long letter: "I have crossed the oceans carrying my ideal of art and the genius of my country triumphed! I have sown the French language in the very centre of foreign literature; this is what has made me most proud. Thanks to the influence of my art, French is still the language of the young generation. . . . In South America, in Brazil, students fought with sabres because some tried to stop them from shouting 'Vive la France!' as they drew my carriage through the streets. In the Argentine republic, students have honoured my country by learning Racine, Corneille and Molière by heart. In Canada, members of parliament and senators pushed my sleigh to the oft repeated cries of 'Vive la France!' and after each performance, students sang out *La Marseillaise* as the English stood up respectfully."[5]

If she felt an impulsion to carry French art and the French language across the oceans, she did not, therefore, necessarily attempt to present the great classic plays of her country. Her repertoire remained rooted in the tastes of her own age. Instinctively she understood both the rôle of theatre as a form of behaviour and the importance of that new medium, the mass circulation illustrated press, in bringing her image into every home. This publicity served to heighten her impact. The age of the international star had finally arrived.

Montreal was only one of the hundreds of cities and towns she played in. Yet among the many places she visited during her triumphal tour of 1880, Montreal came to have a special significance. In her memoirs she states: "Since my childhood, I dreamt of Canada."[6] Also, she alludes to the feelings of the audience and the electricity that flowed through her first house in Montreal during the singing of *La Marseillaise*. For those thousands of Montrealers who crowded the station in sub-zero weather to greet her, Sarah Bernhardt represented *la France*, the country of the heart, "'la mère-patrie". Such an outpouring of emotion had gripped the province a generation earlier in 1855, on the docking of "La Capricieuse", the first French warship to visit Quebec since the conquest of 1760. As Louis Fréchette wrote:

> Salut donc a vous tous, ô Français, ô nos freres!
> Nous vous serrons la main avec un doux émoi.

> Nos rives ne sont plus à la France étrangères,
> Et qui vient de chez elle est parmi nous chez soi.[7]

Twenty years ago, I witnessed a similar manifestation of the intangible, almost spiritual tie between Quebec and France. In 1958, Quebec City celebrated the three-hundred-fiftieth anniversary of its founding. Many events had been planned, such as a huge parade with allegorical floats and marching bands. How can I describe the strong emotion that ran through the crowd when they saw the parade advance slowly forward with a contingent of French marines at the front led by an officer on a white stallion!

Yet there has always been an ambivalent attitude towards France among Quebecers. During the nineteenth century, the strong churchmen felt that republican France and all it stood for since the French Revolution was the enemy of God. In order to keep the purity of a Catholic Quebec, they were driven to attack the literature, the culture and especially the theatre coming from France. These repeated condemnations certainly played a large part in the difficulties experienced in implanting this form of cultural activity in Quebec. It is not, therefore, surprising that the visit of Sarah Bernhardt to Montreal in December 1880 evoked strong emotions. On the one hand, Honoré Beaugrand, editor of *La Patrie*, and Louis Fréchette, poet and ardent francophile, saw her visit as a renewal of the cultural ties with the mother-country; on the other hand, the bishops and the ultra-Catholic journalists viewed her performances in Montreal as a direct attack on the spiritual authority of the Church. For them, Sarah was a messenger of "la France impie" and as such she had to be condemned. However, the curiosity aroused by the arrival of the great star who had made such an impact in the United States, impact noted in the illustrated press of the Province, overrode any spiritual qualms for many Montrealers.

By 1880, the population of Montreal had reached 140,000, an increase of 30 percent since 1870. The French element in the city was beginning to show those signs of dynamism that would make it the centre of French culture in the Province. In 1878, Honoré Beaugrand, a well-known republican and freemason, had founded *La Patrie*, which soon became the largest circulation daily newspaper in the city; and that same year the University of Montreal opened its doors. During the summer of 1880, Louis Fréchette came to symbolize this new confidence. On June 7 and 8, a group of amateur players put on his two patriotic dramas, *Papineau* and *Le Retour de l'Exilé*; then, on August 5, he received le prix Montyon of the French Academy, in Paris. On his return, he was invited to banquets all over the province. On December 21, he led a crowd of over 5,000 to welcome the arrival of Sarah Bernhardt at Windsor Station. The impact of Sarah's first visit on the theatrical life of Montreal is hard to measure in concrete terms, for it did not lead to the immediate creation of a professional French theatre in that city. However, in an intangible way her triumphal visit symbolised the renewal of contacts between France, French culture and New France (Quebec). Nowhere else would the great French actress attain so well the goal she stated in her letter of December 1896, of carrying French art and culture throughout the world.

At the end of her long life, she would remember once again those few days spent in Montreal during the Christmas season of 1880. In her posthumous book, *L'Art du théâtre*, she writes: "In Montreal, I also discovered audiences full of enthusiasm, possessed of a particular charm of youth and gaiety that struck me. Baskets full of flowers and doves were sent down to me from the balconies on wires. Songs were sung in my honour, especially *La Marseillaise*. The Bishop of Montreal had fulminated against me and my colleagues as well as against French art itself. As an answer to these hurtful statements those who admired France and her art unbridled the horses from my sleigh and drew it through the city in triumph."[8]

Sarah was the first truly great French performer to appear in Montreal. Soon others would follow: Coquelin in 1888, 1889 and 1893; Mounet-Sully and Jane Hading in 1894; Réjane in 1895. French Canada was coming of age as more and more of its intellectuals visited France, and as more and more French artists, actors and writers visited Montreal and the province. In the popular imagination, Sarah Bernhardt came to symbolise this new dynamism, arousing passions as no one other person could. These different forces clashed head-on in 1905, when some seminarians in Quebec City threw eggs at her carriage. Immediately, her admirers in Montreal came to her defence; and Wilfrid Laurier, the prime minister of Canada, himself a French Canadian, sent her a telegram of apology.

By the turn of the century, the attitude of the Catholic clergy towards theatre softened, at least in Montreal, and several French professional repertory companies were established in 1898. Montreal, the only cosmopolitan centre in the province, being so close to the important theatre cities in the United States, had been able to attract American touring companies since the end of the eighteenth century. Thus, English language theatrical productions flourished in Montreal, and, during the first half of the nineteenth century, over 1,400 English language theatrical performances have been discovered. On the other hand, the few French amateur companies produced only some 100 performances. This imbalance, attributable to social, political and economic constraints, as well as to the religious scruples of the Church, would not be corrected until well into the present century.

Sarah Bernhardt and her different companies visited Montreal on eight occasions during her six tours from 1880 to 1916. A perusal of the itineraries of these six tours makes it clear that, of all the cities she visited in Canada, Montreal was the most important to her; not only is this demonstrated by the number of visits but also by the length of stay and the number of performances. This period of thirty-six years saw the first attempts at establishing French professional theatre in Montreal. For a few months in 1887, "Le Conservatoire" in its small "Bijou-Théâtre", rue Bonsecours, gave performances six days a week with three matinées, all for the price of ten or twenty cents. Blanche de la Sablonière, known as the Canadian Bernhardt, made her professional début with this group in *Marie Jeanne ou la femme du peuple*. In August, this first French repertory company disbanded to be formed again briefly in 1893 as "La Compagnie Dramatique Nationale".[9]

The year 1898 saw the début of "Le Théâtre des Variétés", and in 1900 "Le National" opened its doors. This company would be the mainstay of French repertory theatre in Montreal until 1917, when the difficulties in recruiting French actors on account of the war and the growing competition of the cinema, forced

Georges Gauvreau, the owner, to close his doors. During its best years, from 1900 to 1910, "Le National" presented almost 400 different plays during its regular seasons, "seasons" lasting forty-five weeks or so each year. Montreal theatre-goers could choose between at least three professional companies presenting French theatre, as well as the different English theatres and the English-language vaudevilles. If Montreal saw the establishment of about twenty French companies during this period, only a small number succeeded in presenting plays with any pretensions to artistic quality. The companies, without any form of financial support other than the admission receipts, and obliged to fill the seats night after night for about forty weeks a year, turned to the melodramas and boulevard plays from the Parisian stage. The few Canadian plays produced during this period were also of the popular type.

If the more discerning journalists often judged severely the quality of the performances, the actors were not any less critical of the audiences and their tastes. Joseph Archambault, known in the theatre as "Palmieri", has left a most interesting account of those years.[10] He tells of the difficulties of the companies, obliged to present a new play every week, and of the directors forced to examine attentively every text in order to avoid any problems with the Church and the police. One night, when his company was performing *Théodora* by Sardou, just as the two lovers embraced one another "dans l'effusion d'une tendresse partagée", the audience broke out in nervous laughter. Palmieri cites this as an example of the small-minded mentality of the times, "pauvre mentalité où domine l'instinct des choses dés-honnêtes" (p. 23).

In spite of the more than 150 rôles performed by Sarah Bern-hardt, she scored her greatest triumphs in the popular vehicles of her day—plays judged severely by theatre critics of today. She did not seriously attempt to influence and change theatrical tastes. Sarah was rather the perfect representative of her age, probing the depths of the collective consciousness and projecting it in full flower on stage. Her repertory corresponded perfectly to the aspirations (and "world-view") of her audiences and her impact in this regard in Quebec was to make the repertory better known. As a certain Francoeur wrote in 1889: "The comedies of

Augier, Dumas and Sardou give the right idea of what dramatic art should be in a cultivated society. No longer do we accept the hearty laughter of a Molière" (*L'Union Libérale*, Quebec: November 22, 1889).

The periodic visits of the Divine Sarah served to remind audiences, too often entertained by second-rate actors and companies, of the heights that a great artist can attain. Her impact on the theatrical life of Montreal cannot therefore be measured solely by the forty-four performances of twenty-three different plays during her eight visits to that city. The magnificence of the spectacle and the magic of her presence reached out and touched the spectators time after time. The reactions to Sarah were of the heart and soul, not of the intellect. Her ability to inspire deep devotion or impassioned hatred can best be symbolized by the attitudes of two of the leaders of Quebec thought in the last decades of the nineteenth century, those of Louis Fréchette, man of letters, and of Jules-Paul Tardivel, an intensely Catholic journalist. Tardivel wrote some of the most virulent articles attacking Sarah that were ever written. These attacks were not the result of any personal contacts with the great actress but were inspired by a desire to protect Catholic Quebec from what were perceived to be evil influences.

The venom that dripped from Tardivel's pen is no more evident than in an article entitled "Paganisme moderne"[11] published in his newspaper *La Vérité* on April 18, 1891. He attacks Sarah not only as an actress who glories in the sensual nature of man, but also insults her as a Jewess. It would be easy to dismiss his comments on the grounds of an implied anti-semitism. However, Tardivel represents a current of thought found not only in Quebec, but in many other countries. These conservative thinkers attempted to isolate their readers and hearers from the social forces at work in the western world. On the other hand, Sarah Bernhardt had no greater admirer or publicist than Louis Fréchette, the most accomplished man of letters in Quebec during the last twenty years of the nineteenth century. Fréchette was the driving force behind the delirious receptions accorded Sarah during her visits from 1880 until 1905. He led the delegation which met her in St. Albans, on the Canadian border, in December 1880 and brought her in triumph to Montreal. Who can forget his oft-quoted poem recited on that occasion and Sarah's light-hearted account of the circumstances?

Poor Fréchette even wrote an historical drama, *Véronica*, which he proposed to her during the 1896 visit.[12] Her answer was evasive and it is not even certain that she bothered to read the text he submitted. However, she always accepted his invitations with good grace when in Montreal and met with those budding writers and actors he presented to her. The poet Jean Charbonneau remembered with gratitude at the end of his life the opportunity afforded to sit at the feet of the greatest French woman of the age;[13] and Juliette Béliveau, who performed on the stage and later on radio and televison almost until her death a few years ago, decided to become an actress after being rocked on Sarah's knees in 1905, thanks to Fréchette.[14]

On each of Sarah's visits to Quebec the same scenario would be played out; on the one hand, virulent attacks upon her morality and that of the theatre in general and, on the other, laudatory articles praising her artistry and the emotions provoked by the contact with the great star. Of course, such articles can be discovered in most of the places she visited. However, the intensity of the passions Sarah aroused in Montreal only serve to remind us that French is the language of the majority of the inhabitants of that city and that, consequently, the impact of her visits there was the greater. Although many Quebecers attended Sarah's performances in Montreal in spite of the condemnations of the bishops, this does not mean that the audiences were not preoccupied with the morality of the plays presented. In 1891, Montreal had an incisive drama critic, a certain de Lorde from Paris. He wrote some balanced articles on the different plays presented by Sarah in April 1891. Well aware of the religious prejudices of the Montreal audiences, de Lorde suggested, after the first performance of *La Tosca*, that the scene in which Madam Bernhardt places a crucifix on the dead body of Baron Scarpia should be suppressed (*La Presse*, April 10, 1891). At the next performance, a plain cross was substituted for the crucifix.

The critics of the time could not help but have an ambivalent attitude when discussing the plays in Sarah's repertory, given the attitude of the Church. A good example can be seen in an enthusiastic article on *Izéil*, a play by Silvestre and Morand, presented on February 26, 1896. After mentioning the extraordinary interpretation of the great star, the qualities of the production and the beauty of the set, the anonymous critic ends his article with a condemnation of the philosophy presented by the play: "We can feel the impiety of the authors by the repeated mention of the inevitable nothingness to which everything must come. This excess of orientalism, translated into French, shocks and repels the audience who, because of their grounding in the Catholic faith, hold as true the morality, strict yet just, which the play casts aside." (*La Minerve*, February 27, 1896)

Can we discover the real art of the actress behind the mask of the stereotypes evoked by the great majority of those who wrote about or told by word of mouth their reminiscences of Sarah Bernhardt's visits to Montreal? It is perhaps significant, in a discussion of her impact, that so few of the newspaper articles examine critically her different performances as *theatre*. How could it be otherwise when every spectator and commentator knew (or had been told) that Sarah Bernhardt was the greatest actress of the day? However, it remains possible to isolate the elements that particularly struck the imagination. Two characteristics of her performances are mentioned repeatedly during her visits, namely the magnificence of the costumes and the marvellous qualities of her voice. This only confirms what so many other critics and essayists have stated. Sarah spared no expense in having luxurious costumes made, as can be seen in the many photographs of her. As for the golden voice which has become the subject of legend, let me quote just one short article published in June 1911: "In the heavy rôle of Soeur Béatrice, Madame Sarah Bernhardt is simply marvellous. Her golden voice, her voice so gripping and supple, fits in admirably well with the poetry of the rôle. In the last act especially, she reaches the summit of her art, bringing shivers to the audience when she speaks out against the love of men and when she declares that genius never ages."[15]

On her last visit to Montreal in October 1916, Sarah confided to a reporter that she wanted to die in harness (*La Presse*, October 7, 1916). On this occasion she did not arouse the virulent passions so evident on her previous visits; in fact, the population greeted Madame Bernhardt with love and respect. *La Patrie* wrote:

"Sarah Bernhardt is eternally young and defies time. She is the most loved actress of the age, representing more than any other the spirit of France. The characteristics of that spirit have never flourished more than they do today: the ardour, the enthusiasm, the courage, the idealism of the French have astonished the world during the present war." (*La Patrie*, September 30, 1916)

NOTES

1.   Quoted by Jules Huret, *Sarah Bernhardt* (Paris: 1899).

2. "Puisque l'acteur représente des passions, on les lui prête toutes, comme si l'on pensait que la figuration de conduites imaginaires impliquait une capacité supplémentaire d'être" (Jean Duvignaud, *L'Acteur: Esquisse d'une sociologie du comédien*, p. 132).

3. A literal, line-by-line translation of the Rostand sonnet would read as follows:

> In these days which are devoid of beauty, you alone remain;
> Pale, descending a bright staircase,
> Head bound by a fillet, carrying a lily as if it were a sword,
> Queen of posture, princess of gesture.
>
> In these lack-lustre days you assert a vehement faith,
> You speak poetry, you die of love, you take flight;
> You hold out dream-arms, then arms of flesh and blood,
> And when your Phèdre appears, we are all of us filled with thoughts
>   of incest.
>
> Avid for suffering, you capture all hearts;
> We have seen your tears flow, and as they flow,
> All the tears of our own souls are on your cheeks.
>
> But then you well know, Sarah, that sometimes
> You secretly feel, as you play,
> Shakespeare's lips kissing the rings on your fingers.

4. Louis Fréchette, *La Legende d'un peuple* (Paris: 1880), p. 292. A literal line-by-line translation would read:

> The voice of blood spoke; the sacred idolatry
> Of country which God puts in the most noble heart
> Was awakened everywhere; in every dwelling-place,

A flood of burning tears flowed from reddened eyes
And amidst the sobs of immense sorrow,
A million voices cried "Long live France!"

5. Quoted by Huret, *Sarah Bernhardt*, pp. 90-91.
6. Sarah Bernhardt, *Ma Double vie*, vol. 2 (Paris, 1923), p. 212.
7. *La Légende d'un peuple*, p. 270. Literal, line-by-line translation:

Hail then to all of you, oh Frenchmen, oh our brothers!
We clasp your hands with deep feeling.
Our shores are no longer foreign to France,
And those who come from her are at home amongst us.

8. Bernhardt, *L'Art du théâtre*, pp. 165-66.
9. John Hare, "Panorama des spectacles au Québec: de la Conquête au XXe siècle" and "Le Théâtre professionnel à Montréal de 1898 à 1937", in *Le Théâtre canadien-francais* (Montreal: Fides, 1976), pp. 59-108, 239-48.
10. *Mes Souvenirs de théâtre* (Montreal, 1944).
11. "La comédienne juive Sarah Bernhardt vient de faire une tournée au Canada. Nous regrettons de le dire, trop de Canadiens-francais oubliant ce qu'exige la dignité chrétienne et les simples convenances se sont traines aux pieds de cette femme qui, si la bêtise ne l'eût décorée du titre d'artiste, porterait un tout autre nom que la pudeur defend d'ecrire. Cet empressement fiévreux autour d'une actrice dévergondée a été un spectacle honteux. L'encens qu'on brûlé en l'honneur de cette comedienne a une odeur fétide. Le paganisme antique n'est pas détruit; ou plutôt, il ressuscite en ce siècle de pretendues lumières. Le joug ignoble de la lubrique Vénus que les siècles de foi avaient brisé, s'appesantit de nouveau sur les peuples, les avilit, les rend mûrs pour l'esclavage. C'est profondément triste! Monsieur Fréchette qui ne manque jamais une occasion de se répandre en injures contre la monarchie française, s'est constitué le cornac de la Bernhardt. Pourtant, au temps de la monarchie française, si l'on frequentait les théâtres, on avait au moins assez de bon sens et de dignité pour mépriser les comédiennes. Aujourd'hui, on les adore!"
12. Paul Wyczynski, "Louis Fréchette et le théâtre", in *Le Théâtre canadien-français*, pp. 137—66.
13. Letter quoted by G. A. Klinck, *Louis Fréchette, prosateur* (Levis: 1955).
14. Denyse Martineau, *Juliette Béliveau* (Montreal: 1970).
15. *Montréal qui chante* (music review).

A Note on the Plates

I am greatly indebted to John Hare, of the University of Ottawa, and to Louis Rachow, Curator and Librarian of the Walter Hampden-Edwin Booth Theatre Collection, New York, for valuable assistance in locating some of these photographs and identifying their sources. My aim has been not only to illustrate points made in the text but also to do this, as far as possible, by using photographs which have not previously been reproduced in books about Bernhardt written in English. And I wanted photographs that illustrated matters of style, in both acting and stage setting, not simply yet another set of portraits of Sarah Bernhardt.

Except in the case of plates 3 and 8, the dates on these plates are the dates of the plays' first productions. Some of the photographs are of revivals at later dates.

E. S.

Plate 1. Bernhardt as Mariette in *François le Champi*, a dramatization of George Sand's novel, which Bernhardt played in 1867. (*From a watercolor by Baudoin*)

"It is naturally the eyes which are most called upon. The actress knew, in making use of such theatrical devices, that the critics would never tire of reporting them." P. 52.

Plate 2. Bernhardt as Phèdre in Racine's play, 1874. (*Photo: Nadar, Paris*)

"In Phèdre, the folds of her gown cunningly arranged...". P. 48.

"...more feminine than Rachel because she appeared more vulnerable". P. 74.

Plate 3. Bernhardt as Gilberte in *Frou-Frou* (Meilhac and Halévy) at Booth's Theatre, New York, April 28, 1881. (*Photo: Sarony, New York*)

"...the very archetype of nineteenth-century femininity...". P. 74.

"...one of the standard rôles for the nineteenth-century emotional actress...". P. 193.

"*Frou-Frou* is a diluted Dodo...". P. 197.

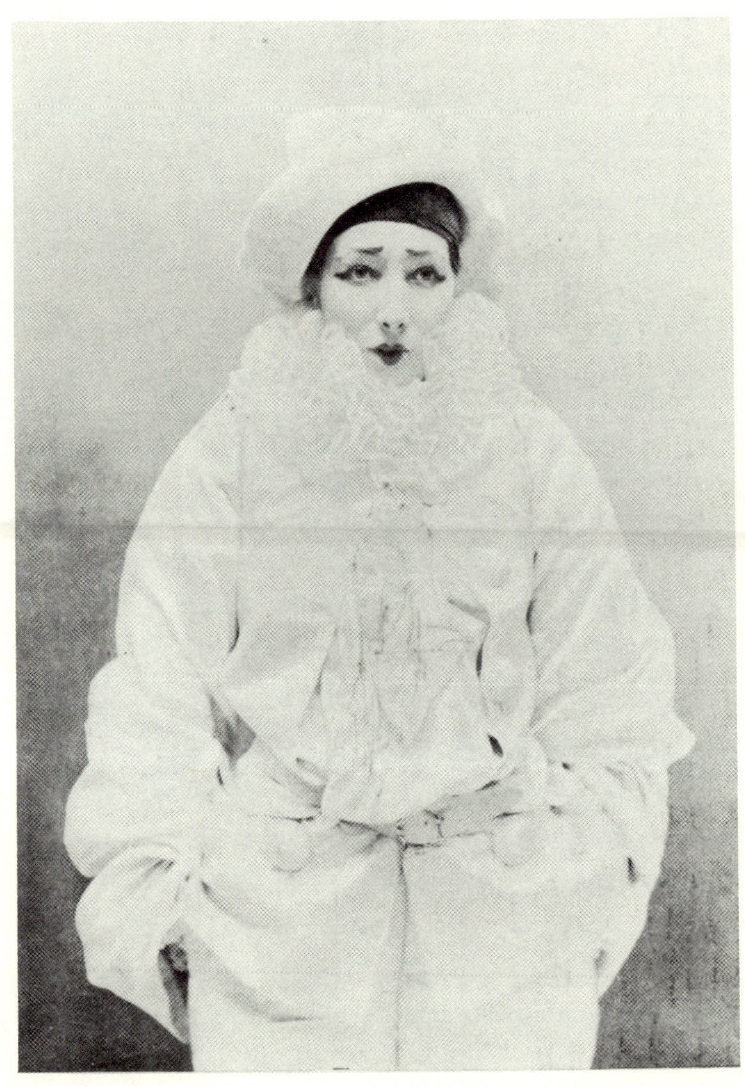

Plate 4. Bernhardt in the title rôle of Jean Richepin's *Pierrot Assassin* at the Trocadero in 1883. (*Photo: Nadar, Paris*)

"It is naturally the eyes...". P. 52.

Plate 5. One of the famous death scenes: the end of Sardou's *Théodora*, first played at the Théâtre Porte Saint-Martin in 1884. (*Photo: Boyer, Paris*)

''Sometimes, at the end of a performance, it has taken me more than an hour to return to life.'' P. 41.

''Her representation of death always proved to be spectacular. . .''. P. 58.

''Sarah's preference for romantic melodramas. . .is instructive.'' P. 246.

Plate 6. *La Tosca* (Sardou), first performed in 1887 but here seen at the Théâtre Sarah Bernhardt in 1908. (*Photo: Nadar, Paris*)

"...her foreshadowing glance when she caught sight of the knife ...".
P. 119.

Plate 7. Bernhardt as Joan in Jules Barbier's *Joan of Arc*, 1890. (*Photo: Nadar, Paris*)

"To indicate penitence, pleading, prayer, or anguish, she would kneel or lie prostrate...". P. 71.

"In 1913 she was back, now in scenes from Sardou's *Théodora*, Barbier's *Joan of Arc*...". P. 128.

Plate 8. Phèdre at the open-air Greek theatre, Berkeley, California, in 1891. (*Photo: Ellis, California*)

"And the frequent reference to statuary shows that this habit of basing her rôles on the perfection of physical form was with her an invariable practice." P. 48.

Plate 9. The title rôle in *Izéil* (Morand and Silvestre), 1894. (*Photo: Nadar, Paris*)

"...the mixture in her of the poetry of an impersonal, mythical being with an almost frightening precision of movement." P. 50.

Plate 10. Bernhardt as Gismonda in Sardou's *Gismonda*, 1894. (*Photo: Falk Studios, Paris*)

"And the picturesque poses...suggested paintings by old masters...". P. 71.

Plate 11. Bernhardt as Francesca in *Francesca da Rimini* (Crawford and Schwob) in 1902. (*Photo: Downey, Paris*)

"The lady sought to please, even seduce, her audience with famous smiles, serpentine movements, flowing gowns...". P. 71.

"In varying degrees...audiences rejected these characters: the last (Francesca da Rimini) with incredible harshness". P. 79.

Plate 12. Bernhardt as St. Teresa in *The Virgin of Avila* (Catulle Mendès) at the Théâtre Sarah Bernhardt in 1906. (*Photo: H. Manuel, Paris*)

"...coordinating sets and costumes for a lavish effect." P. 73.

Plate 13. Bernhardt's second representation of Joan of Arc, this time in a play by Emile Moreau, at the Théâtre Sarah Bernhardt in 1909. (*Photo: H. Manuel, Paris*)

'''' . . . an acceptable framework for an actress capable of stunning displays of personal magnetism . . . ''. P. 246.

Plate 14. Bernhardt in *Jeanne Doré*, by Tristan Bernard, at the Théâtre Sarah Bernhardt in 1913. (*Photo: Bert, Paris*)

"Her plays, like many of those in Sarah Bernhardt's touring repertory, gave the appearance of modernity while remaining comfortably old-fashioned. . . .". P.197.

". . . with their diet of magniloquent and moralizing social dramas . . .". P. 244.

162

Plate 15. Another scene from Tristan Bernard's *Jeanne Doré*: although the play was a contemporary piece and, relatively speaking, naturalistic—as the stage setting indicates—the acting style was certainly not what would be regarded as realistic or naturalistic in the late twentieth century. (*Photo: Bert, Paris*)

"Her tendency toward melodrama…". P. 58.

7

Chekhov's Response to Bernhardt

Laurence Senelick

Biographers of Sarah Bernhardt spend little time on her three Russian tours (1881, 1892, and 1908). For the most part, they are taken to be stations of the triumphal procession through barbaric provinces that followed her success at the Odéon. The American tours have been productive of the most anecdotes; the English tours have been exhaustively covered by memoir literature. But Bernhardt's first visit to Russia in 1881-1882 may be worth closer examination than it has received, both for what it tells us of the development of Russian taste a decade before the founding of the Moscow Art Theatre, and because of the comment made upon it by Antosha Chekhonte, a young journalist who was to become better known under his real name, Anton Chekhov.

In seeking a new audience in Russia, Bernhardt was following a long tradition of European artists who saw in that exotic hinterland illimitable largess waiting to be tapped. Politically, Franco-Russian relations were growing more cordial and would result, at the height of the entente, in a mass purchase of Russian bonds by French capitalists, an investment that they would rue well before 1917. Culturally, the Russian aristocratic fashion for speaking and reading French had been maintained, despite the unmannerly intrusions of Napoleons I and III. The critic Pavel

Annenkov recalled in the 1850s that all men of taste of his generation had cut their teeth on Corneille, Racine and other classics of the *grand siècle*.[1] Abroad, Russians were reputed to be munificent and enthusiastic in the welcomes extended to distinguished foreign performers. After all, had not Rachel managed to make 300,000 francs in a few weeks?[2]

Bernhardt's expectations were not disappointed, and both her vanity and her bank balance were gratified by the results of the venture. Russia proffered her what Louis Verneuil was to call "une réception grandiose".

Every day, for some hours, the crowd waited for her to leave the hotel to give her an ovation. Every night, when she reached the theatre, a wide red carpet was swiftly unrolled on the pavement so that in getting out of her sleigh she needn't put her foot in the snow. Special trains from Moscow had been laid on to allow the residents of that city to attend her performances [in St. Petersburg]. The Grand Dukes, all the members of the Imperial family, were daily in the auditorium where all whom Petersburg deemed most illustrious congregated.

Twice she was commanded to the Winter Palace, home of the Tsar, before whom she played first *Le Passant* and the death scene from *Adrienne Lecouvreur*, and the next time two acts of *Phèdre*. The evening that she was presented to Alexander III, whom she had positively bowled over, he hastily halted her in her curtsey and said, in the presence of all the Court:"No, Madame, it is for me to bow to you!"[3]

Whether or not such stories are to be ranked as *haute* press-agentry, it is noteworthy that they are set in St. Petersburg, seat of the government and most Westernized of Russian cities. In the Russian mind, Petersburg acted as its founder Peter the Great had intended, as a "window on Europe". Its tastes, amusements and predilections were, in the upper echelons of society, French, German, and English. Since the eighteenth century, it possessed a French theatre with its own company, a kind of Comédie Française East; its audiences were familiar with the standard Gallic repertoire, fluent in the language and rather given to that reverse chauvinism that believed that art is best when imported from the West. Moreover, St. Petersburg had been the climax of Bernhardt's Russian tour, the excitement generated by reports of her appearances elsewhere. As usual, her arrival had been heralded by a carefully and lavishly laid train of publicity.

Less cosmopolitan centres were more erratic in their reception. In Odessa, crowds shouting "hurrah" had thrown pebbles into her carriage, hitting a member of her troupe in the eye with a shard of window glass. Moscow blew hot and, mostly, cold. Priding itself on being the mother of Russian cities, Moscow was more impatient with foreign foppery, and steadfastly loyal to its own heritage of purely Russian acting and play-writing. The advance publicity campaign had disgusted many critics, who supposed that the public's delight in the French star was more the result of pre-conditioning than of any inherent excellence in her abilities. A leading newspaper, *Russkie Vedomosti (The Russian Intelligencer)* did not even bother dedicating a special article to her touring activities, but simply carried items in its gossip column. On the whole the items were favorable, but they hardly suggested that a marvel was in their midst.

Bernhardt opened at Moscow's Bolshoy Theatre, a house primarily devoted to opera, ballet and spectacle, on 26 November 1881 in *La Dame aux camélias*, and the first reports were temperate and measured. *Russkie Vedomosti* benignly declared, "Yesterday instead of a pompous heroine we saw the living image of a deeply loving, deeply suffering woman from a notorious milieu—who grappled to herself the audience's sympathy and attention with irresistible force."[4] The perfection of her technique, the flexibility of her voice and the careful plotting of the rôle's details were all noted with favour. But other papers were not so charmed. S. Vasil'ev, the influential critic for *Moskovskie Vedomosti (The Moscow Intelligencer)*, after granting that Bernhardt's Marguerite Gautier had something of the eternal feminine about her, even if she was "a Parisienne from top to toe", went on to complain: "everything is deliberate, everything is accurate, everything is typical; all the intonations are in place; all the gestures and movements are truthful. But truthfulness *[pravlivost']* is not truth *[pravda]*, eternal truth".[5] His later reports emphasized the same deliberate sophistication of Bernhardt's acting and its accompanying lack of candour. A viewing of her other rôles revealed that her vocal tricks and poses were constantly repeated, well-wrought gimmicks. Bernhardt, Vasil'ev summed up, "is very talented, but not an actress of genius. She gives us remarkably clear, so to speak really palpable, almost chiselled types. They are splendid statuettes, which one would gladly place on one's mantelpiece. But a statuette, not a statue".[6] Similar opinions were echoed by the *Russkiy Kur'ër (Russian Courier)*, *Sovremennye Izvestie (Modern Tidings)* and *Novoe Vremya (New Times)*, whose critic V. P. Burenin remarked that Bernhardt's affected gesticulation, pseudo-tragic sobs, and cardboard romanticism made her moments of truth and power all the more surprising for being unexpected.[7]

Among those who found Sarah Bernhardt grist for their journalistic mills was twenty-one-year-old Anton Chekhov, a medical student who had begun to contribute squibs and anecdotes to various humour magazines solely with a view to increasing his income. From childhood, Chekhov had been stage-struck, first performing in various amateur productions at home and in school, later religiously attending the Taganrog Civic Theatre, a solid provincial company with a broadly-based repertoire. In Moscow, Chekhov mingled with the Bohemian world of the greenroom and the pressroom: he rapidly became *au courant* of the latest scandals, knew the ins and outs of backstage intrigue, and avidly followed the fluctuations of the box-office.

The two articles that Chekhov devoted to Bernhardt are written in the flippant, know-it-all style that "Antosha Chekhonte" practised in those post-adolescent days: the writer's tongue is firmly lodged in his cheek and one eyebrow is permanently cocked. But for all that, the aesthetic concerns that lie behind these grimaces both reflect the serious connoisseur's interest in acting and strike a chord that can be heard throughout Chekhov's later, important work—the question of an artist's integrity and diligence in the creative act.

His first article, "Sarah Bernhardt", appeared in *Zritel' (The Spectator)* on 30 November 1881, before he had seen her perform. His piece is in the nature of a news item *cum* potted biography, derivative of the sketches by Sarcey and others, that had already appeared in the Moscow press; the others included Evgeniya Tur' who wrote under the elegant *nom-de-plume* of Saliasse de Tournemire. Chekhov intends to inform his readers of the diva's arrival, her impact on the average Muscovite, and her background; but, because his essay is satirical, he dwells on the hyperbole of her publicity campaign. With sardonic deadpan, reminiscent of Mark Twain, he begins with the astonished discovery that the divine Sarah has, after traversing all the world, deigned to call in at Belokammenaya Street.

Two days ago Moscow knew only four elements; now it won't stop talking about a fifth. It knew seven wonders; now a fraction of a second doesn't go by without it discussing an eighth. Those who had the luck to get even the worst ticket are dying with impatience for nightfall. Forgotten are foul weather, poor roads, expenses, mothers-in-law, debts. Not a scurvy coachman sitting on his box but will give lectures about the new arrival. The reporters forget to eat and drink, they run around and make a fuss. In short, the actress has become our *idée fixe*. We feel that something is going on in our heads much like the onset of *dementia praecox*.

A frightful amount has been written about Sarah Bernhardt and is still being written! If we were to pile together everything that has been written about her and were to sell it by the ton (at 150 rubles per ton), and if we were to dedicate the receipts from the sale to the "Society for the Protection of Animals", then—we swear by our quills!—we could at least give dinner and supper to the horses and dogs at Olivier's and the Tatar's [a very exclusive and a very seedy restaurant, respectively: L. S.]. Much has been written and, of course... many lies have been told. She's been written about by Frenchmen, Germans, blacks, Englishmen, Hottentots, Greeks, Patagonians, Indians. . . . We'll even write something about her, we'll write and try not to lie.[8]

This last statement is followed by a footnote which remarks, "It's incredible, gentlemen! No sooner does one begin to write about Sarah Bernhardt, than one has a desire to tell a few lies. The respected diva, it must be stated, has bewitched the loveliest of human passions."[9] Chekhov then proceeds to recount some of the celebrated incidents in Sarah's early life, her intention to take the veil, her recitation of a La Fontaine fable which procured her admission to the Conservatoire. "Had she not recited a fable with feeling, had she flunked," Chekhov surmises sarcastically, "she probably would never have got to Moscow."[10] Obviously following the standard press release, Chekhov continues to chronicle her career: the fiasco of her début at the Comédie, her abandonment of the Théâtre de Gymnase and flight to Spain, her return to Paris and obscurity, and her eventual success at the Odéon. At this point, the humourist gets the upper hand over the reporter, and despite his avowed intent, Chekhov begins to spin yarns after the fashion of Sarah's advance agents.

"Her success was so spectacular," he proclaims, "that the commander-in-chief of literature, Victor Hugo, wrote the rôle of the queen in *Ruy Blas* specifically for Sarah Bernhardt. . . . Hitherto-microscopic dramatists began, thanks to Sarah's acting, to creep forward and attain visibility."[11] As he expatiates on her motto, "Quand même", and her passion for publicity, Chekhov's prose accelerates and his exaggerations burgeon, as if the legend of Bernhardt impels him willy-nilly to hysteria. "Sarah's 'Quand même' is straightforward and urgent. With it Sarah Bernhardt rushed headlong into the sort of ghastly messes that only an extraordinary mind and a will of, at least, iron could break through. She strode, as the saying goes, through fire, water and copper pipes."[12] After touching on her skill at sculpture, painting and literature, which make her the rival of all the muses, he moves on to her recent trips to England and America:

In America she performed miracles. . . . She flew on her journey through a forest fire, fought Indians and tigers, and so forth. There she visited, among others, the professor of black magic, the wizard Edison who showed her all his telephones and phonophones. According to the French artist Robidà, the Americans drank up all of Lake Ontario in which Sarah had swum. . . . In America she gave (horribile dictu) 167 performances! The total sums of the box-office receipts were so long that no professor of mathematics could read them. . . .[13]

He congratulates her on ignoring the Germans on her European tour, but notes that " 'tis an ill wind blows nobody good, an extra hundred thousand rubles will remain at home in German pockets, and the little children can use the hundred thousand for milk money."[14] Finally, Chekhov promises his readers to keep them impartially informed of Sarah's exploits in Moscow. "We shall compliment her as a guest and criticise her up and down as stringently as we can as an actress."[15]

Clearly, Chekhov, like his colleagues, had been put off by Bernhardt's fondness for *réclame*, and could hardly believe that any performer could stand up to claims made so extravagantly. "More about Sarah Bernhardt", his second article, published in *Zritel'* on 6 December 1881, after he had seen her on stage, begins on a note of exasperation.

What the hell is going on! We wake up in the morning, trick ourselves out, draw on our swallow-tail coat and gloves and round about twelve we head for the Bolshoy Theatre. . . . We return home from the theatre, gulp down lunch without chewing it and do some scribbling. At eight at night, it's back to the theatre; from the theatre back home and more and more scribbling till about four. And it's like this every day! We think, speak, read, write about nothing but Sarah Bernhardt. O Sarah Bernhardt! All this folderol will end with our straining our reportorial nerves to the maximum, our catching, thanks to irregular mealtimes, a most virulent stomach catarrh, and sleeping soundly for two straight weeks as soon as the eminent diva departs.[16]

The reason for all this theatre-going is to discover whether the actress in any way corresponds to the rhetoric used to describe her, but, Chekhov confesses, he can find in her no resemblance to the Angel of Death or any other epithet bestowed on her by her admirers.

In amusing detail, Chekhov limns the crush at the theatre for *Adrienne Lecouvreur*, the boxes filled to bursting with families sitting on one another's laps. He observes the curious phenomenon of an audience made up not only of the regular playgoers, the *aficionados* of acting, but the sensation-seekers, who do not know the difference between the Bolshoy and the Salamonsky Circus, the businessmen who ordinarily have no time for the theatre, the deaf and paralytic who have not been seen in public since 1848. Astutely, he recognises that the attraction of beholding a sacred monster is only part of the explanation; it is the fact that the entertainment smacks of Paris that has drawn this audience together. The three knocks that announce the show (in lieu of the Russian bell), the eighteenth-century décor familiar from reproductions of salon paintings in illustrated magazines, the luxurious costumes and the incomprehensibly guttural language conjure up for Chekhov all the clichés about Paris.

You dream, and before your eyes flash one after the other, the Bois de Boulogne, the Champs Elysées, the Trocadéro, Daudet with his long hair, Zola with his round beard, our Turgenev and our "heart-throb" Mme. Lavretskaya, carousing, tossing Russian gold-pieces hither and yon.[17]

The first act ends in silence, no applause even from the gallery.

In the second act Sarah Bernhardt herself appears. She is handed up a bouquet (it can't be called a bad one, but it's not exactly, no offence meant, a good one either). Sarah is nothing like the postcards you bought. . . .

The curtain falls—and the audience applauds, but so listlessly! Fyodotova and even Kochetova are applauded far more energetically. But the way Sarah Bernhardt takes her bow! With her head cocked somewhat to one side, she comes out the door centre, walks slowly and grandly down to the apron, looking in no particular direction, much like the *pontifex maximus* at a sacrificial offering, and with her head describes an arc in the air not visible to the naked eye. "Here you are, take a look!" seems to be written all over her face. "Take a look, wonder, marvel, and say thank you for being allowed the honor of seeing 'the most original of women', 'notre grande Sarah'!"[18]

The coolness of the Muscovite audience, Chekhov imagines, may provoke in the minds of the French actors the belief that it is composed of brute beasts, insensitive to the subleties of refined performances and ignorant of French. But this would be a misconception: for the most part, the audience is made up of experts ready to debate heatedly every nuance of an interpretation and quite fluent in French. No, declares Chekhov, this audience has been spoiled by the mellow acting of Sadovsky, Zhivokini, Shumsky, Samarin and Fyodotova, sensitized by the socially responsible writing of Turgenev and Goncharov, and keenly attuned to real emotion and pathos on the stage. "No wonder," he concludes, "it doesn't fall into a swoon the moment that Sarah Bernhardt lets the audience know a moment before her death by the most energetic convulsions that she is now about to die."[19]

His summing-up of Bernhardt as an actress is worth quoting at length, because it distills the general opinion in Moscow while underlining certain important features of Russian critical thought on the subject of acting:

We are far from worshipping Sarah Bernhardt as a talent. She has none of the stuff that makes our most respected audience love Fyodotova; she has none of the spark that alone is capable of moving us to bitter tears or ecstasy. Every sigh Sarah sighs, every tear she sheds, every antemortem convulsion she makes, every bit of her acting is nothing more than an impeccably and intelligently learned lesson. A lesson, reader, and nothing more! As a very clever lady, who knows what works and what doesn't, a lady of the most grandiose taste, a lady deeply read in the human heart and whatever you please, she very deftly performs all those stunts that, every so often, at fate's behest, occur in the human soul. Every step she takes is profoundly thought out, a stunt underscored a hundred times. . . . She remakes her heroine into exactly the same sort of unusual woman she is herself. . . . In her acting, she goes in pursuit not of the natural but of the extraordinary. Her goal is to startle, to amaze, to dazzle. . . . You watch *Adrienne Lecouvreur* and you see not Adrienne Lecouvreur in her but the ultra-clever, ultra-sensational Sarah Bernhardt. . . . What shines through all her acting is not talent, but tremendous, strenuous hard work. . . . That hard work comprises the whole key to this enigmatic artiste. Not the slightest trifle exists in any of her rôles great or small that has not been put through the purgatory of that hard work a hundred times. Extraordinary work. Were we as hard-working as she is, what wouldn't we write! We would scribble all over the walls and ceilings just in revising the most paltry scrawl. We envy and most respectfully kowtow to her hard work. We have no objection to advising our first- and second-rate artistes to learn how to work from our guest. Our artistes, no offence meant, are dreadfully lazy! For them, study is harsher than horseradish. We deduce that they, the majority of our actors, work at practically nothing from the simple fact that they are at a standstill: they go neither forward nor . . . anywhere! Were they to work as Sarah Bernhardt works, were they to know as much as she knows, they would go far. . . . We watched Sarah Bernhardt and derived indescribable pleasure from her hard work. There were brief passages in her acting which moved us almost to tears. But the tears failed to well up only because all the enchantment is smothered in artifice. Were it not for that scurvy artifice, that premeditated tricksiness, that over-emphasis, honest to goodness, we would have burst into tears, and the theatre would have rocked with applause. . . . O talent! Cuvier said that you are at odds with facility! And Sarah Bernhardt is monstrously facile![20]

These remarks come as the climax of a century of tension within the Russian theatre between native impulses and foreign examples. The first great Russian actor, Ivan Dmitrevskiy (1734-1821) had founded his technique on Western models: personally acquainted with Garrick and Lekain, he had introduced the declamatory mode back home. Dramatists and actors were hard pressed to warp Slavonic sounds and rhythms into the formal diction and constraints of the hexameter, and to pare down generous emotions to suit histrionic decorum; but they tried. To the unconditioned observer, however, the results were often ludicrous and out-of-keeping; French modes sorted ill with the growing nationalism of writers, popular interest in Russian culture and mores, and the development of self-taught native actors. A sharp distinction developed between the state theatres in Petersburg and those in Moscow. The Petersburg company aped its French colleagues: the accepted manner in tragedy was cool, restrained and, in its opponents' view, punctiliously bureaucratic. Karatygin (1802-1853), for many years the city's leading tragedian, playing his tortured heroes with chill precision; "he commits suicide by numbers", complained the radical writer Herzen. The polished technique of Petersburg actors was exemplary and mirrored the manners of its aristocratic audience.

Moscow, on the other hand, considered its theatre to be "the second Moscow University": the audience was variegated, a mixture of officials, merchants, students and artisans. Its star tragedian Mochalov (1800-1848) has been characterized as the Russian Kean, erratic and impulsive, uneven in his performances because dependent on inspiration steeped in vodka, but always genuine and always exciting. The Moscow theatre's actors had, in many cases, received irregular training; some of them were even of serf origin. They knew life better than they knew the rules of art. Chief among these was Mikhail Shchepkin (1788-1863), who had been redeemed from serfdom by his admirers after he had become the most famous actor in the provinces. Realism and naturalness were Shchepkin's keywords, and he propagandized tirelessly, through his teaching in the dramatic academy, his correspondence and his own sedulously prepared performances, for emotional truth on stage. Shchepkin was no naturalist insistent on the photographic reproduction of everyday details, but he demanded observation of life and the selection of general traits from it that would harmonize with a playwright's conception. Subordination to character was a prime desideratum.

The years that the French tragedienne Mlle. George had spent in Russia at the beginning of the nineteenth century (1802-1812) had imprinted the neo-classic style of declamation on her epigones, a style which Shchepkin strove to uproot. When Rachel arrived in 1853, playing classical tragedy and romantic melodrama in Petersburg and Moscow, she offered a later generation the opportunity of contrasting an accepted European style, executed by a specialist, with the home-grown approach. Pavel Annenkov, the dean of Petersburg critics, devoted three lengthy and detailed essays to Rachel's performances, concluding that her finest moments were those outbursts of passion which owed least to art, and that her failures came when she embroidered most. In a correspondence with Annenkov, Shchepkin considered the question of Rachel's natural talents, and suggested that, had she not been corrupted by the French school of artificial acting, her genius and understanding of human nature might have preserved her from mechanical gimmickry. Both Annenkov and Shchepkin were convinced that Russia was following the right path in forgoing the French elocutionary manner, and in pursuing goals of emotional authenticity.[21] (However, it should be pointed out that the French artists who visited Russia were luminaries of the Comédie, wedded to the academic style and, as *prime donne*, to self-aggrandizement. Had Shchepkin encountered Frédérick Lemaître, he might have revised his negative appraisal of French actors.)

The same dichotomy between French craftsmanship and Russian values was apparent in the repertory that Chekhov beheld in the early 1870s as a boy in Taganrog. The local theatre alternated the neatly-tailored melodramas of Scribe and Dennery with comedies and dramas of Russian life, accurate in reproducing real dialogue and recognizable types. Because dramatists like Ostrovsky and Potekhin viewed the theatre as a means of educating and reforming public opinion, Russian actors in their rôles sought to move the audiences by touching their hearts. And the audiences responded in kind by favoring those actors who displayed the greatest depth of feeling. It was axiomatic that any actress worth her salt could cry real tears. The actors whom Chekhov mentions as Muscovite favorites—Sadovsky, Zhivokini, Shumsky and Samarin—were distinguished by the realism of their impersonations and the ability to create a character from within. Their own identification with the character aroused an empathy in the audience.

Bernhardt's opposite numbers at the Moscow state theatre, Mariya Ermolova and Glikeriya Fyodotova, excelled at this. Ermolova (1853-1928), a *grande dame* not much liked by Chekhov, was apportioned the heroic parts, such as Laurencia in *Fuente ovejuna* and Schiller's Maria Stuart and Jeanne d'Arc, in addition to flashy rôles in an undistinguished repertoire, which she was able to endow with considerable nobility. She combined the highly-colored romanticism of Mochalov with the emotional authenticity of Shchepkin to work upon the spectator's loftier feelings; young audience members would leave the theatre aglow with revolutionary fervor after one of her classical renditions, illustrating once again the performer's importance in Russia not simply as an entertainer but as a social impetus. (This function was of special significance in the politically repressed 1880s, when outright protest and criticism were stifled.) Those close to Ermolova recalled that she had no private life, but dwelt in the lives of the characters she incarnated, retiring into the rôles she created.

Fyodotova (1846-1925), whom Chekhov greatly admired, had an even wider range than her colleague, playing in tragedy, drama, romantic spectacle and comedies of manners; a student of Shchepkin, she was noted for the warmth and pathos with which she imbued her characters. The novelist Pisemsky stated that in his travels throughout Europe, visiting all the best theatres and seeing all the most celebrated actresses, nowhere had he found anyone with the emotional range and depth of Fyodotova.

These women, of unimpeachable moral character, profoundly involved in the progressive social and literary movements of the time, held in affectionate esteem by their public, were the yardsticks by which Bernhardt was measured. It was natural, then, that the enlightened Muscovite impression was of a mountebank and an exhibitionist whose behaviour on stage bore little correspondence to life as it is lived. What must be emphasized, however, is that the Russians were not asking for the kind of true-to-life behaviorism sought by Zola and Antoine. A certain M. N. R. writing in *Gazeta A. Gattsuka (Gattsuk's Gazette)* after Bernhardt's departure sharply criticized her depictions of Marguerite Gautier's demise from consumption and Adrienne Lecouvreur's death by poison. "The essence of dramatic art," he opined, "is to show and interpret what causes a person's death, what spiritual and not what corporeal motions accompany his removal from life."[22] Curiously, the same charge of sensational naturalism had been levelled by Annenkov at Rachel a generation earlier, when her writhing and hysteria in Adrienne's death throes sent women screaming from the auditorium; in his opinion, such melodramatic devices made no statement about the character. Rather, the Moscow public hoped that Bernhardt would drop the mask of star and let the woman appear; wielding the upper hand on stage at every moment, in complete control of each vocal modulation, Bernhardt lacked vulnerability. "Let me whisper my general impression in your ear", confided Spectator in *Sovremennye Izvestie*: "It is all clever, pretty, detailed, with forceful and appropriate expression, but . . . but not once did any of it make my heart beat any the faster, not in the least."[23]

Along with Chekhov, several critics advised young actresses to ignore Bernhardt's example, except in regard to her firm grip on the rôle in all its details, her disciplined work habits and her ability to listen on stage. Chekhov's friend, the powerful editor Suvorin, suggested that Russian actors pay close attention to her pauses, for "she performs her rôle like a piece of music [for] she knows that certain mimic moments on stage should be more pronounced than they are in life".[24] It may be that the famous Moscow Art Theatre pause derives in part from Bernhardt, filtered through Maeterlinck to Chekhov and Stanislavsky. But the consensus remained that Sarah Bernhardt was less the product of genius than of puffery. For the Moscow *cognoscenti*, the press campaigns had resulted in overkill. Chekhov, returning to his analysis of *Adrienne* at last, finally bursts out:

Or else, look here, reader! You're fed up reading my gibberish, and I want awfully to go to bed. The clock is striking four, and the cock is bawling at my pretty neighbor-lady's place. . . . My eyelids are sticking together as if smeared with glue, my nose is grazing my writing-d. . . .

Tomorrow, back to Sarah Bernhardt . . . ugh! However, I won't write any more about her even if the editor pays me fifty kopeks a line. I'm written out! I quit![25]

He meant it. One can examine Chekhov's writings and letters from this point on and find very few references to Bernhardt, except as a commonplace for an internationally known actress. His full-length portrait of a spoiled, capricious leading lady, Arkadina in *The Seagull*, was modelled after Russian stars with whom Chekhov was better acquainted, among them his mistress Lidiya Yavorskaya, whose favorite rôle was Marguerite Gautier. Arkadina, her son Konstantin tells us, cannot stand being compared to Bernhardt or Duse; but this is vanity, not criticism.[26]

Actually, Duse was the foreign actress who, ten years later, attracted Chekhov at a time when his outlook on the Russian stage had been soured by first-hand involvement in it. After he had seen her in Petersburg in *Antony and Cleopatra*, he wrote to his sister (March 17, 1891): "What an actress! I've never seen anything like her. I watched Duse and worked myself into agonies thinking that we have to cultivate our temperaments and tastes through the medium of such wooden actresses as Ermolova and her ilk, whom we consider great because we haven't anyone better. After Duse I can understand why the Russian theatre is so boring."[27] Once again, the moral uplift provided by art, the refining influence of a sensitive performance, are the main criteria for aesthetic evaluation.

Such an attitude, which somewhat parallels that of Bernard Shaw and Max Beerbohm in their contrasting of Duse and Bernhardt, was not uncommon among experienced judges in Russia, who found it revealing to compare visiting stars in the same rôles. Speaking of the scene in act three of *La Dame aux camélias*, in which Armand flings his packet of banknotes in Marguerite's face, the Baron Drizen, an official of the Petersburg state theatre, recalled that;

Sarah Bernhardt at that moment hid her face in her hands and sobbed deeply. Tina di Lorenzo automatically fell into an armchair and simply gnawed her lips in silence. Duse reacted quite differently. She could not believe her eyes. What, was this her Armand? He who had sworn eternal love to her, pleaded and wept at her feet? No, it is some other. And with half-closed eyes and outstretched arms, she repeats in different tones but one word: "Armando! Armando!" . . . I have never experienced a keener sensation in the theatre.[28]

The Baron's impressions are seconded by the shrewd critic A. R. Kugel' ("Homo Novus") who was unimpressed by Bernhardt's emotional grasp of the rôle. He considered Marguerite Gautier to be her masterpiece in many ways; he admired the feminine tenderness of the first act, the sophisticated style of the interview with Armand's father, the expressiveness of her hands and her moaning. But Kugel' was left utterly cold by any scene that required of her "inner life and great sorrow".[29] These were the very qualities that the Russians esteemed most highly in an actor. The word I have translated as "inner life"—*perezhivanie*—actually means "experiencing, reliving, living *through* an emotion" and was to become the touchstone of Stanislavsky's approach to acting. For him, the performer had to exploit his emotional memory and re-create, within himself, the feelings of the character he undertakes to impersonate. Stanislavsky codified and formalized what was already the common direction and predilection of the Russian theatre. So it is little wonder that Sarah Bernhardt, ultimate exemplar of the cult of personality, past mistress of *métier*, should have seemed to the informed Russian spectator an irrelevant throwback to an obsolete and superseded form of exhibitionism.

NOTES

1. P. V. Annenkov, "Pis'mo iz Petersburg o Rashele (k M. S. Shchepkinu)", *Moskvityanin*, vol. 22, no. 7 (1853), pp. 86-87.

2. She did, according to Madame de B[arréra], *Mémoires de Rachel* (London, 1858), pp. 147-50.

3. Louis Verneuil, *La Vie merveilleuse de Sarah Bernhardt* (New York, 1942), p. 165. Unless otherwise indicated, all translations in this article are my own.

4. *Russkie vedomosti* 321 (November 27, 1881).

5. *Moskovskie vedomosti* 330 (December 28, 1881).

6. Ibid., 337 (December 5, 1881).

7. *Novoe vremya* 2087 (December 18, 1881).

8. A. P. Chekhov, "Sara Bernar", *Zritel'*, 21 and 22 (November 30, 1881), pp. 11-14, illustrated by the author's brother Nikolay. This article also appears in Chekhov, *Polnoe sobranie sochineniy i pisem v tridtsati tomakh*, vol. 16 (Moscow, 1979), pp. 7-11. A later sketch by Nikolay Chekhov of the orchestra seats at the Bolshoy and the crush outside the theatre during one of Bernhardt's performances is reproduced in A. P. Chekhov, *Vokrug Chekhova* (Moscow, 1964), p. 107.

9. Ibid., p. 8.

10. Ibid.

11. Ibid., p. 9.

12. Ibid.

13. Ibid., p. 10.

14. Ibid.

15. Ibid., p. 11.

16. Chekhov, "Opyat' o Sare Bernar", *Zritel'*, 23-24 (December 6, 1881), pp. 11-13. Also available in Chekhov, *Polnoe sobranie sochineniy*, vol. 16, p. 52. A complete English translation can be found in *Russian Dramatic Theory from Pushkin to the Symbolists: An Anthology*, ed. and trans. Laurence Senelick (Austin, Tex., 1981), pp. 83-88.

17. Ibid., p. 14. Madame Lavretskaya is an affectedly Francophile character in Turgenev's novel *A Nest of Gentry*. Incidentally, Turgenev himself was anti-Bernhardt. In a letter to his protégée, the actress Savina, he wrote from Paris (December 15, 1881), "I am annoyed by my compatriots who behave so foolishly over the intolerable Sarah Bernhardt. She has nothing to boast of but a charming voice—everything else in her is falsehood, coldness, affectation—and a repulsive Parisian swank. This charlatan, this publicity-seeker, has taken the absurd step of writing—she herself, you understand!—all the newspapers about how the firemen rescued *her* things from the unfortunate theatre. What do you think of that? A thousand people perish—let them! It seems that so long as Sarah's things are saved there is no need to grieve over anything else. This kind of thing makes the ancient blood of my serf-owning ancestors stir in me. Honestly, I could whip this buffoon of a woman with my own hands—only, it's a pity she is so thin". *Letters to an Actress: The Story of Ivan Turgenev and Marya Gavrilovna Savina*, trans. and ed. Nora Gottlieb and Raymond Chapman (London, 1973), p. 83.

18. A. P. Chekhov, *Polnoe sobranie sochineniy*, XVI, 14.

19. Ibid., p. 15.

20. Ibid., pp. 15-16. Compare Evgeniya Tur': "There was not a single note in her voice, not a single turn of her head, not a single movement

or step, which she made *unknowingly*, as something necessary and requisite. Much passion, much strength did Sarah Bernhardt display in this rôle, but even more study and schooling." "O Sare Bernar i ee repertuar na moskovskoy stsene", *Russkaya mysl'* 2 (1882), p. 44; and A. S. Suvorin, "Sarah Bernhardt is becoming boring as an actress or, more accurately, boring as Sarah Bernhardt, for she is always Sarah Bernhardt." Neznakomets, "Teatr i muzyka", *Novoe vremya* 2086 (December 17, 1881).

21. See Laurence Senelick, "Rachel in Russia: The Shchepkin-Annenkov Correspondence", *Theatre Research International* (February 1978), pp. 93-114.

22. *Gazeta A. Gattsuka* 50 (December 12, 1881), pp. 838-39. For favourable reviews of her Marguerite, see *Russkie vedomosti* 321 (November 27, 1881) and V. Chuyko, "Sara Bernar", *Nablyudatel'*, vol. 1 (1882).

23. Zritel', *Sovremennye izvestie* 328 (November 27, 1881).

24. Neznakomets, "Teatr i muzyka", *Novoe vremya* 2086 (December 17, 1881).

25. A. P. Chekhov, *Polnoe sobranie sochineniy*, XVI, 18.

26. See Laurence Senelick, "The Lakeshore of Bohemia: *The Seagull*'s Theatrical Context", *Educational Theatre Journal*, vol. 39, no. 2 (May 1977), pp. 199-213.

27. Chekhov, *Polnoe sobranie sochineniy* (Moscow, 1976), Pis'ma 4, p. 198.

28. Baron N. V. Drizen, *Sorok let teatra: Vospominaniya 1875-1915* (Petrograd: 1916?), p. 81.

29. A. R. Kugel', *Teatral 'nye portrety* (Petrograd: 1923), p. 80. Kugel's essays on Sarah Bernhardt and Eleanora Duse are probably the best analyses of their acting to be found in Russian.

8

Mademoiselle Rhea—An American Bernhardt?

Alan Woods

On 14 March 1892, dedicated theatregoers in Cleveland, Ohio, found themselves facing a difficult decision: the city's two major touring houses were presenting similar star performers in superficially similar plays. One actress was an old acquaintance, having made regular appearances in Cleveland for more than a decade. The other was making her Cleveland début, although she was a highly publicized, world-famous star. As the débutante was performing in French and the old favorite played in English—even though an English heavily accented by French—not surprisingly, the larger audience opted for their native tongue.

The débutante was, of course, Sarah Bernhardt. According to the *Cleveland Plain Dealer*, the audience had assembled to judge her coldly and critically, but her performance overwhelmed them so much that, by the end of the evening, the audience was beside itself with pleasure.[1] Bernhardt continued her triumphal Cleveland début with performances of Sardou's *Fedora* and *Cléopâtre*. Her success was complete when her final performance (as Cleopatra) succeeded in attracting a sold-out house.

Bernhardt's rival was Mademoiselle Hortense Rhea, an actress now virtually forgotten. But Rhea (as she was customarily billed) also did well in Cleveland, even competing against the redoubtable Bernhardt: Rhea's performances were sold out from the beginning of her engagement, and she was regarded as a great actress fully the equal of her rival. Rhea filled the auditorium despite plays which the newspaper reviewers found inadequate (an adaptation of Scribe's *La Czarina* and an unpleasant little farce called *Gossip*, purportedly based on one of Dumanoir's comedies) and despite local criticism of her accent:

Rhea herself was always Rhea and no one else. There would be little fault to find with her if it were not for that ever-present French accent. The longer Rhea stays in this country the broader does that accent become. Sometimes she is not really understood because of it.[2]

Rhea's career in the United States initially paralleled that of Bernhardt, with whom she was frequently (and often favorably) compared. Like Bernhardt, Rhea was brought to North America as a star performer, accompanied by reams of press releases praising her abilities. Like Bernhardt, Rhea was particularly noted for the splendor and number of her costumes, long accounts of which preceded her wherever she toured. And like Bernhardt, Rhea specialized in the chastely-pure fallen woman, or permutations of that rôle. Rhea's death scenes were as frequent and as highly praised as those of the Divine Sarah.

Unlike Bernhardt, however, Rhea never became a major international star. Indeed, in North America she never succeeded in gaining the acceptance of the New York City theatregoers. She conquered most of the rest of the continent, however, and did so during a lengthy career. Her successes provide an interesting example of an actress of limited talent who, carefully building upon the publicity generated by Bernhardt early in her career, carved a place for herself in the commercial theatre business of the late nineteenth century. In the process, she became a major touring star who could be hailed in Atlanta as "the living incarnation and personification of the dramatic muse!"[3] and evaluated in Pittsburgh as "more thorough than Modjeska, and every way more attractive. Rhea is genuine where Bernhardt was a wonderful specimen of art."[4]

Rhea's North American career was not brief; it spanned seventeen years, from her Brooklyn début on 14 November 1881 to her final appearance in Hagerstown, Maryland, on 26 March 1898. Between those dates she toured the United States from Maine to California, from Texas to the northern reaches of the country, as well as playing regular engagements in Canada.[5] Her annual seasons normally began in late August or early September, continuing until June or early July. The actress normally gave approximately two hundred and forty performances each season. These figures are hardly unusual for the period, but do indicate that Rhea was something more than a successful imitator of Bernhardt, even though she was regarded initially as such. She was also more than a one-season wonder, as were so many of the other European "stars" hastily imported to capitalize upon Bernhardt's astounding success during the 1880-1881 season.

The modern conception of Mademoiselle Rhea, for those few who know her name, comes from Geoge Odell's massive *Annals of the New York Stage*, the only readily available source which provides any detailed discussion of the actress. What one finds there does not encourage further examination of her career. Odell described the actress at her American début as ". . . Mlle. Rhea, a handsome, ambitious actress, who never quite fixed herself in our affections, though on the 'road' she attained a certain vogue".[6] Announcing her second (and last) New York appearance, Professor Odell termed her "better liked in the 'provinces' than in New York . . .".[7]

Rhea was indeed liked in the "provinces". In Buffalo, New York, for example, the Buffalo *Courier* summed up the city's reaction in 1882 by saying "she came almost unheralded and within three days brought the town to her feet. . . . [She is] a lady of very remarkable personal charms and a dramatic *artiste* of uncommon power".[8] In Fort Wayne, Indiana, it was observed that "the sweet touches of holy and unselfish love that comes too late, are all delicate shades of a powerful and realistic masterpiece of feminine acting which prove her a consummate artist in emotional rôles",[9] while Kansas City's *Evening Star* found her Lady Teazle "a superb interpretation of the character even when hampered with the incongruity of a strong French accent to an English country girl's words".[10] And in Peoria, Illinois, she had become the measure of excellence for other actresses by 1883, the *Daily Transcript* there maintaining that "while Madame Modjeska is a great actress, she is not the equal of Mary Anderson, and certainly not the superior of Mlle. Rhea".[11] A reviewer in Allentown, Pennsylvania, termed her "with the exception of Neilson, the greatest actress ever seen in our city",[12] while in Boston she was favourably compared with several other foreign actresses for her performance as Adrienne Lecouvreur:

Slender in figure, like [Bernhardt and Modjeska] . . . in the rôle [of Adriennne], she has a more winning beauty of face than either, and her whole style is of distinctly sympathetic quality, winning surely and deeply upon the audience. . . . She does not practise coolly reserving the effects of her power like Janauschek, but generously expends it all along the course of the drama.[13]

The "provinces" cited by Odell included even Brooklyn: the reviewer for the *New York Mirror* there commented in 1884:

In Camille and Adrienne, Rhea stands unexcelled, and is a tragedienne of the highest order; for she is intense in her action and peculiarly happy in tone and expression. . . . She is a perfect artiste, and uses her intuition . . . in the interpretation of the author's words in [*sic*] a wonderful degree. . . .[14]

Even at the end of her career, playing seasons of one-night stands in small towns, Rhea could still garner notices such as "her appearance was certainly that of the best artist in histrionics for whom the curtain ever rose in Ravenna [Ohio]. Her acting was supreme in its simplicity and expression of character genius".[15]

Hortense Rhea was born Hortense Barbe-Loret in Brussels.[16] She made her stage début there in 1871, then appeared for several years in Paris and in the French provinces. In 1876, she became the leading lady of the French Imperial Theatre in St. Petersburg, Russia, where she remained until the assassination of Czar Alexander II in 1881 closed the theatres. She performed Beatrice in Shakespeare's *Much Ado About Nothing* at a matinée at London's Gaiety Theatre during Bernhardt's June, 1881, engagement. Rhea claimed to have studied English for only two weeks prior to her début.[17] After her 1881 Brooklyn début, she remained on the North American stage uninterruptedly until 1898, returning to Europe only for short vacations between her annual tours. She apparently did not perform in Europe at any time after 1881.

Rhea failed to impress Professor Odell because she failed to gain acceptance in New York City, the American theatrical capital. She played Manhattan only twice: in 1881, during her début season, and again in 1890. Of her first appearance, the *New York Times* wrote:

Mlle. Rhea is not, it may be useless to say, an actress of exceptional force. . . . Her talent is not conspicuous, and is of a common quality; her art is simple experience, modified by apt intelligence and good taste. There is no marked individuality, no expressive originality, no delicate and searching subtlety in her acting.[18]

In 1890, the same newspaper termed Rhea's production of *Josephine, Empress of the French* "a novel theatrical and millinery exhibition", and went on to observe,

Rhea is a competent actress, and were it not for her speech she would be an unusually interesting one. She is a shapely, handsome woman, with a noble head and a striking face. Her motions are graceful, and the eye follows her with pleasure as she paces the stage. Her acting is cold, and she never moves the spectator; but it is always well considered, and she has very impressive moments, when her playwright is agreeable.[19]

The *New York Herald* merely noted, "If the real Josephine had been like the lady who stalked through the play last night Napoleon's divorce would have needed no justification."[20]

As reviews from other cities indicate, however, reaction to Rhea was markedly different elsewhere on the North American continent: she was extravagantly praised throughout her career. Negative reviews outside New York were few, most of them attacking her accent or, later in her career, her supporting company and her repertory. For most audiences in North America, she was a glamorous star whose periodic visits were eagerly awaited and who provided, on a regular basis, distinctly Continental sophistication. To understand her appeal, it is essential to examine the reactions of newspaper critics across the continent and to explore her repertory.[21]

Several adjectives recur with regularity in journalistic reactions to Mademoiselle Rhea, and did so throughout her career in both positive and negative reviews. She was consistently referred to as "charming", "feminine", "bewitching", "free from ranting", and "finished". Her personal attractiveness—and she was regarded as a radiantly beautiful woman—was mentioned invariably, frequently in conjunction with her gracefulness on stage.

Rhea possessed natural grace, and was certainly beautiful. Her managers capitalized upon both personal aspects in their publicity, reinforcing the manufactured image of her elegance and sophistication through the time-honored device of praising her costumes. A playbill for her production of *The Widow* (performed during the 1886-1887 tour), for example, includes among its praising passages the notation,

"The Widow" affords M'lle Rhea ample scope for the display of her varied talents, and an opportunity to wear her most gorgeous dresses. Incidental to the comedy, M'lle Rhea will wear her famous QUEEN OF HOLLAND DRESS, which she purchased in Paris for ten thousand francs.[22]

The playbill devoted far more space to the dress than the synopsis of the play's plot. Newspaper reviewers obligingly devoted equally vast amounts of space to Rhea's costumes; after a full description of the "Watteau robe of peach bloom and white brocade" worn during the first act of *The School for Scandal*, the *Denver Tribune* informed its readers that

the toilet worn in the last two acts was a pannier and train of gold leaves on pale blue satin worn over a petticoat of gold lace. The distinguishing feature of this costume was the panniers which were so immense as to seem inflated. The dresses were elegant and in perfect taste.[23]

Press releases describing her costumes and jewelry were frequent, and apparently proved highly effective in providing both publicity and material for journalistic reviews.

Rhea also carefully cultivated her audiences, at least those who might be classified as the social élite in each city visited. The columns of the *New York Dramatic Mirror* attest to the number of social engagements she filled in major cities, while in smaller towns she pleased local inhabitants by well-publicized events such as her tour of the Mollie Gibson mine in Aspen, Colorado; the residents of Aspen responded by filling the theatre for her performance.[24] In Winnipeg her fans presented her with a silver loving cup;[25] while in Los Angeles, where she opened a new theatre in 1884, she was presented a solid gold orange leaf "with raised orange blossoms in silver and engraved 'Welcome' on one side and on the other a raised green emerald laurel wreath with the word 'Rhea' in diamonds . . . ".[26]

These few examples are not unique in the press coverage of Rhea's career. Neither, of course, are they particularly startling in the context of rampant theatrical press-agentry late in the nineteenth century, when unbridled commercialism was supreme.[27] Rhea and her managers made a conscious effort to create an image of Continental sophistication and glamor for the actress; in large measure, the effort succeeded.

Press notices such as those cited are helpful in forming an idea of Rhea's impact upon her audience, but provide little assistance in determining the nature of her appeal and the range of her abilities. It is therefore essential to examine Mademoiselle Rhea's repertory and audience reactions to it. Only six plays were performed for more than two seasons. These six plays presumably contained her most popular, and probably most successful, characterizations. She acted *Frou-Frou* for four seasons; *Adrienne Lecouvreur* and Hester Grazebrook in Taylor's *An Unequal Match* for five seasons each, Beatrice in *Much Ado About Nothing* for six seasons, the title rôle in A. R. Haven's *Josephine, Empress of France* (sometimes subtitled *Empress of the French*) for eight, and the title rôle in *Camille*, as the play was called in America, for ten seasons.[28] She was highly praised in each of these parts and was identified especially closely with Josephine in the latter half of her career. Haven's play was sufficiently popular—despite the reactions of the New York critics already cited—to be the sole piece in Rhea's repertory during the seasons of 1889-1890 and 1890-1891; she played it each year thereafter with the exception of 1894-1895.

Rhea's *Camille* was, along with *Josephine*, her most popular vehicle. Although the play was certainly familiar to North American audiences—it was, after all, a staple for emotional actresses from Jean Davenport through Nance O'Neill—Rhea apparently brought a fresh interpretation to the part, with a performance described most frequently as "moral". It is a commonplace of nineteenth-century theatre history that *Camille*'s popularity throughout the latter half of the century stemmed not a little from its tantalizing naughtiness. The play both attracted and repelled: reviews for other actresses frequently regretted that the performer's genius found expression in, as *The Herald* (New York) once put it, "the five acts of specious but ingenious morbidity which Dumas the younger devoted to the deification of a consumptive strumpet . . . ".[29] This common reaction rarely occurred in reviews of Rhea's *Camille*.

In the absence of a promptscript it is impossible to determine precisely how Rhea approached *Camille*. It seems certain, however, that she did not stress Marguerite Gautier's background, focusing instead upon the character's distaste for her current life; as one reviewer put it, "she nicely portrays a woman who, cloyed with the superficialities and vanities of a giddy life; finds inexpressible peace and rest in reciprocated love . . . ".[30] Rhea's Camille, another newspaper noted, "is more sinned against than sinning. The dissolute adventuress is tenderly converted into the erring and unhappy woman, who, having fallen a victim to the allurements of vice, is mastered by a noble love".[31] In Pittsburgh, the *Gazette* reported approvingly that Rhea

brings most prominently into view her impatience at her disgraceful surroundings, her longings for pure and noble love, and finally, her surpassing generosity and glorious self-abnegation, by which she proves her love in renouncing it, and finds in death the happiness which was denied her in life.[32]

From these and other comments, it is evident that Rhea presented Marguerite as an essentially pure woman trapped by circumstance and disgusted with her current life from the very beginning of the play.

Rhea's performance was apparently not only moral, but also highly polished. Reviewers constantly emphasized her "naturalness" and "plausibility" in *Camille*, comparing her favorably with other actresses who played the rôle. The *Manchester* (New Hampshire) *Mirror American*, for example, declared that "The spectator forgets M'lle Rhea and sees and hears only the Lady of the Camellias. The interpretation differs very essentially from Bernhardt's and the others, and there are numerous passages in which she rises superior to Bernhardt, Morris, or Modjeska".[33] The Cleveland *Herald* observed that "Modjeska or Bernhardt cannot equal the finish of her work, while Clara Morris, with all her intensity, cannot show such power as M'lle Rhea threw into her part . . . ".[34]

Rhea's other major rôle, Josephine in Haven's *Josephine, Empress of France*, shared many of the qualities of her Marguerite. In Haven's play, written in six acts,[35] Napoleon's empress was also depicted as "cloyed with the vanities of a giddy life" in her first appearance at a ball, before her marriage to Bonaparte. Like Marguerite, Josephine selflessly surrendered her lover, in this case giving Napoleon to Marie Louise so that an heir to the French throne might be born; the play's fourth act depicted Josephine's patient waiting for Marie Louise to give birth, while her joy at the news of a male baby provided the act's tableau. And, like Marguerite, Josephine took the entire final act to die, doing so as Napoleon, returning from St. Helena, raced into her chamber to declare his mistake in ever leaving her. The play, as might be expected of a drama starring the Josephine rather than the Napoleon (although William S. Hart, then beginning his career, was highly praised in the rôle), contained some historical inaccuracies, and managed to suggest that had Napoleon listened to Josephine he would never have gone to Russia and certainly would have avoided Waterloo.

Again, reviews of Rhea's Josephine provide an impression of her performance. Her charm, her careful attention to detail, her power and force in Josephine's confrontation with the giddy Marie Louise were all mentioned frequently, as were the splendour of the costumes and the stage settings, several of which reproduced famous Napoleonic paintings. Much the same comments were made of her Beatrice in *Much Ado About Nothing*. Extended reactions to her performance tended to discuss the charm, however inappropriate, of French-accented Shakespearean lines. The only scene consistently singled out for attention was the first scene of Act IV, the "Kill Claudio!" scene. Most newspaper comments praised Rhea's ability to switch from her "bewitching manner" to the sternness of the command.[36] The Cleveland *Herald* was most impressed by her "portrayal of the many extremes of womanly character, grace, wit, petulance, waywardness, tenderness, devotion and power which go to make up this wonderful creation . . . ".[37] Much of Rhea's appeal as Beatrice seemed due to the notion that Shakespeare's heroine lacked consistency: the Pittsburgh *Chronicle-Telegraph* called Beatrice "contradictory" and termed much of the play's humour "repellent", but then added that Rhea had performed the part in "an irresistible style peculiar to herself".[38]

Like Beatrice, Hester Grazebrook in Tom Taylor's *An Unequal Match* was somewhat incongruous when played with a French accent. But as had been the case with the Shakespearean heroine (and with her Lady Teazle), Rhea apparently charmed most critics as Hester. The play was used regularly as a matinée piece during the five seasons it remained in Rhea's repertory, and consequently was rarely reviewed. The few surviving newspaper reactions mention the difficulty of accepting Rhea's strong accent as appropriate for an English country girl; most would agree, however, with the assessment of the *Evening Star* of Kansas City: "Rhea . . . was charming, and made the transformation from a gushing, careless country girl . . . to a haughty, heartless woman of the world, [which] served to show in a very short time the variety and range of her talents".[39]

Adrienne Lecouvreur also remained in Rhea's repertory for five seasons, and was the rôle chosen for her North American début. The character bears certain similarities to several of those already discussed: like Hester, Adrienne comes from humble origins; like Josephine and Marguerite, she wearies of the superficial life of high fashion and society in which she finds herself, yearning instead for a quiet life supported by pure, selfless love. Like both Josephine and Camille, Adrienne sacrifices her happiness for the man she loves. Maurice returns, as did Napoleon and Armand, to his lover's deathbed. And like Rhea's Beatrice and Hester, her Adrienne demonstrated the actress' versatility: as the *Daily Picayune* of New Orleans succinctly put it, "she shows the actress enthused with her art, her love, hate, jealousy, despair, death. The gamut is run".[40] Since Bernhardt had included *Adrienne Lecouvreur* on her first American tour, Rhea was frequently compared with the French star; in Baltimore, *The Sun*, after finding Rhea more believable than Bernhardt in the part, described the characterization in terms strikingly similar to the comments about her Marguerite Gautier: "The surroundings may be impure and the atmosphere tainted, but she moves through all unharmed—the lustre of her purity and the white flower of her love undimmed and untarnished. And yet she is always the woman; as subject to storm and turmoil as the ocean."[41] The actress clearly made her Adrienne an innocent victim of circumstances by her approach, itself a notable, if somewhat dubious, achievement.

The last of Rhea's major rôles, that of Gilberte in *Frou-Frou*, represented no change from the pattern already established. Gilberte was, of course, one of the standard rôles for the nineteenth-century emotional actress (see Plate 3). The character's striving for fashion during the first two acts, her struggle to recapture the affection of her husband and child in the third, and her elopement followed by the requisite suffering and death as the final curtian fell, accompanied by the forgiveness of a repentant male—in this instance the husband—all provided innumerable actresses with the chance to run through a range of emotions. Rhea was no exception, and press comments sounded familiar themes. In Toledo, Ohio, it was noted that she displayed "all the emotions of life, from extreme gaiety and unrestrained happiness to . . . death. In scenes of hatred and anger, where the soul is swayed with intense emotion, she is truly grand, and in the death scene there was scarcely a dry eye in the house".[42] The reviewer in Fargo, Dakota Territory, found Rhea's performance "magnificent, showing careful study of the rôle and an abandon to its requirements that made every gesture and word a part of the mosaic making up the complete play".[43] *Frou-Frou* also permitted Rhea to wear lavish gowns, dutifully noted and praised wherever she played.

Her most standard rôles, and the press reaction to them, permit a relatively clear portrait of Rhea's talents and appeal to be drawn. Were it not for many of the newspaper comments, those six rôles would have earned Rhea, quite inaccurately, the label of an emotional actress. Her complete repertory was dominated by the plays of Scribe and Sardou, and the other rôles she performed were quite similar to the six just outlined. In most of Rhea's parts the characters strove in the early acts for fashionable status, then found the fashionable life hollow; in the standard variant, the character was in the midst of cosmopolitan life at the play's beginning. Only Beatrice deviates from the pattern; the other rôles all included some permutation of this characteristic. Rhea's characters suffered and repented at length, frequently enduring painful illnesses. Most died at their plays' conclusions. It is intriguing, and perhaps significant, that Rhea's parts did not include some rôles from the standard emotional repertory, notably *East Lynne, Leah the Forsaken,* and *Oliver Twist.* To be sure, these plays were, in the versions most often played in North America, of a distinctly English tone, which could have deterred Rhea from attempting them. Her heavy French accent did not deter her from successfully playing Beatrice, Hester Grazebrook, and Lady Teazle, even though one commentator noted that her Lady Teazle was not English, "but a mixture of the French and Russian".[44] Perhaps more importantly, the standard rôles Rhea chose not to play demanded intense and sustained emotions from their leading ladies, and did not provide the opportunity to juxtapose a glittering social life with personal anguish. Rhea's accustomed rôles, by contrast, uniformly called for sudden shifts in emotion in one or two brief scenes. The characterizations were otherwise limited in range, at least as the star actress played them.

Most of Mademoiselle Rhea's parts included that wide range of emotions: she ran the gamut in almost every performance, usually to the applause of her audiences and to printed praise from local newspapers. She prepared carefully for her performances: time after time, her attention to detail was mentioned in reviews, and Rhea herself in an interview with the *New York Dramatic Mirror* maintained that she approached her rôles through extensive and painstaking study, a legacy, she indicated, of her claimed early study with Coquelin.[45] The stress given her preparation and her polish implies a somewhat studied and mechanical performance style.

Throughout her career, Rhea retained her strong French accent, to the delight and dismay of her audiences. Press reaction was divided, ranging from the San Francisco *Wasp's* "she can shout and she can chant, but she cannot speak English so as to be understood . . . "[46] and the Laramie (Wyoming) *Boomerang's* "Rhea has an accent that makes one wonder why she don't stay in France where people can understand what she says . . . "[47] to praising notices which found that her ". . . English . . . was the sweeter by the pretty French brogue that rested on every word, and gave a charm to every sentence she uttered . . . ",[48] found her accent "piquant",[49] and spoke of the "music of [her] entrancing voice".[50] An assessment late in her career provided the best overall summary of the differing opinions: "Devotees at the Rhea shrine do not all object to the peculiarities of accent which seem to become the more pronounced as the years go on; and while others may not regard it in the same light, that is entirely a matter of taste."[51] Other reviews indicated that she could be difficult to understand when she spoke rapidly, while the general press reaction found her voice acceptably melodious.

After 1890, Rhea tended to play royalty: in addition to Josephine, *Catherine Howard, Czarina Catherine I, Princess Andrea, The Queen of Sheba,* and *Mary, Queen of Scots* all appeared in her repertory, most for a single season only. She also played a *Nell Gwynne,* a character certainly close to royalty if not herself royal. All these rôles, it should be noted, shared the general characteristics of Rhea's parts as outlined above. She briefly played Mercy Merrick in *The New Magdalen,* a distinctly unregal rôle which otherwise fits Rhea's established range, demonstrating, according to one newspaper, "the passions of love and hate . . . sympathy and pity".[52] The presence of the royal rôles in her repertory would imply a regality or aloofness in Rhea's stage presence, perhaps made more obvious by the actress' advancing age; she was in her late forties when she first attempted these more queenly characters.

Rhea seems to have been, therefore, a skilled and technically proficient performer. To her personal beauty she added immense charm and femininity, which she emphasized by taking care with both her characterizations and her wardrobe. She apparently could convey with power the emptiness and shallowness of court or high society life. Although many reviews praised her scenes of powerful or intense emotion, such scenes were surprisingly rare in the plays of her repertory: they were generally brief, presumably startling audiences by their suddenness. Rhea was unstintingly praised for her versatility, for her polish, for her grace of movement—even by journalists who found her performances unsatisfactory. She was not praised for her warmth or for her sympathetic portrayals, but for her clearly delineated and carefully (if obviously) constructed characterizations. These qualities made her a major touring star on the North American continent; they proved insufficient to provide a place for her in New York's theatrical world.

Rhea's survival as a touring star for seventeen years provides an interesting view of the popular theatre during the last two decades of the nineteenth century. Rhea looked, dressed, and behaved like a star, removed from the middle-class world of most of her audiences, but graciously condescending to be entertained by the social élite of the cities she played. Her smooth and polished performances not only were modern in that they often treated fashionably risqué topics but, perhaps most importantly, the relatively unsophisticated audiences of the North American "provinces" could see the carefully chosen details which constituted her characterizations. She made, in short, the actor's work comprehensible without it seeming uneven or obvious.

Her ability to shift from emotion to emotion with grace and ease excited breathless praise from provincial newspaper reviewers and, no doubt, was responsible in part for the many indications of thrilled audiences. So many of her reviews stressed Rhea's skill in this area, generally in connection with what was praised as versatility or wide-ranging flexibility, that it would seem apparent the actress possessed the technical capacity to run quickly through a series of emotional states, startling audiences through both sudden contrast and the rapidity of the change. Such rapid shifts of emotion were, of course, a hallmark of the "old school" of acting as defined by recent scholarship; so also were Rhea's painstaking attention to detail and her demand that interest be focused on the star, to the occasional detriment of her supporting company.[53] With a repertory carefully tailored to her audiences' tastes, Rhea titillated without offending, invariably showing fallen women whose repentance, always total and always sincere, elicited forgiveness through touching and extended death scenes. Her plays, like many of those in Sarah Bernhardt's touring repertory, gave the appearance of modernity while remaining comfortably old-fashioned for most of her career (see Plates 14 and 15).

By the end of her life, Rhea's popularity waned, if the record of her last two seasons is any indication. During those final tours, from 1896 through 1898, the number of one-night stands in small towns was appreciably greater than long engagements in major cities. In 1891-1892, for example, ten weeks of Rhea's tour—nearly a third of her time that season—were spent in large cities, playing at least eight consecutive performances. Her last season, by contrast, shows only two weeks in large cities (Montreal and Washington, D.C.) and a proportionately large number of single performances in small towns. The actress may have been ill; after the ignominious disbanding of her company in 1898, Rhea signed to co-star (with Frederick Warde and Louis James) in a "Grand Star Triumvirate" for the 1898-1899 season, but instead retired to France where she died in May, 1899, after a lengthy illness which had required surgery. Although the obituaries which appeared did not specify the nature of the illness, they left the indication that it had been long-term.[54] Rhea's age may also have been a factor in her lessening popularity: her Marguerite Gautier may have seemed a bit superannuated at fifty-four.

Even when age and possible illness are included, however, the nature of Rhea's repertory looms larger as a key element in her gradual loss of drawing power. Her 1897 engagement in Montreal provides a clear example: Rhea opened with *Frou-Frou* to an audience packed with Laval University students. Response was tumultously favorable, particularly after Rhea recited the Marseillaise in French after the first act. The local newspaper, while reporting the favorable reaction, also sternly reprimanded her choice of vehicles:

It is true. . .that Madame Rhea had exquisite gowns, a beautiful peroxide-golden wig, lovely teeth and coquettish French accent. But. . .she had an abominable. . .play, and a part to which she was nowise adapted. *Frou-Frou* is a diluted Dodo. . .without a backbone. . . .A long-suffering theatrical world is...sick and tired of this eternal apotheosis of adultery....We have already had too many plays founded on unfortunate violations of the seventh commandment. *Frou-Frou* should have remained in the twilight of its well-merited oblivion.[55]

The shift in audience taste over the span of Rhea's career is apparent in this reaction. Her repertory of lightly-tarnished heroines who paid for their sins with their lives, highly attractive in 1881, was much less so in 1897, having become old-fashioned and tedious for sophisticated audiences. In response, Rhea spent far more time toward the end of her career in small towns where audiences were more tolerant of older styles. Her popularity was fading, and she made no apparent effort either to expand her repertory or to develop new areas of strength to appeal to changing audience tastes.

Mademoiselle Rhea's North American career began in conscious imitation of Sarah Bernhardt's successful 1880-1881 tour. Rhea's publicity, while studiously avoiding direct comparisons with the French star, stressed the same elements of exotic Frenchness, elaborate costumes, and piquant personality which had provided much of Bernhardt's initial appeal. Rhea's early repertory was similar to that of Bernhardt, and much of the critical response compared the two actresses. Unlike Bernhardt, Rhea remained in North America from 1881 until her final year on the stage. During those seventeen years she carved a place for herself as a glamorous star highly regarded by her audiences, at least outside a few major cities, and became an accepted part of the theatrical world across the continent.

Rhea may not have been the American Bernhardt, matching the Divine Sarah in either talent or press-agentry, but she provided audiences with many of the same qualities as did Bernhardt, even if in diluted form, on a far more regular and dependable basis. Although she is now virtually forgotten, Rhea's career is almost a model of commercial enterprise making the most of modest talent, which was sufficient in the era of the touring star. Graham's summation of her in *Histrionic Montreal* provides perhaps the clearest image of her achievements and shortcomings:

She was personally a woman of great beauty, but of little artistic quality. Her managers used her reputation, which was purely artificial, to give her an eminence she never deserved. She was a hard-working woman, an indifferent actress and had public successes . . . created by good advertisements which gave importance to her interest and do not belong to her death.[56]

NOTES

1. *Cleveland Plain Dealer*, March 15, 1892, p. 2.
2. Ibid.
3. *The Constitution* (Atlanta), February 23, 1886, p. 5.
4. *Chicago Tribune*, March 5, 1882, p. 16, citing Pittsburgh *Chronicle*.
5. Rhea's career has been reconstructed from data appearing in the *New York Dramatic Mirror*'s weekly issues from 1881 through 1898 and several dozen published and unpublished sources. It is impossible to list them all here; specific references will be found below.
6. George C. D. Odell, *Annals of the New York Stage*, vol. 11 (New York, 1939), p. 452.
7. Odell, *Annals*, vol. 12 (1940), p. 360.
8. *Courier* (Buffalo), January 23, 1882; republished in the *Cleveland Plain Dealer*, January 25, 1882, p. 4.
9. Fort Wayne *Journal*, April 16, 1895, p. 1.
10. *Evening Star* (Kansas City), September 12, 1883, p. 1.
11. *Daily Transcript* (Peoria), December 15, 1883; as cited by Marion Moore Coleman, *Fair Rosalind: The American Career of Helena Modjeska* (Cheshire, Conn., 1969), p. 317.
12. *New York Mirror*, October 14, 1882, p. 5.
13. *Boston Evening Transcript*, December 13, 1881, p. 8.
14. *New York Mirror*, April 26, 1884, p. 4.
15. *Democratic Press* (Ravenna), March 4, 1897, p. 3.
16. Rhea's career is detailed most thoroughly in "The Death of Rhea", *New York Dramatic Mirror*, June 3, 1899, p. 13.
17. See, for example, "M'lle Rhea—The Actress," *The Sun* (Baltimore), April 1, 1882, p. 1. Much of the press material published in North America is suspect at best; of the biographical data above, only the single matinée at the Gaiety can be verified in American and English sources. See bill, Gaiety Theatre, June 2, 1881, Enthoven Collection, British Theatre Museum (Victoria & Albert Museum); and *The Era* (London), 43 (May 28, 1881), p. 8.
18. *New York Times*, November 29, 1881, p. 5.
19. Ibid., March 18, 1890, p. 5.

20. *New York Herald*, March 18, 1890, p. 10.

21. I have been unable to locate any prompt books, accounts, correspondence, or other materials pertaining to Mademoiselle Rhea except for scattered collections of playbills and the newspaper accounts.

22. Playbill, Collection of Professor John Marsh, Edinboro, Pennsylvania.

23. *Denver Tribune*, June 10, 1884, p. 5; as cited by E. S. Crowley, "The History of the Tabor Grand Opera House, Denver, Colorado 1881-1891" (Thesis, University of Denver, 1940), p. 221.

24. *Aspen Times*, June 18, 1889; as cited by K. B. Riker, "Theatrical Activity in Aspen, Colorado, from 1881 to 1900" (Thesis, University of Colorado, 1964), p. 71.

25. "Telegraphic News", *New York Dramatic Mirror*, October 13, 1883, p. 10.

26. *New York Dramatic Mirror*, June 21, 1884, p. 2.

27. See, for example, my "James J. Corbett: Theatrical Star", *Journal of Sports History*, vol. 3 (1976), pp. 162-75.

28. Rhea appeared in the following plays for two seasons each: *Diane de Lys*, *The Power of Love*, *Fairy Fingers*, *Pygmalion and Galatea*, *A Dangerous Game*, and *The New Magdalen*.

29. *New York Herald*, January 15, 1878; as cited by Coleman, *Fair Rosalind*, pp. 160-61.

30. *Cleveland Plain Dealer*, January 24, 1882, p. 8.

31. *Zanesville* (Ohio) *Daily Courier*, February 3, 1882, p. 4.

32. *Gazette* (Pittsburgh), February 7, 1882; as cited by J. A. Lowrie, "A History of the Pittsburgh Stage (1861-1891)" (Ph.D. Dissertation, University of Pittsburgh, 1943), p. 162.

33. As published in the *Zanesville* (Ohio) *Daily Courier*, January 31, 1882, p. 4.

34. *Herald* (Cleveland), January 24, 1882, p. 4.

35. The play has not been published. According to a bill in the Players' Collection (13,557), Theatre Collection of the Library for the Performing Arts, New York, the play was initially performed in five acts but "owing to the construction" it was "sometimes necessary to divide it into six acts". However many acts were performed, the play always concluded "with the death of Josephine".

36. *Aspen Daily Times*, June 18, 1889, p. 4; as cited by B. L. Shaw, "History of the Wheeler Opera House, Aspen, Colorado 1889-1894" (Thesis, Western State College, Gunnison, Colo., 1965), p. 103.

37. *Herald* (Cleveland), January 27, 1882, p. 4.

38. *Chronicle-Telegraph* (Pittsburgh), December 18, 1888; as cited by Lowrie, "History of the Pittsburgh Stage," p. 202.

39. *Evening Star* (Kansas City), September 14, 1883, p. 4.

40. *The Daily Picayune* (New Orleans), February 20, 1884, n.p.

41. *The Sun* (Baltimore), April 4, 1882, p. 4.

42. *New York Dramatic Mirror*, December 8, 1883, p. 8.

43. *Fargo Daily Argus*, May 17, 1887; as cited by R. J. Browning, "A Record of Professional Theatre Activity in Fargo, Dakota Territory, from 1880 through 1888" (Thesis, North Dakota Agricultural College, 1958), p. 225.

44. "Provincial—Boston," *New York Mirror*, May 20, 1882, p. 4.

45. "Mirror Interviews," *New York Dramatic Mirror*, August 10, 1895, p. 3.

46. *Wasp* (San Francisco), May 10, 1884; as cited by J. S. McElhaney, "The Professional Theatre in San Francisco, 1880-1889" (Ph.D. Dissertation, Stanford, 1972), p. 246.

47. *Boomerang* (Laramie, Wyoming), May 14, 1890, p. 4; as cited by L. Bruskern; "History of the Laramie Theatre, 1881-1890" (Thesis, University of Wyoming, 1961), p. 131.

48. *Seattle Daily Press*, June 7, 1887; as cited by E. L. Nelson, "A History of Road Shows in Seattle from Their Beginnings to 1914" (Thesis, University of Washington, 1947), p. 46.

49. *The Constitution* (Atlanta), March 1, 1884, p. 8.

50. *The Sun* (Baltimore), April 1, 1882, p. 1.

51. *The Constitution* (Atlanta), February 12, 1895, p. 3.

52. *The Daily Picayune* (New Orleans), January 13, 1895, p. 7.

53. See especially Attilio Favorini, "The Old School of Acting and the English Provinces", *Quarterly Journal of Speech* 58 (1972), 204-5.

54. *New York Times*, May 23, 1899, p. 7; "The Death of Rhea," *New York Dramatic Mirror*, June 3, 1899, p. 13.

55. *The Herald* (Montreal), December 6, 1897, p. 5.

56. Franklin Graham, *Histrionic Montreal* (1902; rpt. New York and London, n.d.), pp. 259-60.

9

Ristori in America

Marvin Carlson

Although Bernhardt unquestionably carried to its peak the image of the international star, she did not create that image. A generation before, two other actresses, Rachel and even more importantly Ristori, established the model upon which Sarah built her dazzling career. The idea of international touring did not, of course, have to wait for the transportation boom of the late nineteenth century. Colleagues of Shakespeare travelled to the low countries, to Scandinavia, and to Germany and for a century thereafter companies criss-crossed the continent, penetrating even deep into Russia. The eighteenth century saw comparatively little of such activity, however, and so the first interchanges between France and England in the early 1800s were, for audiences and actors alike, a new experience, unlike anything within memory. The arrival of English actors in Paris in the 1820s caused a sensation and contributed significantly to the development of romanticism in the French theatre. In 1832, Covent Garden found itself for the first time in the hands of a foreign director, M. Laporte, who during his one-season administration imported a series of continental stars. During July and August Mlle. Mars and other actors from the Comédie Française offered to enthusiastic London audiences Scribe, Molière, and Marivaux. They shared the bill with ballets by Taglioni and alternated with Paganini.

These cross-channel visits were followed by the more ambitious tours of Rachel, the first true international star. In 1841 she and a French company dazzled London and were lauded and entertained by the highest society, even by Queen Victoria. Rachel returned to London four times, but she toured elsewhere as well—to Brussels, Amsterdam, Budapest, Prague, Rome, Vienna, Berlin, and finally even to Moscow and New York. Everywhere, commoners and royalty joined in her praise. Never had an actor or actress achieved such widespread renown—and yet within only a few years Rachel was to be surpassed by new stars following a similar path.

In the spring and summer of 1855, Rachel was challenged on her home ground in Paris by a new touring star, Adelaide Ristori from Italy. Ristori was by this time one of the best known and most popular actresses in Italy, the leader of Italy's best troupe, the Royal Sardinian Company. This by no means guaranteed her any reputation elsewhere, however. As Professor Bradbrook has pointed out,[1] the nineteenth-century theatre world looked to Paris, and the international stars had to capture that citadel before making claim to the first rank of performers. Italy was, of course, known for the production of opera, but aside from that it was considered, with some justification, a cultural backwater, hopelessly divided into minor states generally dominated by foreign powers. In 1830 the Duchesse de Berry had invited an Italian company to Paris which might have countered this impression, but the time was ill-chosen. Scarcely had the actors arrived when the Revolution of 1830 toppled the government, drove the Duchess into exile, and sent the actors scurrying home. Ristori and her company therefore came upon the Parisians unaware, and took them by storm. Critics and authors united in her praise, and the general public followed their lead. The success of the challenger was so great that it was widely and falsely believed that the triumph drove Rachel into the unprecedented expedient of an American tour. In any case, the two actresses were never pitted in direct competition again. The American tour, exhausting and ill-organised, was catastrophic for Rachel's delicate health. She gave her last benefit in Charleston, South Carolina, on December 17, 1855, and soon after returned to Europe, though never again to the stage.

Ristori, left in undisputed possession of the title of Europe's leading actress, lost no time in solidifying her pre-eminence. After her success in Paris she toured France and Germany before returning home, to the unparalleled acclaim of her countrymen. In the years that followed she continued the tradition of international touring established by Rachel—to Spain, England, the Low Countries, to eastern Europe and Russia, then to Greece, Turkey, and Egypt. Inevitably, she set her sights on the goal that had destroyed her predecessor: the New World.

Ristori's first American tour, in 1866-1867, was nevertheless anything but a repetition of Rachel's. Actress, public and circumstances were so different as to create a totally new dynamic. Surely the most striking difference was in the New World itself. In the eleven years between Rachel and Ristori's visits, the United States had experienced its devastating Civil War and had emerged on the other side of that conflict strikingly changed. That period of staggering expansion which Mark Twain named the Gilded Age had begun, the age of great industrial empires, of mushrooming railroads and cities, of the Carnegies, the Morgans, and the Goulds. That perceptive observer of the period, Henry Adams, wrote of his family's homecoming to America in 1868: "Had they been Tyrian traders of the year B.C. 1000 landing from a galley fresh from Gibraltar, they could hardly have been stranger on the shore of a world so changed from what it had been ten years before." A new order with a new focus on energy and capital was rapidly, even ruthlessly, changing the face of the nation.

The international actress was admirably suited to this new order, and Ristori was the first to profit from it. Rachel had aroused interest, even enthusiasm, but she could not have achieved the impact of the later international stars who satisfied a new need, that of conspicuous consumption. The Gilded Age required the best of everything, and the same motives which drove the great private collectors to accumulate paintings of the European masters to hang in their Newport mansions led America's cultural leaders to pay unprecedented sums for performances by the period's acknowledged leading dramatic geniuses—Ristori, and later Bernhardt and Duse. Ristori, in addition to her reputation as the vanquisher of Rachel in Paris, had aristocratic credentials her predecessor lacked, since she was married to a Roman nobleman. She could thus satisfy status seekings on both aesthetic and social grounds.

America, in short, was ready for Ristori as it had not been ready for Rachel, and perhaps even more important, the readiness which existed was exploited for Ristori as it had never been for Rachel. The sort of press agentry commented on by Laurence Senelick, which was so central to the Bernhardt tours, began with Ristori. Rachel's father and brother, who arranged her American tour, were the most avaricious of entrepreneurs, but the power of publicity was unknown to them. The only devices they could apparently imagine for increasing their profits were to raise prices, perform in large halls, and ruthlessly exploit Rachel. With Ristori it was a different matter. She was invited to America and her tour was arranged by Jacob Grau, a manager who had a very clear idea of how to market a new attraction.

Grau had received his training from some of the most imaginative and determined entrepreneurs in New York's theatrical history, that small band of impresarios who during the 1850s struggled to establish and maintain Italian opera in the city with largely unknown imported artists. Grau began his career selling libretti outside Max Maretzek's opera house in 1850. It was Maretzek's second season and his prospects were not good. P. T. Barnum, having made a fortune with curiosities and freaks, was now turning his talents to high culture by sponsoring an American tour for the Swedish singing star Jenny Lind. Maretzek, in desperation, engaged a soprano with a modest reputation, Teresa Parodi, and saved his venture by challenging Barnum with publicity in the same style. His most effective device was leaking to the newspapers wholly fallacious reports that Parodi was going to cancel her American tour in order to marry the Duke of Devonshire.

During the 1850s Maretzek's major rivalry came not from Barnum, however, but from Bernard Ullman and Maurice Strakosch, co-directors of the New York Academy of Music. These profited from the lessons of Barnum and Maretzek, relying on extravagant publicity for certain stars. Strakosch used to say in a manner reminiscent of Barnum that out of a thousand persons ten might laugh at the puffs and fraudulent biographies of his stars, but 990 were fools enough to bite at the hook. He proved his point by attracting substantial crowds in 1857 to hear the tenor Tiberini, billed as linear descendant of the Roman Emperor Tiberius, and in 1858 he announced his prima donna Marlette Piccolomini as the granddaughter of Schiller's hero and a lineal descendent of Charlemagne. Grau, who in the meantime had graduated from selling libretti for Maretzek to speculating in tickets for Strakosch, learned the trade well enough to follow as manager of the New York Academy in 1862. His venture did not prosper during the war years, but in 1866 he made a new start by taking over the Théâtre Française (opened the previous year for the production of French plays in New York) and arranging for a season dominated by the appearance of Ristori.

The venture was a far more risky one than it might appear. The public was becoming accustomed to the importation of Italian operatic stars, but leading actors performing in languages other than English was another matter, and the single precedent of Rachel ten years before had not been a notable success. Most astute observers frankly predicted financial disaster for Grau, especially when it was learned that he had made an unprecedented advance outlay of $50,000. However Grau soon confounded his critics by launching a publicity campaign as unprecedented as his investment. For months before her arrival, the public was treated to reports on the new actress, stressing the concerns that would most appeal to the *nouveaux riches* of the 1860s—the sumptuousness of Ristori's wardrobe, the expense of bringing her, the fact that she had been fêted by European royalty and was herself a Marchesa and of course the fact that Grau was exhibiting an artistic champion, the successful rival of Rachel.

The success of Grau's campaign was clear as soon as tickets went on public sale. The line began to form at 4 p.m. the previous day and by 9 a.m. when the box office opened police were necessary to control the crowd. More than 2,000 persons were in line, not counting some 500 messenger boys dispatched by those unwilling to appear in person. By noon the first week was sold out and speculators were beginning to work the end of the line. It was two days before this line disappeared. The tickets sold for between one and four dollars, the highest prices ever charged in New York, but speculation soon drove prices far higher. One prominent entrepreneur boasted of selling *Medea* tickets for $50 each and the New York *Herald* began running as many as thirty advertisements per issue from disappointed patrons offering fabulous prices for seats. At the first matinée, even standing room was being sold for $5.

Ristori arrived and settled in aristocratic elegance into a suite at the Fifth Avenue Hotel. With her were her husband, son, daughter, manager, secretary, and four servants. Her company was housed in nearby, less ostentatious hotels. During the several days before her opening, Grau had her escorted about the city—to Central Park, to the museums, to Brady's gallery—for the delectation of the newspapers. She did not attend any public place of amusement, however. Grau wanted the public's first official glimpse of the new star to be in his Théâtre Française. The well-prepared opening there on September 20 was a triumph. The play was Legouvé's *Medea*, Ristori's standard opening piece. Thanks to Grau's publicity the audience was prepared to be swept from its feet before the actress even appeared. "New York is really experiencing a sensation," observed the *Tribune*. "You feel it in the air as you approach the theatre—it bursts upon you fully as a calcium light—one of Mr. Grau's marvellous conceptions—and makes its brightest apology for the wretched state of the weather." The audience was worthy of the occasion: "Fashion crowds the balcony in jaunty attire. Newport has returned to give the Tragic Queen a fitting welcome—*prima donne*, literateurs, and artists sit in state, looking unutterable things. How much they understand of Italian; how much they love dramatic art, and long for a worthy exponent of it, is not for us to say. All New York is there in fine feathers and flutter; and Ristori will appear before the best intellect that this commercial city can furnish."

Ristori made her first appearance in the fourth scene, carrying and leading her children down an artificial hill at the rear of the stage. The entrance was one of Ristori's most striking, and was doubtless one of the reasons that *Medea* was usually her opening production in a new city. Professor Coe, in Chapter 3, has noted the period's proclivity for the reproduction of poses from art works on the stage, and Ristori utilized this method to reinforce her long-anticipated appearance. "Having reached the top of the mountain", she remarks in her *Artistic Studies*, "I stop suddenly as if exhausted. This attitude, with many others, I had adopted from my study of the stupendous groups of Niobe which are in the famous Uffizi Gallery of Florence". For the benefit of those who might not appreciate this quotation of classic statuary, Grau added the aid of a strikingly modern medium—photography. Reproductions of this striking tableau were widely circulated in New York as part of the advance publicity, and the thunderous standing ovation which greeted Ristori on her appearance was thus a demonstration not only of the audience's acclaim for the new star but also of their recognition of a significant tableau. *Medea* was neither the most popular nor the most typical of Ristori's offerings, but it allowed her to give ample demonstration of a style which critics, at least for the purposes of contrast with Rachel, characterized as "passionate", "realistic", and "psychological". Descriptions of her acting show that all the critical set-pieces we have encountered so frequently in other chapters were already in place. To let one example stand for many, here is Legouvé, the author of *Medea*, describing Ristori upon her first appearance in Paris:

I was immediately struck with the sovereign beauty of her eyes. And what eyes! I only saw their equal in Talma and in Malibran. . . . They were liquid when their glance darted soft and luminous like a ray of sunshine across a cloud. But under the stress of passions, when that cloud gave place to fire in the pupil, what lightnings! Her voice had a surprisingly great range, velvety, caressing, profound; it made shivers whether of joy or terror run over the spine.

Tumultous applause followed each act, and the performance was followed by twenty curtain calls. Later, Ristori's coach was pulled to her hotel by a mob of her countrymen who continued to cheer and to serenade her until she reappeared late that night to make an impromptu speech of gratitude for her reception.

The opening engagement in New York lasted for five weeks,

during which Ristori performed twenty times in Manhattan and five times at the Brooklyn Academy. *Medea* was followed by *Mary Stuart*, Giacometti's *Elizabeth, Queen of England*, and *Judith, Phaedra*, and *Macbeth*. All were presented in Italian and thus libretti were an essential part of the event. Although there were frequent complaints about their inaccuracy and their illegibility, these guides were bought and faithfully followed by the vast majority of patrons. Critics complained regularly of the distraction this caused—more heads bowed over the text than turned toward the stage and twenty times during a performance such a turning over of leaves as to drown even Ristori's powerful voice.

There were other complaints as well. The Théâtre Français was far too small to accommodate the crowds generated by Grau's publicity. This encouraged speculation in tickets, and although the season was completely sold out, there were often many empty seats, the tickets being held by the speculators. Ristori's costumes were dazzling, but the theatre's scenery was poor and shabby and the staging crew inexperienced. The curtain would, on occasion, drop in the wrong place and intermissions were so long that the *Tribune* critic suggested one could "begin and end a three-volume novel" in them. Grau had employed an orchestra to play during the entr'actes but they were so inferior that they only made matters worse. Finally, the company Ristori brought with her was far from outstanding, some wooden and unconvincing, others offensively melodramatic.

These flaws were duly noted by the critics, but little else mattered when Ristori appeared. Audiences and critics alike judged that all the rest was to an extent superfluous. The version of *Macbeth* she presented was a clear illustration of this. The witches were seen no more after the first scene. Banquo, Macduff and even Macbeth were severely cut, and most of the final two acts disappeared entirely, so that the sleepwalking scene came shortly before the final curtain and Lady Macbeth was moved to the center of the play. Having thus eviscerated the text, Ristori somewhat paradoxically treated the lines which were left with the greatest care, seeking how to achieve from each the richest effects. Consider her description of the action with which she accompanied the reading of the line "You lack the season of all natures, sleep," when she and Macbeth are left alone on stage:

I take hold of his left hand with my right and place it over my right shoulder, then painfully bending my head in deep reflection and turning toward my husband with a look filled with the remorse which is agitating my mind, I drag him toward our chamber in the same manner that one leads an insane person. When reaching the limit of the stage Macbeth, frightened by the tail of his cloak trailing at my feet, again shudders suddenly. Then, with a quick turn, I pass on the other side of him, and try to master the terror with which I am also seized in spite of myself. Using a little violence I succeed in pushing him behind the wings, while quieting him with affectionate gestures. This mode of acting was not contradictory to the logic and reality of the situation, and always produced a great effect.

It was clear even before the New York engagement was completed that Grau was going to win handsomely on his $50,000 gamble. Ristori's second week in the city brought an income of $15,000 for five nights, not counting $3,900 for a performance of *Mary Stuart* at the larger Brooklyn Academy. At her benefit in Moscow, Ristori had gained the largest amount ever recorded in a single evening at a European theatre—$3,600—but she would break that record many times during her American tour. Even at the smaller Théâtre Français, the Brooklyn figure was surpassed for a matinée of *Elizabeth* on October 20, when demand for seats was so great that over a hundred ladies were seated on the stage.

On Sunday, October 28, Ristori departed for Boston, where she gave eleven performances with equal success. Her fame had preceded her to the extent that the Boston firm of Davis and Co. made a handsome profit selling Ristori kid gloves at $1.50 a pair. The audiences were larger than in New York, since a larger auditorium was available. The Boston papers complained, however, that while a large stage was more suitable to Ristori's "commanding figure and breadth of action", the beauty of her facial expression was lost in the vast hall. As Phèdre, Ristori was judged inferior to Rachel, but her other rôles were universally praised, and the *Post* observed that one could readily judge the relative popularity of the two artists in Boston by comparing the "handsome returns" of Ristori with Rachel's "meagre receipts". Some $4,200 was gained at the final matinée and again on the last evening.

In mid-November Ristori returned to New York for another two weeks before continuing to Baltimore, Washington, and Philadelphia. The demand for seats was as great as before, but the productions were this time less well received by the New York critics. Ristori had already offered her greatest rôles, and the new pieces added now were somewhat disappointing. In *Adrienne Lecouvreur* she was pronounced distinctly inferior to Rachel, her interpretation crude and melodramatic. Even the death scene, which Professor Horville has reminded us[2] was so important a part of the nineteenth century grand manner, came in for attack. "Never was so much dying given for the same amount of money", sneered the *Tribune*. "We have seen Forrest die in *Hamlet*, when it appeared as if he meant to make a night of it, and die all over the stage in every known style, but he was not at all equal to Ristori." Marengo's *Pia di Tolomei*, which featured Ristori dying in a dismal swamp, reviving at the last minute, and then dying again, drew similar criticism. Not until she returned to Elizabeth, Mary Stuart, and Medea did the chorus of approbation resume.

It was on these rôles that she relied during her week in Washington and Baltimore and two weeks in Philadelphia. Then she returned for two more weeks in New York before departing on the most extensive part of her tour. She offered two more new works, *Deborah* and *Camma*, with little success and then returned to the tested Elizabeth and Mary Stuart.

So far, Ristori had not much departed from the tour projected by Rachel a decade before, though the ailing Rachel had been forced to cancel her performances in Washington and Baltimore. Now, however, Ristori struck out into new territory, the expanding American West. As far as the Mississippi, the major cities were now easily if not especially comfortably accessible by railroad, and on January 10 Ristori's company headed west to Detroit, Cincinnati, and Chicago.

Grau's advance agent preceded the company by a week to ten days, organizing publicity and the sale of tickets. The same enthusiasm shown for the actress in New York was repeated as she travelled west. Tickets were placed on sale in Chicago on January 15 for five performances, at unprecedented prices, double those commanded by Edwin Booth earlier this same season. Nevertheless, more than half of the available tickets had been sold by the evening of the first day of sales. Ristori and her company were travelling by private train, which protected her from many of the discomforts and uncertainties of rail travel at this period, but not all eventualities were prepared for. A blizzard stopped the train near Michigan City and the company arrived at last in Chicago the morning after their scheduled opening. This served, however, simply to heighten expectations, and the scheduled five performances were given beginning a day later, with receipts surpassing even those of Boston. Only one offering, *Camma*, gained under $4,000, and the total receipts were an astonishing $20,794. The Chicago papers called the series "the greatest dramatic triumph on record" and this quotation, with the Chicago receipts, was duly reported in the newspapers of those cities where Ristori was next scheduled to appear.

Everywhere, other entrepreneurs were quick to capitalize upon Grau's success, so that a whole series of Ristori endorsements helped to swell the tide of publicity. On the front page of the Chicago *Tribune* of January 23 under the bold heading RISTORI, the manufacturers of Dr. Chaussier's "Empress" for the hair quoted in full a letter of thanks from the actress, who had received a bottle of their preparation in New York and spoke warmly of its usefulness. The article concluded: "If any other testimony than that of the fashionable world, who universally use this incomparable preparation to the exclusion of all others, were necessary, it would be found in this most strong and positive endorsement of this preparation, from the Italian Queen of Song". The "Queen of Song", repeated several times in the article, does not suggest that the copywriter was very familiar with what Ristori was actually doing. Perhaps he confused her with Jenny Lind.

From Chicago, Ristori turned south to St. Louis and Memphis, for a week in each city, then went on to New Orleans. Earlier touring companies had generally descended by the Mississippi

River, but Ristori made the entire trip in her private train. She arrived at New Orleans on February 10 and was given a grand reception at one of the city's most sumptuous hotels by the Italian community. The Italian reception had by this time become a standard feature of Ristori's arrival in any large city, and the papers usually remarked on the actress' warm welcome by her countrymen. This should not be taken to suggest, however, that there was anywhere in America a large enough body of Italian speakers to make up a significant percentage of her audience. Immigration figures show that in the fifty years before Ristori's arrival, a total of less than 20,000 Italians had preceded her to America. The American public had nevertheless a keen interest in Italy at this period because they saw in the emergence of the new Italian state a republican manifestation parallel to their own struggle for independence nearly a century before. John Hare suggests in Chapter 6 that we must not overlook Bernhardt's rôle as a representative of France. Neither must we overlook Ristori's rôle as the representative of the new Italy. Italian flags were often presented to her along with the inevitable bouquets, and a frequent part of the publicity which attended her visits was the printing in the local paper of a letter to her from Cavour, the architect of the new Italian state, praising her as the outstanding foreign representative of the emerging nation.

Richard Findlater has remarked on the importance of respectability to English actresses, particularly in the generation just prior to the triumphs of Bernhardt. Another aspect of the Ristori publicity clearly responds to this concern, particularly in the cities of the southern United States. Her brilliance as an artist was of course stressed as always, along with her aristocratic marriage and her rôle as a symbol of modern Italy, but special emphasis was now placed on the more domestic side of her character, as we see in a typical front-page story in the New Orleans *Times-Picayune* of February 12, which cites the actress's "wonderful industry" as the true source of her greatness, and continues:

She carries her own cook with her and superintends the preparation of all her meals. She arranges the economy of her own household, like any other good housewife. She watches, like a mother, over her son and daughter, and like a good wife, loves her husband. She personally attends to the wants of her servants, and sees they are well fed and housed. When she travels abroad, she packs her own trunks. She likes, above all things, to have her own house. If she resides long in any city, she always does have it. She has one in New York, and is looking out for one in New Orleans. She is fond of domestic life, its quietude, its honesty, its purity, and though very fond of society, desires to be the mistress of her own household. Thus, true and honest and natural in all the relations of life, fond and capable of studying tragedy at its fountain sources, she has become the queen of tragedy, not by any wonderful transformation, but by the simple laws of nature.

There had always been a certain shadiness, if not actual scandalousness, in the background of Rachel, for all the classic purity of her style. Richard Findlater has noted that Helen Faucit dropped her acquaintance. But Ristori was eminently respectable when the mid-Victorian passion for respectability was at its height. In another decade and a half Bernhardt would find seemingly unending publicity value in being surprising, and even outrageous. But in the mid-1860s Ristori could stimulate publicity simply by being respectable, as we see in a *Times-Picayune* story of February 15:

Yesterday Signora Ristori held a rehearsal of *Maria Stuart* in her private parlor, all the artists in the cast being present. The rehearsals are strictly private. It may be interesting to know that none of the abandon, customary at theatrical rehearsals, is permitted, but that all is dignified and in strict accordance with the rules of polite society.

Ristori remained in New Orleans for almost a month, through the carnival season, and gave eighteen performances, almost invariably to over–flowing houses. In her farewell on March 11 she closed with her first non-Italian offering, the farewell speech of Joan of Arc in French.

From New Orleans she went to Mobile, Alabama, then turned northward again. She arrived in Nashville on March 18, too ill to perform and with more than $1,000 of advance tickets sold. The authorities threatened to impound her trunks, but Grau settled with a payment of $500 and a promise of a delayed performance. That obligation satisfied, Ristori returned by way of

Louisville, Kentucky, to Chicago. After another five performances, with no decrease in audience enthusiasm, she toured the cities of the lake shores to Buffalo, then crossed upstate New York, playing each successive night in mid-April in a different city. After another brief pass through Boston and Providence she returned to complete her tour in New York and Brooklyn. Elizabeth, the most popular of her rôles, now dominated her repertoire, and wisely so, for the New York critics remained less willing than those of New Orleans or Chicago to acclaim her in every rôle. "In both *Angelo* and *Adrienne Lecouvreur*", the *Tribune* observed on May 7, "Ristori's conception is fine, her execution less so. She is somewhat too mature and massive readily to invest herself with a character so spiritedly poetic." The Théâtre Français was condemned as before for being small and cramped with poor shabby scenery, bad stage management and an atrocious orchestra.

The tour ended with a series of benefit performances—a matinée on May 15 for the American Dramatic Fund and an evening performance in Brooklyn for the Italian Schools of New York, a performance May 16 for the Ladies' Southern Relief Association, and Ristori's own farewell benefit of *Medea* on May 17. The capacity audience brought the actress back with cheers after every act and sprang to their feet, waving hats and handkerchiefs at the end. Ristori expressed in English her gratitude for her reception in America, the high point of her artistic career, and was presented with an Italian flag amid continued cheering. She departed for France the following day and the *New York Times* offered statistics on her remarkable tour. She had given 370 performances during her eight month tour in thirty cities, travelling 18,000 miles in all. Her receipts totalled $430,000.

The enormous success of this first tour ensured that Ristori would return, and that other European stars would follow. Grau had won his gamble, and he and others were quick to pursue the new profits. Even before Ristori left, Grau had made arrangements for her to return the following fall. This second tour was somewhat longer and even more successful than the first, lasting from mid-September of 1867 until the end of June 1868, and including a two-month trip in mid-winter to give fifty-seven performances in Cuba. The repertory remained much the same, with more than half of the performances devoted to *Elizabeth, Mary Stuart,* and *Marie Antoinette.*

Few complaints had been voiced during the 1875-1876 season about Ristori herself, but the relative weakness of her supporting actors and Grau's lack of care in scenery and costumes had drawn frequent negative comments, especially from the critics in New York. With the handsome profits from this first season, Grau sought to meet all objections. He completely remodeled the Théâtre Français, which many found crowded and uncomfortable. He hired a new conductor to improve the orchestra. He arranged for a new leading male actor, Antonio Bozzo, who drew universal praise in America. And, most importantly, he arranged for Ristori on her second tour to be accompanied by a large number of settings and costumes executed by some of Europe's leading theatrical designers. It was well he did so, for while critical enthusiasm for Ristori remained high, the intense public interest of the first tour was not recaptured until Grau produced his new *tour de force,* Giacometti's *Marie Antoinette.* The play had been especially created for this tour, and Grau had spared no expense in mounting it. The settings were designed by Recanatini and Venier of the San Carlo in Venice, by Giannini of the Pergola in Florence, and by Colvina of the Carlo Felice in Genoa. The costumes for the huge cast were designed by Wortz of Paris and were dominated by eight striking costumes for Ristori. There was even a new drop curtain for the production, the work of du Cerri of the Paris Opéra.

Between her first performance, in *Medea,* on September 18, and October 2, Ristori appeared most often in *Elizabeth,* which also had new scenery. Attendance was good, but not outstanding; the New York *Post* called the first part of her season "more triumphant artistically than pecuniarily". Particularly unsuccessful was her first attempt at Alfieri's gloomy *Myrrah* in New York. The *Post,* normally among her warmest supporters, declared: "the play, which could never have been written save by an Italian, is simply horrible, and is only saved from being revolting by the superb acting of Madame Ristori". Audiences disappeared, the play was cancelled, and the company began full-time on *Marie Antoinette,* their central hope for saving the season. This was one of the first of the huge historical spectacles which achieved such popularity in the nineteenth century, a visual pageant covering most of the major events of the French Revolution and running almost six hours, from 7:30 p.m. until 1:15 a.m. "I took particular pains", said Ristori, "in order to produce it with a splendid effect. I was especially careful that the execution of the play should be historically correct, and the costumes and scenery should portray exactly the time it represented."

The opening on October 7 magnificently fulfilled her expectations. The enraptured audience reportedly showed not the slightest sign of fatigue. The acting of Ristori and Bozzo as the king and queen was lavishly praised, but it was the visual spectacle which most impressed the public. The old "Ristori fever", as the papers called it, returned. Audiences at subsequent performances overflowed the seats into the aisles, into the orchestra pit, and onto the stage. The streets surrounding the theatre were once again blocked with triple rows of carriages, and travel on the Sixth Avenue cars had to be suspended. The dazzling success of *Marie Antoinette* assured that it would be Ristori's staple offering on this tour as *Elizabeth* had been the previous year, and guaranteed also that later travelling stars, most notably Bernhardt, would make historical spectacle in scenery and costuming an important part of their appeal to American audiences.

Aside from her appearances during February and March in Havana, Ristori concentrated on the cities of the northeastern United States for her 1867-1868 tour. She appeared most often in New York—to open her tour, before and after the appearances in Cuba, for a set of farewell appearances in May and then for another set in June before actually departing for Europe. She made two two-week tours, one in the fall and one in the spring, to Boston, Philadelphia, and Washington, and in December she went west as far as Cincinnati, but did not continue on to Chicago or to the southern cities she had visited the year before. Everywhere, *Marie Antoinette* attracted the greatest attention. *Season* magazine predicted accurately in September that "Ristori's personal wardrobe for this play cost a royal price and will itself create a sensation", but added, probably with more optimism than conviction, that "the acting will have greater charm for the true lovers of the drama". Grau knew well enough what brought audiences flocking to *Marie Antoinette*. After the opening performance in New York he cut the production so that it ran only four hours, but not a bit of the visual spectacle disappeared. In Boston and elsewhere the programs for *Marie Antoinette* stressed the "lavish outlay" and "historical accuracy" of the production, and even included, instead of the customary plot summary, detailed descriptions, scene by scene, of what Ristori was wearing, a practice continued by later leading actresses. Ristori had come a long way from *Mary Stuart*, which drew a complaint from a Boston reviewer in 1866 concerning her appearance in the same plain black satin dress from beginning to end. One measure of the success of *Marie Antoinette* was the rapidity with which it was copied. Even before Ristori left America, Mrs. W. F. Lander was touring to New York, Boston, Philadelphia, Chicago, and Detroit with productions of her versions of *Elizabeth* and *Mary Stuart*, which were advertised as "authentic reconstructions of the Elizabethan era" with "imported costumes and scenery".

Neither of Ristori's two subsequent trips to the New World generated the enthusiasm of these first two nor proved so influential for the international stars which followed, but Ristori nevertheless continued in each to break new ground. It was not until 1875 that she returned for a third visit, though during the intervening years she had toured South America and most of Europe. Her old producer, Jacob Grau, was dead, victim of a traffic accident in Vienna where he had gone to book Anton Rubenstein for an American tour. His business had been inherited by his nephew Maurice, who had begun his own career selling libretti for Ristori's first tour, and who gladly undertook the arrangements for a new series of appearances. The 1875 tour was part of Ristori's most ambitious project, a theatrical tour around the world. After touring South and Central America she arrived in New York on February 26, where she performed until the end of March. Ristori was again hailed by the critics as the greatest living exponent of tragedy, but the audiences which braved the severe winter of 1875 to see her were normally what the papers characterized as "small but distinguished". Shortly before her departure for Boston, the *Herald* summed up the prevailing attitude in this way:

The return of Ristori to America at this time has offered to this public the opportunity of seeing and studying the magnetic personality and the trained art of a great actress, and likewise of observing a dramatic curiosity—a famous relic of a storied past—that may soon vanish altogether from the stage. Ristori is fifty years old, and it is some time since she reached both the head of her profession and the summit of her career. Nothing that she does now presents either her nature or her art in a new aspect; and everything that she does has been many times canvassed and described.

Clearly, such an attitude encouraged Grau to utilize the popular device of claiming that each appearance of Ristori in New York would be positively her last, but it is difficult to imagine that audiences were fooled for long since, after the end of her season on March 27, she returned for a series of farewell performances in mid-April and once more for the actual farewells in early May. In this final series, Grau unveiled Giacometti's new historical spectacle *The Huguenots*, but the Saint Bartholomew's Day Massacre proved less attractive a subject than the French Revolution, and neither Ristori's acting nor the lavish setting could bring large houses to this offering. The *Herald* called it "the most stupid, tiresome, and inexcusably dull drama that the prosy mind of Signor Giacometti has produced; and it ranks well with the rubbish of all literature. It was observed with patient attention and mild sorrow."

Ristori's major innovation during this tour was her first performance in English. She had occasionally used the sleep-walking scene from *Macbeth* as an afterpiece during previous tours and for 1875 prepared it in the original language. The public found it less than impressive, however, and it was praised, if at all, more as a gesture to English-speaking audiences than as an artistic achievement. The San Francisco *Chronicle* comments are typical:

Her look is truly enough that of a cataleptic somnambulist; her labored breathing is true to nature so far as it correctly portrays the physical signs of approaching dissolution. Her English is perfect, scarcely a trace of a foreign accent being noticeable; but this said, all is said. She stands in the center of the stage and glares; she exhibits no sign of the remorse and mental misery that tortured the miserable Queen.

Still, Ristori did well enough on the East Coast to launch Maurice Grau on a successful career as a producer. When she left New York for the west on May 9 she had given fifty-eight performances in the northeast, with average receipts of nearly $2,000.

She embarked for Chicago on the first stage of a trip that would take her across the continent over the recently opened rail lines to the Pacific. It was a long and arduous trip, but Ristori was spared the discomfort most early travellers experienced in changing trains and seeking adequate hotels *en route*. Her own private Pullman provided her not only with coast-to-coast transportation, but also, except in the largest cities, with accommodation. It was a completely equipped little studio apartment on wheels, with heavy silk curtains, a library, paintings on the walls, flowering plants and even a piano. Only a few performances were given en route—six in Chicago, four in Cincinnati, three in St. Louis and one each in Indianapolis and Louisville, but the company performed for three weeks in San Francisco before setting sail on June 21 for Australia.

Ristori, now fifty-three, truly meant this "farewell tour" to be her last, but five years later she became fascinated by a new project, mastering English and presenting the great works of her repertoire in that language. By 1882 she was sufficiently confident to undertake *Macbeth* at Drury Lane itself, and, although the critics were anything but pleased by the grotesque adaptation she employed, her ambitious experiment was generally approved. The audience response was warm and enthusiastic. Encouraged by this experience, Ristori soon after began arrangements for her final American tour, which began in November of 1884. This was her longest and most extensive tour in the New World, including sixty-two cities ranging from coast to coast and into Canada and lasting seven months, a major feat for an actress in her sixty-third year. One naturally wonders what made America so attractive to the international stars, with its huge distances and its multiplicity of communities offering only brief engagements. Ristori's countryman Salvini in his autobiography suggests several possibilities:

The actor's life in North America can be summed up in three words, "Theatre, railroad, hotel." Very few are the cities in which a stop of two or three weeks is made. Away from the large centers, sometimes theatre and town are changed every night, with the intervening weariness of packing and of sleeping-cars. . . . But with all that . . . one can endure in America what would not be endurable in Europe, and especially in Italy. I do not know whether this is due to the air, or to the material comforts of life, or whether it is that the example of industry animates, fortifies, and spurs one on: but it is certain that so continuous a strain in Europe would prostrate a man in a single year, while in America, one undergoes it with resignation and resists it with courage. I will not deny that the anticipation of a satisfactory profit had some influence in maintaining my vitality; although my strongest incitement came from knowing that I was appreciated and loved.

The anticipation of a satisfactory profit doubtless had some influence in maintaining Ristori's vitality, too. Like Sarah, she gained her greatest financial rewards from her American tours, and her final American appearances were the most profitable of all, thanks to an agreement with Maurice Grau which returned to her 40 percent of her gross receipts. The demonstrations of love and appreciation, however, were much less impressive than they had been for her first appearance. She was welcomed everywhere with respect but without great enthusiasm, rather with what the *New York Herald* called "noble-hearted sympathy". Her power had not greatly declined, but her style now seemed rather old-fashioned and her English, while generally accurate, proved no real aid to her art. The Chicago *Tribune* noted that she spoke distinctly in calmer moments, but her English "fell like tangled underbrush in her path when she rose to higher endeavor". The Boston *Globe* reported that her English showed less trace of a specific accent than had been noticeable in other foreign touring stars, but that she had little feel for the natural stress pattern of English sentences. Individual words were therefore clear, but it was "infinitely difficult" to understand entire phrases.

Public interest was now clearly directed toward a new generation, with a different style. In 1866 Ristori had stood almost alone, but now the international star was a familiar phenomenon. During the 1880s, Modjeska, Janauschek, Irving, and many lesser figures challenged Ristori's position, and, more than anyone else, Bernhardt was gaining the dominance Ristori had once held. Even when she was not in America, the dazzling French actress was able, by 1885, to dominate the interest of the public on this side of the Atlantic. A single striking example of this may be seen in the Chicago *Tribune* of November 23. Ristori was then completing a week of performances in Chicago and in this issue was accorded her longest review, a full column on her three productions. In the same issue, however, two full columns were devoted to recent reports on Sarah's activities in Paris. The columns were headed "Bernhardt's Vagaries" and the three sub-headlines give an idea of the whole: "The Notorious French Actress Still Occupying the Public Attention in Paris", "Scenes and Incidents Consequent upon Her Attempt at Theatrical Management", and "Playing the Lunatic to Gratify a Morbid Passion—Her Probable End as Told by a Member of Her Troupe". After such rhetoric, a review describing Ristori's acting as "methodical and correct" must have seemed bland indeed.

With this final tour Ristori ended her acting career. She returned to a quiet life among the Italian aristocracy and enjoyed twenty years of retirement. She remained concerned with the theatre, however, and followed with interest, though with some disapproval, the careers of her successors Bernhardt and Duse. To her, they seemed representatives of a new and disturbing approach to acting. In a letter of 1893, she conceded to Bernhardt "great talent and great artistic perspicacity" but associated her with the art "of modern tendencies, based on neurosis and verily *à tout prix*". Duse, she said elsewhere, had a great talent, "but she is ill, neurotic, like our century. Everything is nerves now." In 1894, she wrote bitterly of what constituted the "famous" actress of the day: "Your striking toilettes, the face of a cunning little soubrette, the friendship of the most noisy newspaper men, a way of reciting by jumps and convulsions, and a great deal of hysterics, christen you as a model and leader in dramatic art." There is some justice in the charge, but there is perhaps more irony, for whatever her misgivings, Ristori must have been well aware that it was she more than anyone else who had marked out the path of the international star which Duse and Bernhardt followed.

NOTES

1. See Introduction, p. 8 and note 1 on p 12.
2. See Chapter 2 and also similar comments in Chapters 3, 5, and 8.

10

Martin-Harvey In Canada

L. W. Conolly

So far as I know, Sir John Martin-Harvey (1863-1944) never met Sarah Bernhardt. If they did meet it could not have been a very memorable occasion, for she does not mention him in her memoirs, and he does not mention her in his autobiography. Bernhardt was only eighteen years older than Martin-Harvey, but by the time the English actor had gained some international recognition she was nearing the end of her career. They both, of course, made professional visits to Canada—Martin-Harvey's first was only four years after Bernhardt's—and in Chapter 6 John Hare describes one aspect of Bernhardt's impact on the Canadian theatre of the period. Martin-Harvey's somewhat later visit of 1914 is the subject of this present chapter. The visit presents, I think, some interesting contrasts with Bernhardt's Canadian experiences.

Martin-Harvey does not receive much attention from today's theatre historians—certainly not as much as Bernhardt receives—nor has he been particularly well served by earlier historians and biographers. The most substantial examination of Martin-Harvey's life and work is still Maurice Willson Disher's *The Last Romantic*, published nearly thirty years ago.[1] Assuming one can cope with Willson Disher's highly idiosyncratic style, there is much to commend his book: it is, to be sure, unscholarly, but it generates an enthusiasm and creates a sympathy for its subject which many scholars might well envy. The book was clearly a labour of love, yet there is something distinctly defensive about it. Martin-Harvey is associated with the end of a tradition; he is seen as a lonely survivor of that romantic style of acting which was on its way out, at least in London, long before even Irving died. Hesketh Pearson, too, pictures an antediluvian Martin-Harvey. The book in which Pearson discusses Martin-Harvey is called *The Last Actor-Managers*, and in it he is described as "the last eminent specimen of a rapidly disappearing class".[2]

Martin-Harvey's career coincided with the return of the playwright as a dominant force in the English theatre, when the audience's attention was increasingly directed to the play rather than the players. Martin-Harvey had little time for Ibsen or Shaw, though he did on rare occasions act in plays by both of them. More to his taste as both actor and manager was the kind of unashamedly romantic costume drama typified by a play he eventually brought to Canada, *The Breed of the Treshams*, written by two American ladies using the pseudonym of John Rutherford.[3] The play gave Martin-Harvey the part of a dashing Royalist officer in the English Civil War who risks his life for love and suffers all kinds of torture in the process—by whipping, stabbing and burning. This, together with what one critic described as the hero's "proclivity for entering and leaving a room by the window instead of the door", made for an exciting evening when the play was performed in London in December 1903. But the critics were not impressed, dismissing Martin-Harvey's efforts as "grotesque mannerisms".[4] In fact, Martin-Harvey's preference for plays which stressed the conventional virtues of service and self-sacrifice, and his taste (and ability) for acting parts which allowed him to dominate a production with an intensely emotional performance, never won him an ardent or durable body of support in London, though in the provinces and abroad he rarely failed. He had scarely reached the height of his powers before he was pigeon-holed as a purveyor of faded glamour, an exponent of well-worn conventional tastes and techniques. At a time of change and experiment in English drama and theatre no one expected Martin-Harvey to be innovative or inventive.

Willson Disher sees his task as one of explaining and defending the tradition which Martin-Harvey espoused. He perhaps does as good a job of this as could be done, but he sometimes misses opportunities to emphasize that Martin-Harvey did have an adventurous side to his character. True, he laboured on and on with performances of his most famous rôle, that of Sydney Carton in *The Only Way*, a play adapted from Dickens's *A Tale of Two Cities*, making of it a kind of Edwardian *Mousetrap*—there were some 5,000 performances during his career and Martin-Harvey claimed not to have missed one. And there can be no denying that his exploitation of popular romantic plays left him precious little time and energy for serious consideration of new ventures. But I think Martin-Harvey deserves more recognition than he is generally given for some of his explorations as an actor-manager. He tried hard, for example, to introduce Spanish drama to London audiences; his production of *Oedipus Rex* at Covent Garden on January 15, 1912 was the first in England since the seventeenth century; his *Hamlet* at His Majesty's during the First World War moved determinedly away from nineteenth-century productions of archaeological exactness to a Poel-like simplicity; and his decision to stage Hofmannsthal's *Jedermann* at the Garrick in February 1923 was, as Willson Disher says, a "bold venture".[5] Now there is nothing here to compare with the new directions being taken at the time by, say, Granville Barker or Gordon Craig, and however hard we search we are not likely to find enough evidence to alter to any significant degree Martin-Harvey's position in theatre history from that of a willing traditionalist to that of a renowned progressive. What his few experiments in the English theatre do suggest, however, is that there was somewhere within him an urge to take chances, to be unconventional, to pursue that which he believed in, regardless of commercial risk—in short, to break new ground.

In England the new ground broken by Martin-Harvey amounted to no more than a few short furrows, but if we look at his Canadian career, particularly the tour of 1914, we can perhaps see more clearly the innovative element in his work, the way in which he broke with well-established traditions in the long history of touring stars in Canada. Willson Disher remarks that "Considering [Martin-Harvey's] unquestioned right to a place in theatrical history he was not closely observed by critics. For the simple reason that he spent so much of his life on tour he did not win a nameable fraction of the descriptive pages devoted to Irving."[6] Perhaps historians have been put off by the relative inaccessibility of sources for a study of Martin-Harvey's Canadian tours; perhaps they have assumed that the Canadian Martin-Harvey was a replica of the English Martin-Harvey. Certainly Willson Disher has little to say about Martin-Harvey in Canada, but both from the point of view of the new insights we get into Martin-Harvey and what we can learn about the state of Canadian theatre and criticism toward the end of the Bernhardt era, Martin-Harvey's Canadian experiences are well worth considering.

In his autobiography Martin-Harvey tells us that when he was a young apprentice shipwright in his father's shipbuilding company in Wivenhoe, Essex, he made plans to run away to Canada and become a farmer in Manitoba.[7] Instead he caught a cold and decided to stay in Essex, and he had to wait many more years before he saw Manitoba. It was as an insignificant member of Irving's Lyceum company that Martin-Harvey first visited Canada in 1884.[8] His impressions of the country on that occasion are not recorded, but later on in the autobiography he devotes two full chapters to the tours he undertook in charge of his own company. Altogether, Martin-Harvey made eight Canadian visits. According to his own account he crossed Canada fourteen times, and he was never disappointed by his reception. For one thing, he made a lot of money in Canada, certainly more than any other previous touring actor. On his 1923 tour, for example, a week of *Oedipus Rex* in Chicago, with its million inhabitants, produced $6,090; a week in "little Winnipeg", as he calls it, grossed almost twice as much, $11,400.[9] On one occasion, at what must have been a quite remarkable theatrical event, Martin-Harvey produced *Oedipus Rex* in Calgary and invited the chief and leaders of the Sarcee Indian tribe to be present. They occupied the boxes, and apparently didn't move a muscle throughout the performance; but they were impressed, for afterward they made Martin-Harvey an honorary chief of their tribe—one is reminded of Edmund Kean's similar honour in Quebec in 1826.

It is worth recalling that even though American and English actors had been regular visitors to Canada for over a century before Martin-Harvey set off with his company in December 1913, a Canadian tour was not an easy proposition. There was far from any guarantee of financial success, theatres in smaller centres were sometimes barely adequate, transportation (especially in winter, when most tours took place) was often hazardous, audiences could be sparse, and hotel accommodation frequently left much to be desired. Crossing the Atlantic at the turn of the century was undoubtedly a good deal safer than crossing the Irish Sea had been for many actors in the eighteenth century, but it was still a long and uncomfortable trip, and disasters did occur. Laurence Irving was one of more than a thousand people who drowned when the *Empress of Ireland* sank in the St. Lawrence in the spring of 1914, the voyage on which Martin-Harvey himself had originally planned to return to England.[10] So far as I know, no English actor visiting Canada ever had to endure the vicious riots encountered by Kean in Boston and Baltimore in 1825, or by Macready in New York in 1849. Long before Martin-Harvey got to Canada there had been incidents in which American actors had suffered or had been threatened with physical violence. A man named Hutchins, a member of John Ricketts's circus company in Montreal in 1797 was once, we are told by John Durang, "obliged to hide himself, else the mob would have kill'd him—though they had some justification, for Hutchins had shot out an eye of a member of the audience.[11] And Solomon Franklin Smith was involved in some fisticuffs at Niagara in the 1880s when a group of Ontario loyalists determined to "drive off the d—d Yankee vagabond actors".[12]

Sarah Bernhardt had to contend with some verbal violence from the Bishop of Montreal in 1880, but in general I think it is fair to say that the major problems faced by a touring actor in Canada in the nineteenth and early twentieth centuries had less to do with opposition and prejudice than with discomfort and inconvenience. Fanny Kemble was once asked by Charles Mathews to describe her impressions of her visit to Canada in 1833. Her reply was unequivocal:

. . . unless Mrs. Mathews's and your own health were tolerably good at the time, the daily and hourly inconveniences which you would have to endure, would, in my opinion, render an expedition to the Canadas anything but desirable. The heat, while we were in Montreal, was intolerable—the filth intolerable—the flies intolerable—the bugs intolerable—the people intolerable—the jargon they speak intolerable. I lifted up my hands in thankfulness when I set foot again in "these United States".[13]

Mrs. Kemble's complaints are perhaps too petulant to be taken entirely seriously, and by the time people like Bernhardt and Martin-Harvey visited Canada standards of hygiene had improved. Nonetheless, in his autobiography Martin-Harvey does complain about "playing the 'smalls' " in Canada: "The accommodation for artists in the theatres of these small towns is often a grave reproach to their citizens. . . . To cover the long distances between the larger towns it is necessary to stop at these small places, and it is such discomfort and unhealthy conditions which often deter good companies from visiting the Dominion."[14]

Martin-Harvey was only one of a long line of English actors who visited Canada. By 1914 there was nothing especially bold or unusual about such a visit, although it certainly was not something to be undertaken lightly. But Martin-Harvey's 1914 tour of Canada was something rather out of the ordinary. In a number of respects it broke with tradition. We get some indication of this from the *Autobiography*, but for a fuller realization of his accomplishments we need more detail. This is provided by a valuable collection of newspaper clippings (which covers the 1921 as well as the 1914 tour) held at the Victoria and Albert Museum. I do not know who collected them, but the clippings represent newspapers from virtually every town visited by Martin-Harvey in 1914 and give as detailed an account of the tour as one could reasonably expect to find.[15]

Martin-Harvey's 1914 tour of Canada was the first to be arranged under the auspices of the newly formed British Canadian Theatrical Organization (BCTO). The organization was sponsored by Francis Pryor and Carl Leyel, and according to Canadian press reports Martin-Harvey's friend William Holles was joint managing director with Leyel. The organizing secretary in Canada was, appropriately enough, a Mr. English of Montreal. Basically, the aims of the company were to encourage and facilitate visits of English theatre companies to Canada and, at the same time (to quote Martin-Harvey), to "relieve Canadians of their dependence upon indifferent companies from the United States".[16] There were other ambitions too. An article in the *Halifax Evening Mail* of January 7, 1914 carried the intriguing headline, "Mr. Martin-Harvey Addresses the Canadian Club and in a Brilliant Lecture Outlines an All-Red Campaign for Dramatic Art". This was not, as one might be tempted to suppose, a plan for a left-wing takeover of the theatre, but rather an idea for extending the influence of the BCTO to Australia, New Zealand, India and South Africa so that, as Martin-Harvey explained to the Canadian Club, "a theatrical company will be able to start from London, travelling over what may be called the 'all red route' thruout the British empire . . .".

A more immediate objective was the establishment of a theatre in Montreal or Toronto where Canadian plays with Canadian casts could be produced (*Fort William Daily Times Journal* , March 2, 1914). This was an objective supported by Martin-Harvey in some of the lectures he gave while on tour. He spoke of it, for example, to the Toronto Empire Club on February 26, 1914, when he actually argued that a Canadian national theatre should be established (*Toronto Globe* ,February 27, 1914). He was thus twenty years ahead of Granville Barker's better-known appeal for a national theatre in 1936.[17]

The idea for a national theatre—for Britain, as well as for Canada—was important to Martin-Harvey. In addition to lecturing on the subject, he put his views in a more permanent form by writing an article while in Canada for the *University Magazine* .[18] Noticing that a "feeling of dissatisfaction with the condition of the theatre in Canada seems to be more and more widely felt", Martin-Harvey claimed that part of the dissatisfaction arose from the fact that drama in Canada lacked the "virile, national expression" emerging in other Canadian art forms, such as architecture and painting. He suggested that Canada needed subsidized national or municipal theatres which, freed from commercial inhibitions, would be able to encourage native drama. "I commend the consideration of this matter to Canadians", he wrote, "with the profound conviction that in their determination to leave nothing undone which shall be to their advantage in the culture or in the education of their people, they will find no force so potent as the maintenance of national theatres throughout their Dominion".

All the aims of the BCTO were well received by the Canadian press. Theatre critics looked forward to more frequent visits of English companies, but they seemed to be even more enthusiastic about the prospect of ridding Canadian theatres of American influence. The kind of influence everyone had in mind was that exercised, for example, by American organizations like the Theatrical Syndicate and the Shubert Theatre Corporation, which controlled the major theatres of eastern Canada and imported into Canada American shows and companies.[19] Margaret Bell, in an article in the *Canadian Courier* on March 21, 1914, expressed a resentment shared by many other critics: "Canadian entertainment," she wrote, "has been so long in the clutches of the big New York syndicates and trusts, that Canada's tastes have had to be governed by the tastes of the syndicates. The discrimination of the Broadway offices begins and ends with the shows which make the greatest appeal to the unthinking public. In short, the artistic perception is influenced solely by financial profits." Miss Bell exempted from her criticism American producers such as Winthrop Ames, George Tyler and David Belasco, but other papers were less discriminating. The *Guelph Herald*, for example, issued a blanket condemnation of American influence. In its issue of February 7, 1914, it wished the BCTO every success, for it promised to "supply Canada with something that will be worth while going to see, and taking the women folks to see without fear of bringing blushes of shame to their cheeks, besides freeing this country of the Americanizing influences with which the stage has been so predominating [*sic*] for years past".

Wherever he went in Canada in 1914, Martin-Harvey never tired of spreading the gospel of the BCTO. He lectured about it and supported its aims at dozens of meetings across the country. He was also practising what he preached, for his own tour was organised very much in accordance with BCTO policy. Most important was Martin-Harvey's determination to make his tour an exclusively Canadian event. Traditionally, English performers had included Canada in their itinerary only to the extent to which it was convenient to fit it in with their American commitments. In practice, this meant that people like Kean, Macready and Irving—and Sarah Bernhardt—limited themselves to brief visits to the few major centres of Ontario and Quebec. Contrary to this custom, it was Martin-Harvey's intention to spend the entire duration of his tour—from the opening night in Halifax on January 8, 1914, to the final performance in Quebec City on May 20, 1914—on Canadian soil. In the event he didn't quite make it, slipping over the border just once for a performance of *The Only Way* in Detroit on April 27. There had, apparently, been an administrative error which caused the loss of a Canadian booking, so Detroit was reluctantly used as a fill-in (*Montreal Daily Star*, May 13, 1914). This was the only blot on the record. In his four-and-a-half months in Canada, Martin-Harvey acted in forty-one towns, gave 140 performances, and travelled 15,000 miles.[20] Nothing of this magnitude had ever been achieved before by an English company in Canada. And what's more, he made it pay. On April 4, 1914, Martin-Harvey told the *Vancouver Daily News* that he was "immensely proud that we have demonstrated to the world that an exclusively Canadian tour can pay".

Another feature of the BCTO's influence was its emphasis on sponsoring companies rather than individual actors. Irving, of course, had brought a full Lyceum company to North America, but he was an exception. Other English actors had merely accommodated themselves with whatever company could be provided by local managements. Martin-Harvey, no doubt partly influenced, as he was in so many things, by his former chief's decisions, but also complying with BCTO guidelines, adopted the more troublesome and more risky plan of taking his own company. The logistical problems of moving performers, scenery, costumes and properties across Canadian distances were enormous. The *Moncton Times* reported on January 9, 1914, that it took five train cars to move everything, and the time taken to dismantle sets and pack costumes meant that more often than not the company could not move on from one booking to another until the early hours of the morning. The acting company itself was not unduly large, consisting of about a dozen performers. Supers were taken on as necessary; many were needed, for example, for the trial scene in *The Only Way* . A group of hopefuls gathered round the Regina theatre at five o'clock on April 16, 1914. A reporter from the *Regina Leader* (April 17, 1914) described them as "a motley crowd": "Young men with lavender gloves and clean collars, out for a lark, rubbed shoulders with out-of-works seeking the price of a meal. Others, rarely seen so far from the bars, were typical of the crowds that may be seen hanging round the theatres in the larger cities, who toil not, neither do they spin; some with the hope that they may be given a minor part in the play and [be] taken on with the company; others caring for nothing else beside the paltry sum they might get for their evening's services." Critics marvelled at Martin-Harvey's success in drilling groups like this into the disciplined crowds which appeared on stage. What Martin-Harvey did, to an extent that was entirely new for an English actor in Canada, was to take full artistic and financial responsibility for his productions. He was rewarded for his efforts with full houses and complimentary reviews. There were, as I shall show, some dissenting voices, but the general tone of hundreds of reviews during the 1914 tour was set by the *Halifax Evening Mail*'s summary of the opening production of *The Only Way* on January 8: "Nothing to equal the performance at the Academy of Music last night has been seen in the theatrical history of Halifax, and Halifax has reason for the keenest satisfaction that it has had the privilege of seeing drama by an English star with an English company and staged with English scenery."

Partly because of the interruption caused by the 1914-1918 war, and partly because of financial recklessness, the BCTO collapsed before it achieved very much of what it had promised.[21] But, as well as Martin-Harvey's 1914 tour, it organized Canadian trips for Laurence Irving, H. V. Esmond and Eva Moore. These were, it seems, successful, and a new group called the Trans-Canada Theatre Society emerged out of the BCTO in 1915 to purchase a chain of theatres across Canada, primarily for the use of English companies. Backed by a capitalization fund of four million dollars and the power of the Canadian Pacific Railway, the Trans-Canada Theatre Society was an honourable but madcap enterprise. Martin-Harvey says it failed because "there were not enough British companies to keep these theatres open for a profitable period of the year",[22] though it is hard to believe that anyone seriously thought that this was indeed possible. One imagines a kind of thespian shuttle service operating across the Atlantic between Liverpool and Halifax.[23]

In supporting the objectives of the BCTO, Martin-Harvey displayed an interest in the development of theatre in Canada which marked him out from most of his predecessors. He was committed to the Canadian theatre to an extent unmatched by any foreign actors of the nineteenth century, and perhaps only by Tyrone Guthrie in this century. Martin-Harvey was to spend a significant proportion of his professional life in Canada, and the state of Canadian theatre was never merely of temporary concern to him. Rather, he consistently tried to do what he could to influence its development. For this reason, criticism of his Canadian productions was especially important, for it helped him to assess Canadian standards and tastes and to plan accordingly for future tours.

In 1914 Martin-Harvey brought three plays to Canada. Predictably enough, *The Only Way* was one of them.[24] The play had received its first production on February 16, 1899, at the Lyceum, and thereafter soon became the mainstay of Martin-Harvey's career. Of course, *The Only Way* brought him wealth and fame, but at the same time it seriously impeded his artistic development. Like an actor who finds himself in a long-running television series, Martin-Harvey was typecast by his rôle as Sydney Carton; Martin-Harvey as Sydney Carton was what the public wanted and expected, and to the end of his career Martin-Harvey too willingly obliged them. *The Only Way* is a short sentimental and melodramatic play based on a long sentimental and melodramatic novel. It reads badly, but there are hundreds of contemporary accounts which attest to its powerful impact on the stage, and even in reading one can recognise the potential of the trial scene in which Charles Darnay is sentenced to death.[25] The two other plays chosen by Martin-Harvey for Canada were *The Breed of the Treshams* which, as I mentioned earlier, was disliked by London critics but was popular with the public and *A Cigarette Maker's Romance*, by Charles Hannan.[26] *A Cigarette Maker's Romance* is not a promising title, and one's doubts are justified by the play itself. It is set in a Munich cigarette factory in 1850 and concerns the life of a Russian count who has lost his memory. For eight years he has been working as a cigarette maker, but during the course of the play his true identity is discovered, his memory returns, and he is able to return to his estates, having meanwhile married the girl who has stood by his side throughout his exile. The plot is predictable, the dialogue is stilted, and the characterization is minimal; but Martin-Harvey, as the count, evidently made something of it.

The weakness of such a repertoire is obvious. It lacked any kind of real variety. What Martin-Harvey gave Canadian audiences in 1914 was a straight diet of romantic costume drama. Probably his estimation of Canadian tastes was based on what went down well in the English provinces, and it was a fairly accurate estimation. A review of *The Breed of the Treshams* in the *Port Arthur Daily News* on March 4, 1914, is typical of the way all three plays were received by the majority of Canadian audiences:

Never was the Orpheum theatre the scene of such enthusiasm as obtained last evening when Mr. Martin Harvey presented The Breed of the Treshams. . . . Spontaneous applause here and there throughout the play testified to the enjoyment of the audience, but for the most part a hushed silence, eloquent of appreciation, greeted the players. As the curtain fell on the last act the wildest pandemonium broke loose. Standing on their feet, the hundreds of auditors gave vent to the emotion evoked by the tense situations, the matchless moments achieved in the play's action and applauded without restraint. Curtain call succeeded curtain call. Then, as the curtain rose for the sixth time Mr. Harvey essayed to thank the audience for their grateful hearing.

Since he had carefully selected three plays which would give him every opportunity to display his talents, it is not surprising that Martin-Harvey's acting received loads of praise. The *Halifax Evening Mail* (January 9, 1914) admired him in *The Only Way*: "There was no ranting. Restraint, but not too great restraint, was always manifest. It was art, and when the play was at its height and magnificent scene piled on yet more striking situation, the reason became evident for the popularity and fame of Mr. Martin Harvey. There was a delicacy and finesse in everything he did . . . ". And in *The Breed of the Treshams* the *Montreal Daily Star* (January 20, 1914) praised Martin-Harvey's "polished elocution, his absolute mastery of gait and gesture, his exquisite sense of humour, his fine poise, and his subtle appreciation of the finesse of character-portraiture". (The point about "polished elocution" can be appreciated by listening to some BBC recordings of Martin-Harvey reading extracts from *The Bells, The Only Way* and *The Burgomaster of Stilemonde;* the recordings are held by the British Institute of Recorded Sound in London.)

So, despite his unadventurous choice of plays—or perhaps because of it—there was praise aplenty for Martin-Harvey himself and his productions. But there were also enough rumblings of discontent to make Martin-Harvey think seriously about raising the level of his offerings next time he came to Canada. It may be that he was surprised by the level of sophistication he discovered in some critics, but what they said persuaded him to start making promises about bringing Shakespeare and Sophocles next time.

On March 28, 1914, the *Calgary Albertan* observed that "There is a possibility that public taste, reacting from problem and sex plays, is beating back to the picturesque absurdities of romantic melodrama" and the *Victoria Daily Times* (March 25, 1914) developed the argument that Martin-Harvey's repertoire did not "impose any great tax on an actor's ability". But the most sustained criticism came from the *Montreal Gazette*. In the issue of January 20, 1914, its reviewer was not over-impressed by *The Breed of the Treshams*. Although he found the play "at all times of absorbing interest, brisk in action, and fertile in incident", he also recognized the "numberless artificialities and inconsistencies which recurred constantly. Frequently the logical and obvious act or word dictated by circumstances is arbitrarily discarded in favour of less natural deeds and speeches, for no apparent reason [other] than that the dramatist looks upon his characters only as a set of puppets to be jigged and shifted at will." What sounds like the same reviewer (*Montreal Gazette*, January 22, 1914) found *A Cigarette Maker's Romance* equally flawed:

. . . there is no reason why some of the outworn tricks which it employs should not be discarded. The long soliloquies, the audible asides, the unconvincing eavesdropping, the clumsy speeches in which the villain conveys information to the spectator, by telling his accomplice at length what the latter already knows and the audience suspects—all these and other antiquated devices could be either eliminated altogether or replaced with more natural and plausible incidents.

Other newspapers, while not being so directly critical of the plays Martin-Harvey had brought with him, did point out that he had gained a reputation in England for his productions of *Hamlet* and *Oedipus Rex*, and wondered if Canadian audiences would ever get the opportunity of seeing them. To his credit, Martin-Harvey reacted positively to criticisms and suggestions. He told the *Toronto World* (February 9, 1914) that next time he would bring *Hamlet* and *The Taming of the Shrew*, and to the *St. Catharine's Herald* (February 11, 1914) he promised *Oedipus Rex* as well, although he did point out that his Shakespeare and *Oedipus* productions were technically very complex, and the Canadian labour laws prevented him from bringing his own technicians and stagehands. He also took to lecturing on his ideas for producing Shakespeare. The *Toronto Sunday World* (March 1, 1914) gave an account of one such lecture in which he described the work of Max Reinhardt and showed photographs of Shakespearean productions without footlights, with few drop curtains, practically no scenery, and scene shifting as part of the action. By the end of the 1914 tour Martin-Harvey still had not made up his mind about which plays to bring next time, but he had certainly raised his estimation of what Canadian audiences would accept. In an interview with the *Montreal Daily Star* on May 13, 1914, he spoke of giving productions "which shall reach, in an ascending scale, from, say, melodrama to the highest tragedy—through romantic drama, mystical drama . . . to the tragedies of Sophocles".

Largely because of the war, it was seven years before Martin-Harvey returned to Canada, and instead of Shakespeare and Sophocles he brought Tom Robertson (*David Garrick*) and Maeterlinck (*The Burgomaster of Stilemonde*), with, of course, *The Only Way*. But again on this 1921 tour he was soon assuring critics and interviewers that more demanding plays were on their way, and indeed Canadian audiences did eventually see—and support—Martin-Harvey's *Hamlet, Richard III, The Taming of the Shrew* and *Oedipus Rex*.[27]

I think it is true to say that Martin-Harvey underestimated the standards of Canadian critics and audiences in 1914. It appears that he also quite seriously misunderstood the *nature* of Canadian theatre audiences. This misunderstanding stirred the beginnings of a controversy which threatened to disrupt the harmonious relationship Martin-Harvey had achieved with Canadians. He was always willing to give lectures while in Canada in 1914, and he received many invitations to do so. He once told a reporter from the *Peterborough Evening Examiner* (February 4, 1914) that "You Canadians seem to like talks and addresses. I think more so than we do in England". His subjects were usually the BCTO, Shakespearean production methods, or the value of drama. But in a lecture to the Ottawa Drama League on January 9, 1914, he got on to the subject of Canadian theatre audiences. "We find," he said, "an absence of laughter. There is a lack of responsiveness. Coming from the rollicking Anglo-Saxon audiences on the other side of the water, these characteristics of Canadian audiences have astonished us. . . . The emotion of the theatre cannot be given from one side of the curtain alone. The audience must come to the theatre as willing to give as to receive, and it is when the audience give, in response, what we have given, that the finest moments of a performance can be given" (*Ottawa Free Press*, January 30, 1914). Not very elegantly expressed, but Martin-Harvey's comments hit a raw nerve. The *Peterborough Daily Evening Review* (February 4, 1914) wanted to blame it all on the Americans: "The reason for this apparent dullness is the adoption of American standards by Canadians as to what constitutes a joke. Anything subtle, obscurely ironical or sarcastic is lost upon the average American. A joke must hit him full in the face or he does not see it. . . . The only thing that can be said about this kind of humor is it is very primitive." Urgent remedial action was required: "our educationalists might well enter into the consideration of the question of humor in regard to the training of our boys. A special lesson upon clean wit and humor would do as much good as one on hygiene, it would give our youth a taste of something better than the stuff that comes over the line and [is] passed off as humor."

Martin-Harvey quickly realized that he had put his foot in it. In Peterborough he hastened to explain that he "was not speaking dogmatically, and that what he [had] said only applied to Ottawa" (*Peterborough Evening News*, February 4, 1914). In Guelph he insisted that "I have never played before more enthusiastic audiences than those before whom I appeared in Canada. There is something very stirring in the way they appreciate British actors . . . " (*Guelph Daily Herald*, February 6, 1914). As he headed west he began to think that Canadian audiences, contrary to what he had believed in Ottawa, might be rather better than English audiences. The *Lethbridge Daily Herald* reported on March 18, 1914, that "The silent manner, reserving itself for an outburst of applause at the end instead of during the performance, was in contrast to that of audiences in some of the provincial towns in the Old Country. This [Martin-Harvey] considered a great help to the players, as it did not tend to embarrass them temporarily while their parts were being played". And finally, by Victoria, he was fully converted: "No man could wish to play to finer and more responsive audiences than we have met with in Canada. Personally I found them better than English audiences in that they are quiet and understanding while the acting is in progress, only letting themselves go at the end of the act, while an English audience sometimes laughs in the wrong place. Canadian audiences are in many ways more reliable, and though just as alive to anything missing in the acting, have more consideration for the feelings of the artists themselves" (*Victoria Daily Times*, March 23, 1914).

One could interpret this remarkable *volte-face* as a diplomatic avoidance of controversy. Perhaps it was. But the whole episode also represents, I think, another phase of Martin-Harvey's developing interest in and understanding of the nature of Canadian theatre. There does seem to have been a marked difference between the behaviour of Canadian and English audiences at the beginning of the century, and it took some getting used to. Martin-Harvey initially mistook quiet attentiveness for bored indifference, and it was some little time before he came to realize that frequent and noisy interruption of a play is not the only mark of an appreciative audience.

I have suggested that an examination of his Canadian tours helps us to recognize a more innovative Martin-Harvey than we are accustomed to think of. If this is true, the innovation is more one of attitude than artistic technique or achievement. Martin-Harvey's attitude as a touring actor in Canada was one of commitment to, of involvement in, Canadian theatre life. For reasons which went far beyond commercial considerations, Martin-Harvey interested himself in such matters as the BCTO, the idea of a Canadian national theatre, the effect of American influences, the place of drama in Canadian society, and so on. Unlike most visiting actors, Martin-Harvey came to Canada not merely to make a few guest appearances in Toronto, Quebec or Montreal; to be sure, he was here primarily to make a living, but his presence was one which stimulated talk and ideas about theatre in Canada. Some of the talk was of relatively small importance— should an audience applaud during or at the end of an act? Some, such as New York's dominance of the Canadian theatre, was of major importance. Canadian theatre benefited significantly from Martin-Harvey, and I think Martin-Harvey benefited from Canada. In England he seemed to be an onlooker on change and development; in Canada he often seemed to be at the centre of affairs. In England he was popular, but never important; in Canada he sensed he was both.

NOTES

1. Maurice Willson Disher: *The Last Romantic: The Authorised Biography of Sir John Martin-Harvey* (London, 1948). George Edgar's *Martin Harvey: Some Pages of His Life* (London, 1912) is a chatty memoir of Martin-Harvey's early life. There is a sympathetic portrayal of Martin-Harvey in Robertson Davies's novel, *World of Wonder* (Toronto, 1975). See also Davies's comments in *Theatrical Touring and Founding in North America*, ed. L. W. Conolly (Westport, Conn., 1982), pp. 48-53.

2. Hesketh Pearson: *The Last Actor-Managers* (London, 1950), p. 47.

3. *The Breed of the Treshams* is unpublished. I base my brief account of the play on newspaper reviews.

4. See Willson Disher, p. 168.

5. Ibid., p. 217.

6. Ibid., p. 265.

7. *The Autobiography of Sir John Martin-Harvey* (London, 1933), pp. 32-33.

8. Laurence Irving, *Henry Irving, the Actor and His World* (London, 1951), p. 444.

9. *Autobiography*, p. 509.

10. Willson Disher, p. 216.

11. *The Memoir of John Durang*, ed. Alan Downer (Pittsburgh, 1966), p. 88.

12. Solomon Franklin Smith, *Theatrical Management in the West and South for Thirty Years* (New York, 1868), p. 41.

13. *The Life and Correspondence of Charles Mathews the Elder*, ed. Edmund Yates (London, 1860), p. 441.

14. *Autobiography*, p. 427.

15. I am most grateful to Heather McCallum of the Metropolitan Toronto Central Library and George Nash, late of the Enthoven Collection, Victoria and Albert Museum, for assistance in providing a microfilm copy of the newspaper clippings.

16. *Autobiography*, p. 419.

17. See his essay in *Queen's Quarterly*, vol. 43 (1936-1937), pp. 256-67.

18. "Canadian Theatres", *University Magazine*, vol. 13 (1914), pp. 212-19.

19. See Murray Edwards, *A Stage in Our Past* (Toronto, 1968), p. 37.

20. *Autobiography*, p. 428.

21. For an extensive account of the BCTO, see Patrick B. O'Neill: "The British Canadian Theatrical Organization Society and the Trans-Canada Theatre Society" in *Journal of Canadian Studies*, vol. 15 (Spring, 1980), pp. 56-67.

22. *Autobiography*, p. 420.

23. Reasons for the failure of the Trans-Canada Theatre Society are discussed by O'Neill, pp. 63-64.

24. *The Only Way* was written by two clergymen, the Reverend Freeman Wills and the Reverend Canon Langbridge. It was published in 1942 with a foreword by Rafael Sabatini and an "Apology" by Martin-Harvey.

25. Robertson Davies saw *The Only Way* in Canada when a young man. He gives an account of the experience in Conolly: *Theatrical Touring and Founding*, pp. 51-53.

26. Published in French's Acting Edition, vol. 160, no. 2389, n.d.

27. A full list of Martin-Harvey's Canadian plays is given in the *Autobiography*, pp. 438-39.

11

Actor as Puppet: Variations on a Nineteenth-Century Theatrical Idea

S. Beynon John

There is a brilliant snapshot of Irving, on his way to be knighted at Windsor Castle, contained in Max Beerbohm's obituary notice which originally appeared in *The Saturday Review* for 21 October 1905:

But as I caught sight of him on this occasion—a great occasion, naturally, in his career; though to me it had seemed rather a bathos, this super-imposition of a smug Hanoverian Knighthood on the Knight from No-where—he was the old Bohemian, and nothing else. His hat was tilted at more than its usual angle, and his long cigar seemed longer than ever; and on his face was a look of such ruminant, sly fun as I had never seen equalled.[1]

This image of contained triumph will conveniently serve to epit-omize the social apotheosis of the actor in late nineteenth century England. The presence of Sarah Bernhardt among the more glamorous lady guests at the coronation of Edward VII provides equally colourful confirmation of the changed status of the ac-tress, even if some irreverent wits of the day, borrowing the language of the turf, were moved to picture these ladies simply as occupants of the "King's Loose Box".[2]

In retrospect, it may not be too fanciful to think of the com-mercial stages of London and Paris in the last decades of the nineteenth century as representing a kind of secular cathedral in which the prosperous middle classes performed one of their favourite social rituals. The gilt and plush of the auditoriums, like the lavish sets, sumptuous costumes and elaborate stage machinery, seem to offer the very image of a materialistic and technical society. And these stages, with their diet of magniloquent and moralizing social dramas (see Plates 14 and 15), "well-made" comedies of high society, farces, historical pageants and pantomimes, foster the cult of star performers. Many of these stars use plays as vehicles for displaying their own personal magnetism, run their own theatres, embark on triumphal and money-spinning tours which resemble royal progresses and, notably in the 'eighties, are lionized in the fashionable drawing-rooms of London and Paris. Their personalities and activities, on and off the stage, are the subject of avid curiosity on the part of the public, and the playgoer is catered for in a great variety of publications, many of them new and devoted exclusively to the stage, some elaborately illustrated. The notices of drama critics are generous in length; theatre programmes are packed with information; and there is a vogue for actors' memoirs and playgoers' reminiscences. There is even a fashion for novels that deal with theatrical life, from Edmond de Goncourt's *La Faustin* (1882) or Mrs. Humphrey Ward's edifying *Miss Bretherton* (1884) to Henry James's *The Tragic Muse* (1890), which bears the imprint of the excitements he had known at the Comédie-Française.

Of course, all this does not imply that actors were the subject of universal adulation and, to confirm it, we do not have to rely on what Arthur Symons recalls Duse saying in an unguarded moment: "To save the theatre, the theatre must be destroyed, the actors and actresses must all die of the plague. They poison the air, they make art impossible."[3] No doubt, the great Italian tragedienne was thinking of the death of others, and, in any event, she was making a statement about art (which Gordon Craig was later to take up and flourish) and not about the social position of actresses. But other injured voices are raised, some obscure, some celebrated. George Moore in his essay "Mummer Worship", which originally appeared in *The Universal Review* for September 1888, launched a sharp attack on the regrettable new fashion for idolizing actors, arguing that it was symptomatic of an age of "facile amusement and parade", and testily concluding:

Our contention is a threefold one; first, that acting is the lowest of the arts, if it be an art at all; secondly, that the public has almost ceased to discriminate between bad and good acting, and will readily grant its suffrage and applause to anyone who has been abundantly advertised, and can enforce his or her claim either by beauty or rank; thirdly, that the actor is applauded not for what he does, but for what he is—that of late years the actor has been lifted out of his place, and that, in common with all things when out of their places, he is ridiculous and blocks the way.[4]

This kind of criticism, which Max Beerbohm objected to, has its vitriolic counterpart in the polemics of the French novelist, dramatist and critic, Octave Mirbeau, notably in two resounding articles: "Le Comédien", which first appeared in *Le Figaro* (26 October 1882), and "Cabotinisme", originally published in *La France* (25 March 1885). The first not only complains of the social prestige accorded to leading actors by an infatuated public, but summarily dismisses the artistic pretensions of the actor, an "inferior being" who simply mimics the actions, gestures and words of invented characters and who has "the face of a vicious eunuch crowned with a silly crown of painted cardboard".[5] The second directs its fire chiefly against actors of the Comédie Fran-çaise, a privileged "band of ignoramuses" who set themselves up as judges of literature, are granted a kind of "official inves-titure" to "trample on our glorious heritage", and who deserve to be treated as hired entertainers, a species of prostitute.[6]

But the voices of dissent tend to be drowned in the chorus of star worshippers and the contemporary admiration for an actor-dominated stage. In the light of this cult it may, at first, seem perverse to speak of the idea of the actor as puppet. However, it is an idea which recurs frequently in the 'nineties, at a time which witnesses the consecration of the actor as "sacred mon-ster", to borrow Cocteau's phrase. Not surprisingly, it forms part of the counter-attack mounted against the prevailing gross conventions of the late-nineteenth-century stage in France and England by a brilliant minority of theorists and reformers for whom the creation of a new aesthetic of the theatre becomes an urgent necessity. Obviously, this notion of the actor as puppet is totally at variance with the practice of the dominant actors of the day and, more specifically, with Bernhardt's own style. Indeed, Sarah's preference for romantic melodramas, like *Fédora* and *Théodora*, is instructive (see Plate 5). The spectacular settings of costume drama constantly threaten to crush the run-of-the-mill player under a mountain of bric-à-brac, but they can be made to seem an acceptable framework for an actress capable of stunning displays of personal magnetism and technical virtuosity (see Plate 13). On such occasions, it is not by losing herself in the part that the actress triumphs, but by asserting her incandescent personality over and above the part. The "incomparable Max" put it memorably: "I said just now that no actress ever tried to disguise herself. I was forgetting Sarah. She does try, and the result is (as I said it must inevitably be) ludicrous. As L'Aiglon and other young men, she loses herself, but becomes no one else: she becomes merely a coruscating thing. The feat is amazing, but it is not serious art: it is showmanship . . ."[7] Shaw wrote something remarkably like, in 1895, in his famous comparison of the styles of Duse and Bernhardt: "She is beautiful with the beauty of her school, and entirely incredible. . . . She does not enter into the leading character: she substitutes herself for it."[8] Duse emerges from this comparison as the essence of naturalness and the opposite of the rhetorical actress like Bernhardt.

All the figures I intend to deal with (Maeterlinck, Jarry, Edward Gordon Craig and Yeats) seem to me drawn to the notion of the actor as puppet not only because it is congruent with the imaginary worlds they create, but also because, in varying degrees, they exhibit distaste for, or disenchantment with, the styles of acting current in their day and the implications which those styles have for the art of the theatre. Here it is necessary to make a distinction between the idea of the actor as puppet and that of *character* as puppet. One has only to recall the practice of nineteenth-century French farce. The spirit of misrule or carnival that presides over the farces of Labiche and Feydeau operates within a closed world in which the characters, caught up in a rigorously complicated plot, are propelled forward at an accelerating tempo so that their actions appear increasingly mechanical and subject to the whims of the playwright. This may well require of the actors heavily stylised modes of playing but, I would argue, this is not the same thing as demanding the surrender of important aspects of the actor's personality and technique—which is what seems to me to be implied in the rôle assigned to actors by Maeterlinck, Jarry, Craig and Yeats.

Maeterlinck peoples his drama with puppets, if one means by that characters who are the playthings of a mysterious fate, and these characters necessarily impose on the actors who play them a stiffly mannered style of performance. When Maeterlinck published his "three plays for puppets" (*Alladine et Palomides, Intérieur* and *La Mort de Tintagiles*) in 1894, he was responding both to personal inspiration and to that cult of the transcendental in the arts which we associate with Symbolist poetry and painting in France in the 1800s and 1890s. It is a cult shaped by the confluence of different forces: Wagnerian aesthetics, the Catholic revival, the penetration of the French educated public by the great spiritual traditions of the Russian novel, the impact of the Scandinavian theatre in its more symbolic forms. Maeterlinck was responsive to these artistic tendencies which go beyond the prevailing conventions of realism and naturalism, and he looked to the theatre to provide a medium of suggestive power that would translate, in words and silence, man's most profound and universal anxieties and aspirations. In this way, he hoped to create a work of art that would bind human beings together in an awareness of their common plight.

At this stage of his development, a kind of spiritual delicacy seems to have prompted Maeterlinck to feel that actors, with their human density and idiosyncrasy, were too obtrusive an instrument for embodying the metaphysical concerns which preoccupied him and which required to be expressed in archetypal figures. By using the deliberate and stylised movements of puppets, he seems to have thought that he might create between play and audience the aesthetic distance necessary to produce an atmosphere of tranquil meditation.[9] His approach has to be seen in the context of the contemporary craze for pantomime, puppets and shadow plays. The figures of Pierrot, Harlequin and Columbine, familiar from the tradition established in the 1830s by the Théâtre des Funambules, find a new lease on life at the Cercle Funambulesque (founded in Paris in 1888). These slight and charming entertainments might already be said to offer the model of a stylised theatre greatly at variance with the dominant forms of the period. Their concentration on action and gesture, their spare lines and economy of effect point to Maeterlinck's own "theatre of silence".[10] But even more significant for Maeterlinck's "plays for puppets" was the success of the Petit Théâtre des Marionnettes established by Henri Signoret in May 1888 at the Galerie Vivienne in Paris. From the outset, the programme of this theatre was extraordinarily ambitious and continued to be so under its subsequent director, Maurice Bouchor. The first plays presented for performance by puppets were nothing less than adaptations of Cervantes, Aristophanes and Shakespeare's *The Tempest*. There were also (1889-1894) performances of works by Marlowe and Ford and of a whole range of plays of a biblical or mystical character. One could already see in these performances an aesthetic of extreme simplicity and high stylisation applied to mythical subjects. In the use of puppets, the principle of the stage mask had been pushed to its limit in order to serve the most primary kinds of human experience: awe, wonder, worship. Here, as a recent critic has perceptively noted, we see a kind of paradox at work. The fashion for masks and marionettes in the 'nineties is both an attempt to "retheatricalize the theatre, to rescue it from a paralysing realism" and to "detheatricalize it, to divest it of the kind of theatricality. implied in the eternal posturing and grimacing of the actors".[11]

Marionettes were never, I believe, used in actual public performances of Maeterlinck's "puppet plays",[12] but they share with Maeterlinck's other early plays a common imaginary universe, characterized by the dream-like quality of its undefined settings and by a brooding sense of disquiet, mystery and fatality that comes from depicting characters as largely passive victims—in spite of moments of struggle—of nameless surrounding forces. As Maeterlinck himself put it in the preface to his collected plays: ". . . vast, invisible and fateful powers, the intentions of which no man can decipher, but which the spirit of the play assumes to be malevolent, heedful of all our acts, and hostile to gaiety, life, tranquillity and happiness . . . ".[13] It is true that the tone is sometimes portentous and that the reliance on silence and enigma, though it often creates the oppressive atmosphere which Maeterlinck intends, can baffle the spectator. The point I wish to make is that these characters, who move like sleepwalkers across a stage frequently in shadow, sometimes in darkness relieved by a shaft of light, are largely symbolic figments whose motions constitute a kind of mystical choreography in which death is a constant, if implied, presence. Arthur Symons, always a sympathetic guide to French Symbolist experiments, expressed it vividly: "Death was always the scene-shifter of the play, and destiny the stage-manager. The people who came and went had the blind gestures of marionettes, and one pitied their helpless-ness."[14] In this sense, the performance of the actors becomes reduced to a very restricted grammar of movements, gestures and tones of voice. They move closer to the style of puppets because only in this way can they be obedient to the atmosphere and vision created by the playwright.

Indeed, specific features of all three "plays for puppets" emphasise graphically that a deliberate display of the actor's personality can hardly be accommodated within the ritualism of Maeterlinck's legendary action or matched with his archetypal figures. For example, *Intérieur*, that remarkable exercise in "static theatre", responds fully to the notion, expressed by Maeterlinck in an essay of the same period, that tragedy may be located in "immobility", and in the "slow, discreet and silent laws" of life.[15] The figures of the afflicted family play throughout in dumbshow, their gestures related, in studied counterpoint, to the spare dialogue of the Old Man and the Stranger in the garden. This device, by dissociating speech and action, tends not only to break the conventional bond between actor and audience,[16] but also, as it seems to me, to intensify the audience's sense of the actor as mechanism or puppet. In *Alladine et Palomides* the maze of Ablamore's palace, the association of Alladine with a lamb and Palomides with a horse, Palomides's worship of Astolaine as the embodiment of spiritual perfection, the sudden radiance bathing the grotto in which Alladine and Palomides are immured, all point to an allegory of the conflict between spirit and animal instinct and transform the protagonists into archetypes moving trance-like in response to promptings they are powerless to resist. Here, too, the exigencies of the allegorical convention impose a hieratic style upon the actors which brings them nearer to the art of puppets. More legendary effects are conjured up in the great struggle between love and death symbolised by *La Mort de Tintagiles*, in which the Destroyer-Queen, from her remote high tower, relentlessly exacts the death of the frail boy, Tintagiles, who lies imprisoned behind a massive iron door in a gloomy vault beneath the castle. The baleful power of the setting and the omnipotence of the queen dwarf the servants and even the sisters who try to save the boy. This kind of dramatic scheme seems positively to invite a more impersonal mode of acting, analogous to that of puppets, if only to emphasise that these characters move to the bidding of the Queen as wooden dolls dance to the strings of their puppeteer. In fact, Maeterlinck's preference for puppets as the medium for rendering these early plays springs naturally from his distinctive vision of the world. Preoccupied only with the great simplicities of life and death, flesh and spirit, he looks to an art of acting which will serve these simplicities. In this sense, his "plays for puppets" surely imply an aesthetic of acting that is also a critique of much of the existing practice and conventions of the Paris stage of the 'nineties.

No one could be further in spirit from Maeterlinck than Alfred Jarry, yet he too must be seen as a playwright whose experiments with dramatic form represent the outcome of a deeply idiosyncratic view of the world and whose revolutionary aesthetic of the stage embraces a conception of acting which extinguishes the kind of actor who succeeds, as Bernhardt so frequently did, through sheer bravura. The startling impact made by the first performance of Jarry's *Ubu Roi* on 11 December 1896 has become one of the commonplaces of theatre history. W. B. Yeats was there and recorded the events with a kind of appalled bewilderment: "The players are supposed to be dolls, toys, marionettes, and now they are all hopping like wooden frogs, and I can see for myself that the chief personage, who is some kind of a king, carries for sceptre a brush of the kind that we use to clean a closet . . . ".[17] What Yeats saw was a play about a gross, cowardly and grotesque buffoon, Ubu, who, egged on by his monstrous wife, a kind of comic-strip Lady Macbeth, turns on his king, murders him and most of the royal family, proclaims himself King of Poland and inaugurates a reign of terror with the aid of a "disembraining" machine. Ubu is eventually defeated by the army of the Russian Czar and forced to take refuge in a cave in Lithuania before escaping to France, presumably to resume his activities there.

The elements of gross slapstick and the frenetic tempo of the action are crucial to the distinctive impression produced by *Ubu Roi*. As a play, it radicalizes the medium by inflating the rôle of violence and making it one of the central and unifying metaphors of the theatrical experience. The stage is used as a weapon for unnerving the polite audience and in this respect *Ubu Roi* may be thought to offer a high-spirited and sympathetic image of the anarchist violence of the early 'nineties, and a ferocious challenge to the optimism implied by the rational, scientific and positivistic ideas which constitute the dominant ideology of the early Third Republic. Jarry's combination of nihilism, levity and schoolboy smut understandably shocked his bourgeois public. In the uninhibited way in which it allows the predatory and destructive instincts to run riot, *Ubu Roi* can properly be called subversive and its vein of infantilism must be seen not simply as an effect of Jarry's own temperament but also as a flash of insight into the nature of human aggression and as a satiric device for demolishing the "serious" world of the bourgeoisie. It is this primitivism which so forcibly struck Arthur Symons when he saw the play performed: "These jerking and hopping, these filthy, swearing 'gamins' of wood bring us back . . . to what is primitively animal in humanity."[18]

This description, while it vividly conjures up the spirit of *Ubu Roi*, also points to the novel conventions embodied in the performance of the actors. The actors move stiffly and jerkily, like puppets, and, in a subsequent performance at the Parisian Théâtre des Pantins (January 1898), are actually replaced by puppets belonging to the painter Bonnard. In fact, Jarry must be seen as one of the earliest of modern theorists of the stage to question the autonomy of the actor, and his conception of the actor's function is inseparable from a larger aesthetic theory. One critic has summarized it neatly: "Behind Jarry's theories lie the general anti-historical bias of the symbolists, their preoccupation with myth and legend, and the arguments advanced by some—such as Mallarmé—for a theatre of *myth* and *symbol*."[19] Seen in this context Jarry's characters, from Ubu himself and Mère Ubu to Bordure and Bougrelas, are purely conventional; that is, stylised images of a colourful, imaginary universe. They do not represent figures rooted in a specific history or society but archetypes who embody, in a dramatic way, primary human impulses. They generate an impression of abstraction and universality, and this is enhanced by the costumes which Jarry has envisaged for them, the setting against which they move and the mode of acting which the playwright, in cooperation with the director, Lugné-Poë, and the principal actor, Firmin Gémier, has contrived for the performers. The costumes are highly fantasticated, from Ubu's metal-grey suit, stick and bowler hat to Bordure's Hungarian gypsy outfit and the Czar's black uniform and massive yellow belt. In addition, all actors wear cardboard masks of a fairly crude kind which emphasise their non-human appearance and contribute to the general impression of macabre oddity. The single painted backdrop designed by Sérusier and Bonnard with the help of Vuillard, Toulouse-Lautrec and Ranson, epitomizes Jarry's view that conventional scenery is an encumbrance which prevents the intelligent spectator from using his imagination to conjure up an appropriate setting of his own. This backdrop, executed in bright flat colours and freely distorted in line and perspective, offers a kind of synthesis of the play's different scenes. Again, Arthur Symons noted how closely it approximated to the convention of child art, as he listed its different facets: apple trees in bloom under a blue sky, a painted bed with a bare tree at the foot of it, a palm tree with a boa-constrictor coiled around it.[20] This is not the illustration of a concrete and literal scene as much as a piece of abstract decoration which synthesizes in line, colour and perspective the spirit of Jarry's imaginary world, though I doubt if the provocative novelty of the design qualified it to perform the rather neutral function which Jarry's theory seems to call for. Here a sort of metaphoric suggestiveness expels literal statement from the stage, helps to frame the action within a vague never-never land, and so reinforce the spectator's readiness to view the characters as mere figments of the imagination.

This readiness is supported by a whole range of stylised devices: a noisy musical accompaniment in the manner of a fairground band; the representation of cavalry by a cardboard horse's head suspended from an actor's neck; scene-shifts conveyed by roughly scrawled placards carried on by an old man with a white beard. Above all, it is supported by a novel mode of acting. Jarry's actors echo the anti-realistic style of the rest of the production: they are animated grotesques, closer to the rigid movements and spasmodic life of puppets than to the actors of the conventional stage of the period. And the blithe cruelty, the coarse and inventive verbal play, the broad parody of revered models like *Macbeth*, conspire to maintain characters and actors alike within the limits of strict artificiality. The energy of Ubu himself is not human; it is the energy of a destructive machine, a dreadful puppet, and to capture and project it, the actor performing Ubu has not so much to subdue his personality to the rôle as to be subjugated and reduced to mere mechanism by the conventions imposed on him by the playwright. The actor's normal range of effects (voice, gesture, facial mobility) are lost behind the false voice ("on two notes") insisted upon by Jarry, the deliberate mimicry of puppet motions, and the rigidity of the mask. Nor is there anything accidental about this. Jarry is perfectly aware of what he is doing. He insists that the play of light on the mask, combined with a very restricted range of movements of the head—up, down and sideways—will afford the actor adequate means of expression.[21] In effect, if the aim of the theatre is to concentrate only on what is permanent and universal in human experience, the actor's mask will serve admirably to embody the "effigy" of the character he is playing, that is the character's essential and perennial nature.[22] This comes close to arguing for the suppression of acting considered as a flexible mimetic art, in favour of acting as a system of ritual gestures. Indeed, the argument contained in the lecture which Jarry delivered in Brussels in 1902 confirms his intention to kill off the actor. Jarry insists that if the playwright's vision is not to be distorted, the actor's freedom to interpret the text must be neutralised: " . . . the more gifted or individual the actor, the more he betrays the poet's conceptions".[23] And this fact is contrasted with the way in which puppets are passively obedient to the will of their master and faithfuly reflect his ideas. Jarry's reference to the "poet" is very revealing: it suggests that his hostility to the actor is born of the literary creator's determination to safeguard the primacy of his text. The preference for puppet over actor could not be more plain.

Jarry's notion of the actor is inseparable from a general view of the function of the stage that owes much to the poetic ideals of the French Symbolists. It is this aestheticism which provides a link between Jarry and a seminal figure like Edward Gordon Craig, who differs from him in almost every other respect. As a disciple of Ruskin and Pater, Craig is acutely conscious of the degeneration of the late-nineteenth-century stage into mere spectacle and vulgar display. He sees the theatre as bleeding to death under the combined assault of the overweening author, the egocentric actor and the pretentious scene painter, and he longs to restore the stage to the dignity of an independent scenic art.[24] It is impossible to divide Craig's revolutionary conception of the actor from his view of the play as a grand artistic design which rests on simplicity and proportion, and which integrates scenery, line and colour with lighting and acoustic effects, and with the costumes, speech and movements of the actors. He conceives of an essentially visual art that will also serve to elicit the poetry of sound and motion and so create a supreme scenic harmony that draws its inspiration from music and architecture.

Early in his career, Craig was temporarily seduced by the fashion for the purely pictorial in theatre productions. It was a fashion already available to him in the work of his father, the architect E. W. Godwin, who modified and simplified the tradition of archaeological accuracy in sets, costumes and properties which had been inherited from the innovations of Charles Kean at the Princess's Theatre (1851-1859). Godwin retained the picturesque elements in that tradition but, in his most successful stage productions, subdued them to a large and harmonious artistic design. This is exemplified in the striking and unified visual scheme created by him for the 1886 production of Todhunter's *Helena in Troas*, with its sumptuous and authentic architectural detail and its accurate and delicately coloured costumes. Some of Irving's Shakespearean productions drew on Godwin's ideas and though Irving's artistic tact sometimes faltered in his pursuit of spectacle, it has been suggested that Craig learned from his productions at the Lyceum something of Godwin's aesthetic principles: "the classical ideal of space and clarity of outline, the use of a restricted colour range, and above all the authoritative placing of the performers within a scenic whole . . . ".[25] Admittedly, this is not the same as Craig's own preference for handling volume, line and colour in an impressionistic and suggestive way, but it points in a similar direction.

Craig also encountered the pictorial in the experiments of Sir Hubert von Herkomer, a fashionable portrait painter who established an art school at Bushey in Hertfordshire in 1883. This contained a theatre for which Herkomer wrote plays, composed music, and designed and built machinery with the aid of his pupils. His theatrical productions were something of a social event and attracted the cream of London's artistic society. There, Gordon Craig saw a "Pictorial-Musical" play, *An Idyl*, produced in 1889, and it seems to have greatly impressed him, as did Herkomer's lecture on "Scenic Art" given at the Avenue Theatre, London on January 28, 1892. No doubt Craig responded to *An Idyl* because it was a stage production deliberately contrived so as to fuse the arts of painting and music and to establish the primacy of the visual and pictorial.[26] More specifically, Craig was impressed by Herkomer's "atmospheric backgrounds" and by his use of a backcloth painted in one colour with a grey gauze stretched on a frame and placed at an angle in front of it. If light of another colour was projected onto this gauze, a striking three-dimensional effect was produced.[27] Some of these effects were borrowed by Craig for his production of Purcell's *Dido and Aeneas* at the Hampstead Conservatoire of Music (May 1900). One isolated effect from this production will serve to illustrate how Craig manages, even this early in his career, to transcend the purely pictorial and to create a subtly poetic statement which underpins the dramatic action and enhances the dominant mood of the scene. It is the scene of Dido's death song. Dido, dressed in black, lies back on the black cushions which have replaced the triumphal scarlet of the opening scene. The lights gradually dim from green to ultramarine. Then a rain of rose-petals, caught in a vertical shaft of light, falls on Dido until she is blotted out. Through the deep indigo night the arms of the chorus of sailors are dimly discerned as they wave farewell.[28]

I stress this strong early feeling for the visual and for the total aesthetic effect because it is central to all that Craig subsequently does in the theatre, and because it conditions his approach to acting. The aim of the art of the theatre, as Craig envisages it, is to convey the spirit of the theatrical work in its different aspects. It is pre-eminently an art of suggestion and evocation which avoids mere decoration in order to concentrate on the central, significant action created by the dramatist in his text. It is, therefore, an art of "simplification, selection and synthesis", involving "determined simplification of the scenic picture, a representation of architecture reduced to its elementary geometry".[29] Such an art is at one with the aesthetic principles of what Craig himself describes as "Symbolism" in an article of 1910: "Symbolism is really quite proper; it is sane, orderly, and it is universally employed. It cannot be called theatrical if by theatrical we mean something flashy, yet it is the very essence of the Theatre if we are to include its art among the fine arts."[30] In this sense, everything in the theatre is intended to be symbolic of the play's central meaning, so that the setting is not just a physical framework for the action but a design calculated to express the significance of that action.

These principles are pungently formulated in the essays brought together in Craig's original and provocative book, *On the Art of the Theatre* (1911), and are illustrated in the great range of drawings and scenic designs which he produced from 1900 onward. These prescriptions and designs constitute an argument which moves progressively toward the extinction of the late-nineteenth-century star actor. The actor is effaced behind the mask, then submerged in some form of animated puppet and finally reduced to a shape moving, with stylised gesture and gait, in front of a monumental scene or a set of flexible screens on which changing coloured lights are allowed to play. The argument of the book begins innocuously with a plea for establishing harmony between actors, setting and text in Shakespearean productions, though, contrary to Jarry, Craig expresses doubts as to whether the *written* play is "of any deep and lasting value to the Art of the Theatre".[31] He is at pains to emphasize the importance of "the large and sweeping impressions produced by means of scene and the movement of figures", and the necessity of producing "general and broad effects appealing to the eye" (p. 21). The scene ought to harmonise with the thoughts of the dramatist and suggest the essential spirit of his work. Hence, Craig proposes a setting for Macbeth which will utilise simplified lines and a simplified colour scheme so as to suggest a dramatic dichotomy that contrasts rock and man with mist and spirit and evokes "a place for fierce and warlike men to inhabit, a place for phantoms to nest in" (p. 22). Clearly, this is not mere pictorial embellishment of the kind favored in nineteenth-century productions of Shakespeare, but a functional use of line and colour to enlarge the dramatic action.

This conception is reinforced by Craig's proposals for the proper design of costume. Just as his scenery for *Macbeth* rests on impressionistic use of colour and tone and calls for the movement and disposition of figures to be congruent with, and expressive of, the mood and action of the text, so costume too is to be seen as part of a great design incorporating acting, movement and voice (p. 31). Craig explicitly depreciates slavish reliance on "costume books" and advocates designing costumes that are suggestive of or imaginatively faithful to the spirit of the piece rather than pedantically authentic in an archaeological or historical sense (pp. 32-33). In Craig's new programme, costumes will be freely imagined *inventions* chosen deliberately so as to form a homogenous part of the mass of colour, light and shade available in the stage design (p. 34). He argued that naturalistic movement would mar the general effect of scene and costume and should therefore be replaced by "a noble artificiality" (p. 35). The aim must be to create beauty rather than mere effect. As the purely pictorial is simply part of the armoury of gross theatrical tricks, it must be subordinated to forwarding the dramatic action, just as the action itself must be meaningfully related to the play's overall conception (p. 36). The goal of the art of the theatre is "perfect balance, the result of movement" (p. 46) and to achieve it, the young artist of the theatre must pass through three stages: impersonation, representation, and revelation. In the first two, he will use the human figure, speech, and physical setting; in the last, he will exploit movement to reveal "the invisible things" (p. 46). This new theatrical art is eloquently summed up by Craig: "No; the Art of the Theatre is neither acting nor the play, it is not scene nor dance, but it consists of all the elements of which these things are composed: action, which is the very spirit of acting; words, which are the body of the play; line and colour, which are the very heart of the scene; rhythm, which is the very essence of dance." (p. 138).

So radical a shift of emphasis toward the play considered as a total theatrical design necessarily displaces the actor from his traditional function as the focus of dramatic activity, and implies a disparagement of his mimetic art. Indeed, the control of so ambitious a design calls for what Craig describes as the "ideal stage-manager". He will be "capable of inventing and rehearsing a play: capable of designing and superintending the construction of both scenery and costume: of writing any necessary music: of inventing such machinery as is needed and the lighting that is to be used" (p. 99). Given a dramatist's text, this paragon will interpret it, decide "the entire colour, tone, movement, and rhythm that the work must assume . . . " (p. 149); invent the scenes in which the play is set (p. 155); seize on the play's dominant moods and impressions and illustrate them visually. In effect, no one is "to rule on the stage except the stage-manager . . . " (p. 174), and only through the "Renaissance of the stage-director" can the theatre become "self-reliant" as a creative art, and no longer merely "an interpretative craft" (p. 178). Hence, Craig's bold forecast that the masterpieces of the theatre of the future will be composed of "ACTION, SCENE, and VOICE." (p. 180).

It is something of a paradox that Craig should be the theorist who goes farthest toward diminishing the rôle of the actor. After all, as the son of Ellen Terry, he was born into the theatrical purple; belonged for eight years (1889-1897) to Irving's company at the Lyceum; and played thirty or forty parts in touring companies, including a much praised performance of Hamlet at the Olympic Theatre, Westminster, in 1897. He idolized Irving, defending him against critics who complained of his peculiar pronunciation, his odd way of breaking up the spoken line and his curious loping stride. In his biography of the great actor,[32] Craig writes categorically: " . . . I have never known of, or seen, or heard, a greater actor than was Irving" (p. 1) and goes on to insist that Irving was " . . . a great actor, speaking perfectly, moving faultlessly . . . " (p. 68). Not content with describing Irving's performance in *The Bells* as "the finest point that the craft of acting could reach" (p. 61), Craig feels obliged to defend melodrama as "a pure product of the theatre" (p. 150) and to confess that the practice of using plays as vehicles for an actor's talent is "too old a custom for a playwright to run counter to" (p. 151). This veneration of Irving, which is also reflected in the numerous drawings, woodcuts and lithographs Craig devoted to him, seems oddly at variance with the strictures he expresses elsewhere about star actors. But it is not an isolated case. Craig can write fulsomely of Bernhardt herself as giving "a perfect exhibition of acting", and of being the "only actress who is complete at all points".[33] In *On the Art of the Theatre* he is generous in his praise of the actors at the Moscow Art Theatre, and singles out Stanislavsky: "You are not to imagine that this actor is cold or stilted. A simpler technique, a more human result, would be difficult to find. A master of psychology, his acting is most realistic, yet he avoids nearly all the brutalities; his performances are all remarkable for their grace." (p. 135)

At one level what one can see at work here is the natural sympathy of an ex-actor for the problems of his craft; at another, Craig's belief that technique and self-discipline, raised to a certain pitch in an actor, can sometimes achieve the kind of supreme detachment he requires, which, presumably, is what prompts him to write that Irving was "the nearest thing ever known to what I have called the Übermarionette" (p. 32). In spite of this, it is evident that the theories of the actor contained in *On the Art of the Theatre* do represent a radical break with the styles of acting prevalent in the 'nineties, even if Craig's own experience of the stage makes him at moments more susceptible to the charms of an actor's mastery of technique than is the case with Maeterlinck or Yeats.

Craig's view of the actor is startling enough. The actor's aim, he avers, should be to become "an artist of the Theatre", which implies using calculation as well as spontaneity, and finding symbolic gestures which will convey the essence of the feelings involved, as distinct from reproducing the external signs of feeling through crude mimicry (p. 11). The actor's face should be a highly controlled system of expressions, a "mask" like Irving's, whose face was "the connecting link between that spasmodic and ridiculous expression of the human face as used by the theatres of the last few centuries, and the masks which will be used in place of the human face in the near future" (p. 13). This mask, described here as "the only right medium of portraying the expression of the soul as shown through the expression of the face", is preferred over the human face for reasons which Craig gives elsewhere, in his comment on the Abbey Theatre's production of Yeats's *On Baile's Strand* in 1911: "The advantage of a mask over a face is that it is always repeating unerringly the poetic fancy, repeating on Monday in 1912 exactly what it said on Saturday in 1909 and what it will say on Wednesday in 1999. Durability was the dominant idea in Egyptian art. The theatre must learn that lesson".[34]

The actor's face, converted into a mask, has a further advantage. It does not compete for our attention with the actor's body as the instrument through which beauty is communicated. Indeed, Craig's ambition seems to be to turn the actor's body into a form of impersonal instrument, comparable to a music instrument, that can be played upon by the stage director (p. 50). In this way, the actor will be quite effaced as a person and may eventually be dispensed with altogether once the theatre has become the supreme art of movement (p. 53). Essentially, Craig's essay on "The Actor and the Über-Marionette" denies acting the status of an art because its primary material (the human actor) is too unstable, too much the prey of emotion to be used as the basis for creating a beautiful design (pp. 55-56). The actor's physical nature unfits him for the perfection of art unless he creates for himself "a new form of acting, consisting for the main part of symbolical gesture" (p. 61). Craig argues that the prevailing conventions of European realism make this impossible. Instead of suggesting the essence of the experience he is conveying, the actor merely copies surface appearances and is content to look on life as "a photo-machine looks upon life" (p. 63). He is satisfied with being a mimic, something comparable to a ventriloquist (p. 63). What Craig implies is that the actor's body can only produce a work of art if it can be converted into a machine totally obedient to the actor's will and intelligence (p. 70). A certain nostalgia for the dance and the ritualised art of the oriental stage seems to lie behind this conception and, connected with it, a profound hostility to the stage regarded as the locus of mere impersonation: "the bringing of excessive gesture, swift mimicry, speech which bellows and scene which dazzles, on to the stage . . . " (p. 75). There can be no revolution in the art of the theatre until the actor's force of personality and talent for impersonation can be tamed. The corollary is plain: "Do away with the real tree, do away with the reality of delivery, do away with the reality of action, and you tend towards the doing away with the actor." (p. 81)

The conventional realistic actor needs to be replaced by the "Über-marionette". This is not just a "superior doll", like present-day wooden puppets which have become objects of fun precisely because they imitate the antics of flesh-and-blood actors, but a figure capable of conveying the "grave grace", "the stamp of reserve" which used to characterize puppets in the remote past (p. 83). Here, Craig appears to imply that the Über-marionette is not so much a doll as a special kind of malleable actor, transcending through some fierce new discipline—"the body in trance", as he expresses it (p. 85)—the limits of common life. Underlying this, and Craig's other references to Asia, Africa and the temple art of Egypt, is a conception of the stage as serving a common spiritual tradition through an art of high stylisation and composure. This admired model of puppets as "a great and noble family of Images . . . " (p. 90) is contrasted with the "gush, emotion, swaggering personality of the artist" (p. 87), and with the crude art of realism, that "frank representation of human nature" which presents experience in "all its actuality" (p. 286). And Craig's aspiration toward his ideal theatre is attested to by the numerous plays for puppets which he writes, notably in 1916 and 1918.

Of course, "The Actor and the Über-Marionette" is a polemic, and its strictures on actors are intended to be provocative, though the disclaimer contained in the preface to the 1924 edition of *On the Art of the Theatre* suggests that Craig regrets having gone so far. Denying that he ever wanted to see "the living actors replaced by things of wood", Craig declares: "The Übermarionette is the actor plus fire, minus egoism: the fire of the gods and demons, without the smoke and steam of mortality" (pp. ix-x). This reaffirms that he is more anxious to transform the actor than to abolish him. In fact, the actor can probably survive Craig's ideas on mask and puppet, but hardly his experiments with light-painting, monumental sets and flexible screens. Lighting used with artistic tact and inventiveness can indeed animate and colour space, freeing the imagination of the audience, but it can also overwhelm the actor and reduce him to a passing shape. Craig's stage designs are on so monumental a scale,[35] with their severe right-angles, their juxtaposed planes of light and shade, their soaring vertical lines, their massive cubes and columns arranged like some abstract architectural composition, that they conspire, whatever the remoteness and dignity they convey, to dwarf or obliterate the actor. Even the grandly simplified colour schemes—for example, the gold surfaces, properties and costumes for the court scene in Craig's *Hamlet* designs of 1912— seem too powerful for the actors in the play. Can Macbeth survive against the great cubes and vertical blocks of Craig's design for a stage set of Act II, Scene I (1928); can Hamlet against the towering blocks of two model sets made around 1911?[36]

Nor do the famous mobile screens seem to me calculated to enhance the actor's function. Craig's invention was a system of hinged screens of uniform height, composed of a number of panels of varying widths and capable of being moved horizontally. These screens were of a neutral colour and could be lit from different angles so as to allow streams of coloured light to play over them. The idea was that these constantly changing lights, falling on the moving screens, would conjure up different scenes and moods and elicit subtle shifts of emotion from the audience. They would in fact provide what Craig himself called " . . . The Thousand Scenes in One Scene".[37] In essence, Craig's screens and moving images seem to me to reflect the ambition to give the physical set a dramatic life of its own and consequently they distract attention from the actor to the changing spectacle which they provide. The correspondent of the *Times* tends to imply this in his report on the operation of the screens at the Moscow Art Theatre's production of *Hamlet* in January 1912: "Mr. Craig has the singular power of carrying the spiritual significance of words and dramatic situations beyond the actor to the scene in which he moves . . . ".[38] Certainly these screens, imaginatively lit, could produce an extraordinary impression of fluidity and variety, and it is not difficult to see them as a form of kinetic art producing a state of aesthetic receptivity in the audience. Nor is it hard to envisage such a theatrical device enhancing plays which embody experiences of a rarefied or intensely poetic kind.

This helps to account for W. B. Yeats's enthusiasm for them. He experimented with Craig's model screens in the summer of 1910 and something of his excitement in the innovation is captured in what he writes at the end of his 1910 essay on "The Tragic Theatre": "All summer I have been playing with a little model, where there is a scene capable of endless transformation, of the expression of every mood that does not require a photographic reality. . . . I am very grateful for [Mr. Craig] has banished a whole world that wearied me and was undignified and given me forms and lights which I can play as upon some stringed instrument."[39] The full extent of Years's passionate interest in this new device may be gauged from a notebook which contains thirty-five sketches of scenes employing Craig's screens: these indicate a variety of settings and give an impressive amount of detail on ground plans, lighting effects, colour schemes and so forth.[40] Craig's full-scale screens were first used by Yeats for performances of his own *The Hour-Glass* and of Lady Gregory's *The Deliverer* at the Abbey Theatre on 12 January 1911. *The Irish Times* noted soberly: " . . . a reduction of the stage furniture to its simplest elements, so that the figures of the players stand out more prominently against the primitive background, and attention is concentrated on the human and truly expressive elements of the drama."[41]

Here is epitomised Craig's conception of the play as a total aesthetic effect, a conception congenial to Yeats, who shares a number of Craig's aesthetic assumptions. Like Craig, Yeats is hostile to scene-painting considered as an elaborate extra effect, and he deals with it severely in his essay on "The Tragic Theatre". Specifically, he complains that scene-painting vitiates the art of the theatre if it is not in harmony with "the characteristics of the stage, light and shadow, speech, the movement of the players", and he adds that "painted light and shadow" are in danger of having no meaningful relationship to the real light, so that the background will be "full of forms and colours" instead of presenting an even surface against which the players can be clearly outlined.[42] Like Craig, he is hostile to realistic conventions, especially as they apply to character, preferring to see tragic drama not as the clash of "characters", in the sense of bundles of surface mannerisms, but as the conflict of "passions and motives".[43] He shares Craig's admiration for the stylised simplicities of the oriental stage: the simplified properties and scenery, the dignified beauty of the masks, the disciplined movement of the whole body. And reflecting on "the high breeding of poetical style" to be found in the formality of the Noh theatre, he argues in 1916 for an imaginative art that distances itself from life: "Verse, ritual, music, and dance in association with action require that gesture, costume, facial expression, stage arrangement" must help in effecting that distance.[44] All this is consistent with Yeats's earliest ideas on the drama, as in his review of Villiers de l'Isle-Adam's play *Axël* in April 1894, where he expressed a preference for "the personages of great art" who are "for the most part too vast, too remote, too splendid for imitation. They are merely metaphors in that divine argument which is carried on from age to age . . . about the ultimate truths of existence".[45]

Such views tend to establish a more ritualised rôle for the actor, in contrast with the individualism and bravura of nineteenth-century star actors, and this preferred formal style matches Yeats's idea of the actor as primarily a speaker. For the Irish poet, it is language which is central to the dramatic performance, so that it is entirely natural that he should wish to relegate the actor to being, as he expresses it on the same page of his review of *Axël*, "a reverent reciter of majestic words". This view is very much in tune with the aesthetics of French symbolism and recalls Mallarmé's preference for a theatre of the mind in which he himself would be the solitary reciter of his masterpiece before an audience of eight people.[46] Yeats's lecture on "Ideal Theatre" delivered to the Irish Literary Society in April 1899 puts the case for the primacy of language even more forcefully: "If we were to restore drama to the stage—poetic drama, at any rate—our actors must become rhapsodists again, and keep the rhythm of the verse as the first of their endeavours. The music of a voice should seem more important than the expression of face or the movement of hands . . . ".[47] The natural end of such an argument comes with Yeats's advocacy, in what might be called his Celtic twilight period, of a special style of intoning verse or prose which will remove the actor from the patterns of everyday speech and avoid variations of pitch and tone without leading to a "monotonous chant".[48] From there it is only a step to envisaging actors as musical puppets, speaking to a system of musical notes and being trained never to deviate from them, as in an early experiment which Yeats tried out on the actress Florence Farr, using a twelve-stringed instrument based on the Greek lyre. However, it is right to recall that Yeats gradually moved away from his 1894 model of the actor as a "reverent reciter of majestic words" to the model of the Japanese dancer (1921), capable of "histrionic expressiveness, emotional truth and precision".[49]

So we may conclude that Sarah Bernhardt's gorgeous pyrotechnics are remote from, and everywhere challenged by, the strange wraiths that people Maeterlinck's early plays, the gross and violent puppets of *Ubu roi*, Craig's ideal Über-Marionette moving against subtly shifting screens, or Yeats's "rhapsodist" serving a high ceremonious ritual. Yet, if the "sacred monster" gradually disappears from the stage in the course of the twentieth century, it is not because the visions of Maeterlinck or Jarry or Craig or Yeats prevail, nor because the improvisatory actor has succeeded in expelling all others but, more plausibly, because of the rise of disciplined ensemble playing, itself in part a reflection of the democratic ethos. And this style of playing, whether embodied in Michel Saint-Denis's Compagnie des Quinze or Brecht's Berliner Ensemble, does not spell the end of the mimetic actor. He survives as one of a team, neither puppet nor sacred monster.

NOTES

1. Reprinted in *Around Theatres* (London: Rupert Hart-Davies, 1953), p. 400.

2. Sir Philip Magnus, *King Edward the Seventh* (London: Murray, 1964), p. 299. (A loose-box is a stable in which a number of horses, untethered, are allowed to move about freely—though they are still locked in, of course, and cannot escape.)

3. In "Eleanora Duse", *Studies in Seven Arts* (London: Constable, 1906), p. 336.

4. *Confessions of a Young Man* (London: Heinemann, 1952), pp. 188-89.

5. Octave Mirbeau, *Le Comédien* (Paris: Brunox, 1883), p. 6.

6. *Gens de théâtre* (Paris: Flammarion, 1924), pp. 52-54.

7. Max Beerbohm, *Around Theatres*, p. 160.

8. "Duse and Bernhardt", reprinted in *Plays and Players*, ed. A. C. Ward (London: Oxford University Press, 1952), pp. 34-35.

9. Marcel Postic, *Maeterlinck et le Symbolisme* (Paris: Nizet, 1970), p. 54.

10. John A. Henderson, *The First Avant-Garde (1887-1894)* (London: Harrap, 1971), p. 122.

11. Jonas Barish, *The Antitheatrical Prejudice* (Berkeley: University of California Press, 1981), p. 344.

12. Though private performances of *Les Sept Princesses*, with sets designed by Serusier and Vuillard and costumes by Maurice Denis, do seem to have taken place. Charming puppets and model sets figure among the exhibits in the Musée du Prieuré (Saint-Germain-en-Laye), devoted to the work of Maurice Denis.

13. *Théâtre I* (Paris: Lamm, 1901), p. III.

14. "Monna Vanna" in *Plays, Acting and Music: a Book of Theory* (London: Cape, 1928), p. 38.

15. "Le Tragique quotidien", reprinted in *Le Trésor des humbles* (Paris: Mercure de France, 1949), pp. 135-36.

16. As Bettina Knapp persuasively argues in *Maurice Maeterlinck* (Boston: Twayne Publishers, 1975), p. 83.

17. "The Trembling of the Veil", in *Autobiographies* (London: Macmillan, 1961), p. 348.

18. "A Symbolist Farce", reprinted in *Studies in Seven Arts*, p. 375.

19. K. S. Beaumont, "The Making of Ubu: Jarry as Producer and Theorist", *Theatre Research*, vol. 12, no. 2 (1972), p. 151. Italics in the original.

20. "A Symbolist Farce", p. 373.

21. "De l'inutilité du théâtre au théâtre", in *Tout Ubu*, ed. Maurice Saillet (Paris: Le Livre de Poche, 1962), p. 143.

22. Ibid., p. 142.

23. "Conférence sur les Pantins", in *Tout Ubu*, p. 495.

24. Denis Bablet, "Gordon Craig and Scenography", *Theatre Research*, vol. 11, no. 1 (1971), pp. 8-9.

25. John Stokes, "An Aesthetic Theatre: the Career of E. W. Godwin", in *Resistible Theatres* (London: Paul Elek, 1972), p. 68. Illustrations of the sets and costumes of *Helena in Troas* are to be found opposite p. 55.

26. John Stokes, "A Wagner Theatre: Professor Herkomer's Pictorial-Musical Plays", in *Resistible Theatres*, pp. 86-87.

27. Edward Craig, "Gordon Craig and Hubert von Herkomer", *Theatre Research*, vol. 10, no. 1 (1969), p. 10.

28. Ibid., p. 13.

29. Denis Bablet, "Gordon Craig and Scenography", pp. 12-13.

30. Reprinted in *On the Art of the Theatre* (London: Heinemann, 1911), p. 293.

31. Ibid., p. 21. All subsequent page references are given in the text.

32. Edward Gordon Craig, *Henry Irving* (London: Dent, 1930).

33. John Balance (pseud.), "Sarah Bernhardt", *The Mask*, vol. 1, nos. 3-4 (May-June 1908), pp. 71-72.

34. Reprinted in Janet Leeper, *Edward Gordon Craig: Designs for the Theatre* (Harmondsworth: Penguin Books, 1948), p. 46.

35. He argues for them in: Louis Madrid (pseud.), "In Defence of the Scene of Vast Proportions", *The Mask*, vol. 7, no. 2 (May 1915), pp. 163-64.

36. Reproduced in: George Nash, *Edward Gordon Craig, 1872-1966)* (London: HMSO, 1967), fig. 61 and figs. 53, 54.

37. *The Mask*, vol. 7, no. 1 (May 1915), p. 139.

38. Ibid., p. 157.

39. Reprinted in *Uncollected Prose by W. B. Yeats, 2: Reviews, Articles and Other Miscellaneous Prose 1897-1939*, ed. John P. Frayne and Colton Johnson (London: Macmillan, 1975), p. 392.

40. James W. Flannery, "W. B. Yeats, Gordon Craig and the Visual Arts of the Theatre", in *Yeats and the Theatre*, ed. Robert O'Driscoll and Lorna Reynolds (London: Macmillan, 1975), p. 99.

41. *The Mask*, vol. 3, nos. 10-12 (April 1911), p. 191.

42. "The Tragic Theatre", in *Uncollected Prose by W. B. Yeats, 2*, p. 391.

43. Ibid., p. 386.

44. "Certain Noble Plays of Japan", reprinted in *Essays and Introductions* (London: Macmillan, 1961), p. 224.

45. "A Symbolical Drama in Paris", in *Uncollected Prose by W. B. Yeats, 1: First Reviews and Articles 1886-1896*, ed. John P. Frayne (London: Macmillan, 1970), p. 325.

46. Haskell M. Block, *Mallarmé and the Symbolist Drama* (Detroit: Wayne State University Press, 1963), p. 78.

47. *Uncollected Prose by W. B. Yeats, 2*, p. 156.

48. "The Play, the Player and the Scene", in *Explorations* (London: Macmillan, 1962), pp. 172-73.

49. James W. Flannery, *W. B. Yeats and the Idea of a Theatre* (New Haven, Conn.: Yale University Press, 1976), p. 208.

Selective Bibliography

The following is a selected list of books on Sarah Bernhardt and on the period in general, some of which are referred to in the text and the notes of the present book. What is here provided is not a bibliography in the strict sense but a reading list of books that may prove useful to readers wishing to pursue the subject further. The list is by no means exhaustive.

Agate, May. *Madame Sarah*, London: Home & Van Thal, 1945.

Archer, William. *The Old Drama and the New*. London: Heinemann, 1923.

————. *The Theatrical World, 1893*. London, 1894; reprinted New York: Blom, 1969.

————. *The Theatrical World, 1894*. London, 1894.

————. *The Theatrical World, 1895*. London, 1895; reprinted New York: Blom, 1969.

————. *The Theatrical World, 1897*. London, 1898; reprinted New York: Blom, 1969.

Arthur, Sir George. *Sarah Bernhardt*. London: Heinemann, 1923.

Ashwell, Lena. *Myself a Player*. London: Michael Joseph, 1936.

Bancroft, Squire and Bancroft, Marie. *Mr. & Mrs. Bancroft On and Off the Stage*. London, 1888.

Baring, Maurice. *Sarah Bernhardt*. London: Davies, 1933.

Barker, Harley Granville. *The Exemplary Theatre*. London, 1922; reprinted New York: Blom, 1969.

Beerbohm, Max. *Around Theatres*. London, 1924.

————. *More Theatres*. London: Hart-Davis, 1969.

————. *Last Theatres*. New York: Taplinger, 1970.

Bernhardt, Lysiane. *Sarah Bernhardt, My Grandmother*. Paris, 1945; translation, London: Hurst & Blackett, 1946.

Bernhardt, Sarah. *L'Art du théâtre*. Paris, 1923; translation, London: Bles, 1924.

Booth, Michael. *English Melodrama*. London: Jenkins, 1965.

Busson, Dani. *Sarah Bernhardt*. Paris, 1900.

Carlson, Marvin. *The French Stage in the Nineteenth Century*. Metuchen, N.J.: Scarecrow Press, 1972.

Coquelin, Benoît-Constant. *L'Art du Comédien*. Paris: Ollendorff, 1894.

Craig, Edith, and St. John, Christopher. *Ellen Terry's Memoirs*. London: Gollancz, 1933.

Craig, Edward. *Gordon Craig: The Story of His Life*. New York: Knopf, 1968.

Craig, Edward Gordon. *Henry Irving*. London: Dent, 1930.

————. *Index to the Story of My Days*. New York: Viking Press, 1957.

————. *On the Art of the Theatre*. London, 1911.

Darbyshire, Alfred. *The Art of the Victorian Stage*. London, 1907; reprinted New York: Blom, 1969.

Disher, Maurice Willson. *Blood and Thunder*. London: Muller, 1949.

————. *The Last Romantic*. London: Hutchinson, 1948.

Dickinson, Thomas. *The Insurgent Theatre*. New York, 1917.

Emboden, William. *Sarah Bernhardt*. London: Vista, 1974.

Findlater, Richard. *The Player Kings*. London: Weidenfeld & Nicholson, 1971.

————. *The Player Queens*. London: Weidenfeld & Nicholson, 1976.

Graham, Franklin. *Histrionic Montreal*. Montreal, 1902.

Granville-Barker, Harley. See Barker, Harley Granville.

Hahn, Reynaldo. *Sarah Bernhardt: Impressions*. London: Elkin Mathews, 1932.

Hart, Jerome A. *Sardou and the Sardou Plays*. Philadelphia and London: Lippincott, 1913.

Henderson, John A. *The First Avant-Garde, 1887-1894*. London: Harrap, 1971.

Hewitt, Barnard. *A History of Theatre from 1800 to the Present*. New York: McGraw-Hill, 1964.

Huret, Jules. *Sarah Bernhardt*. Paris, 1899; translated, London: G. A. Raper, 1899.

Kahn, Gustave. *Sarah Bernhardt*. Paris, 1901.

Maeterlinck, Maurice. *The Treasure of the Humble*. Translated A. Sutro. London: Allen, 1897. Also, a new edition in the original French, Paris: Mercure de France, 1949.

Matthews, Brander. *These Many Years*. New York: Chas. Scribner's Sons, 1917.

Moses, Montrose J., and Brown, J. Mason. *The American Theatre as Seen by Its Critics, 1752-1934*. New York: Cooper Square Publishers, 1967.

Nemirovitch-Dantchenko, Vladimir. *My Life in the Russian Theatre*. Translated J. Cournos. London: Bles, 1937.

Pearson, Hesketh. *The Last Actor-Managers*. London: Methuen, 1950.

Peter, René. *Le Théâtre et la vie sous la Troisième Republique*. Paris: Marrot, 1947.

Poinsot, E. A. *La Comédie Française à Londres*. Paris: Ollendorff, 1880.

Postic, Marcel. *Maeterlinck et le Symbolisme*. Paris: Nizet, 1970.

Richardson, Joanna. *Sarah Bernhardt and Her World*. London: Weidenfeld & Nicholson, 1977.

Robins, Elizabeth. *Both Sides of the Curtain*. London: Heinemann, 1940.

Rowell, George. *Victorian Dramatic Criticism*. London: Methuen, 1971.

Salvini, Tommaso. *Leaves from the Autobiography of Tommaso Salvini*. New York, 1893; reprinted by Blom, 1971.

Sarcey, Francïsque. *Quarante Ans de Théâtre*. Paris: Bibliotheque des Annales, 1900.

Scott, Clement. *The Drama of Yesterday and Today*. London: Macmillan, 1899.

————. *Some Notable Hamlets of the Present Time*. London, 1900; reprinted New York: Blom, 1969.

Shaw, Bernard. *Our Theatre in the Nineties*. London: Constable, 1932.

Skinner, Cornelia Otis. *Madame Sarah*. New York: Houghton Mifflin, 1967.

Stoker, Bram. *Personal Reminiscences of Sir Henry Irving*. London, 1907.

Stokes, John. *Resistible Theatres*. London: Elek, 1972.

Taranow, Gerda. *Sarah Bernhardt and the Art within the Legend*. Princeton, N.J.: Princeton University Press, 1972.

Trewin, J. C. *The Edwardian Theatre*. Oxford: Blackwell, 1976.

————, ed. *The Pomping Folk in the Nineteenth-Century Theatre*. London: Dent, 1968.

————. *Benson and the Bensonians*. London: Barrie & Rockliffe, 1960.

Towse, John Rankin. *Sixty Years of the Theatre*. New York, 1916.

Verneuil, Louis. *The Fabulous Life of Sarah Bernhardt*. Translated by Ernest Boyd. New York: Harper, 1942.

Waxman, Samuel M. *Antoine and the Théâtre-Libre*. New York, 1926; reprinted by Blom, 1968.

Wilson, A. E. *Edwardian Theatre*. London: Barker, 1951.

Witkowski, Georg. *The German Drama of the Nineteenth Century*. Leipzig, 1909; reprinted, in translation of L. E. Horning, New York: Blom, 1968.
Woon, Basil. *The Real Sarah Bernhardt*. New York: Tudor Publishing Co., 1937.

Index

In general, references in the Notes at the end of each chapter and titles in the Bibliography are not included in the Index unless they are directly referred to in the main text.

Contributors

DOUGLAS ARRELL is Assistant Professor in the Department of Theatre and Drama at the University of Winnipeg. He is the author of several articles on Canadian theatre history, but his major interest is in dramatic theory and aesthetics. He is currently working on a major study of the nature of audiences and the audience-artist relationship.

MARVIN A. CARLSON is Professor and Director of Graduate Studies in Theatre and Drama at Indiana University and was previously Professor of Theatre Arts at Cornell University. His most recent books in the area of European theatre history are *Goethe and the Theatre in Weimar* and *The Italian Stage in the Nineteenth Century*.

MARGUERITE COE is Associate Professor of Speech Communication and Dramatic Arts and member of the Honors Faculty at Arkansas State University in Jonesboro. She has written several articles on theatre history and dramatic criticism and is currently at work on a biography of Coquelin.

L. W. CONOLLY is Professor of Drama and Chairman of the Department at the University of Guelph. He has published articles in a wide variety of British, American and Canadian journals, and has written entries on Canadian theatre and drama for the *Oxford Companion to Canadian Literature* and the *New Canadian Encyclopedia*. His books include *The Censorship of English Drama 1737-1824, English Drama and Theatre*

1800-1900 (with J. P. Wearing) and *Theatrical Touring and Founding in North America*. Professor Conolly was co-founder of the publication *Nineteenth Century Theatre Research*, and now serves as advisory editor, a position he also holds with *Theatre History in Canada*.

RICHARD FINDLATER's books on theatrical history include *The Player Queens* and *The Player Kings*, and he has written biographies of Grimaldi and of Lilian Baylis of the Old Vic. His most recent publication is *At the Royal Court*, which he edited for the English Stage Company as a record of its first twenty-five years. Formerly theatre critic of *Tribune, Time and Tide*, and other publications, he is an assistant editor of the *Observer* (London) and editor of *The Author*, the journal of the Society of Authors.

JOHN E. HARE is Professor of French and Quebec Studies at the University of Ottawa. Drama critic for *The Ottawa Citizen* since 1970, he has published several studies on the history of theatre in French Canada, especially in *Le Théâtre canadien-français* (Montreal: 1976). He is a co-author of the *Dictionnaire pratique des auteurs québécois* and is currently preparing a repertory of Quebec theatre from its beginnings to the twentieth century.

ROBERT HORVILLE, titulaire d'un doctorat de troisième cycle et d'un doctorat d'Etat, est maître assistant de Littérature française à l'Université de Lille III. Spécialisé dans l'analyse dramaturgique et dans l'étude des conditions de représentation, il est l'auteur de nombreux ouvrages, parmi lesquels des monographies sur *Dom Juan* (édition Larousse), *Tartuffe* (édition Hachette), *Le Misanthrope* et *Lorenzaccio* (édition Hatier).

S. BEYNON JOHN is Reader in French at the University of Sussex, of which he is a founding member of faculty. He has held appointments at the universities of London (England), Western Ontario, and the Humanities Research Centre (Australian National University); he has also been a Leverhulme Research Fellow. He has published essays on Anouilh, Camus, Sartre and Balzac, as well as on French Romantic drama and the theatre of the Second Empire. He contributed most of the entries on French nineteenth and twentieth-century playwrights in the *Penguin Companion to Literature: European*.

LAURENCE SENELICK is Associate Professor of Drama at Tufts University and a member of the Russian Research Center at Harvard. His most recent books are *Gordon Craig's Moscow Hamlet, Russian Dramatic*

Theory from Pushkin to the Symbolists, and (in collaboration) *British Music Hall, 1840-1923: A Bibliography and Guide to Sources.* He is at present completing biographies of Mikhail Shchepkin and George L. Fox.

J. C. TREWIN, a Cornishman, is the senior London drama critic (*Illustrated London News* since 1946). Formerly literary editor of *The Observer,* he has written fifty books, mostly on the theatre—among them *Benson and the Bensonians, The Edwardian Theatre,* and *Going to Shakespeare.* The first volume of his autobiography, *Up from the Lizard,* has been reissued. He received the OBE in 1981 for services to drama criticism.

ALAN WOODS is Director of The Ohio State University Theatre Research Institute and Associate Professor of Theatre at Ohio State University. He is a former editor of *Theatre Journal,* and has served on the American Theatre Association's Commission for Theatre Research and the American Society for Theatre Research's Research Committee. He has published extensively in the area of North American popular theatre.

About the Editor

ERIC SALMON is Professor of Drama at the University of Guelph in Ontario, Canada. He is the author of *Another Morning Coming, The Dark Journey: John Whiting as Dramatist,* and *Granville Barker: A Secret Life,* in addition to numerous articles on European and American theatre. He is currently at work on an edition of the Letters of Granville Barker and also has a forthcoming book, called *Is the Theatre Still Dying?,* on the present state of the English-speaking theatre.